MY LIFE IN PIECES

MY LIFE IN PIECES

PIECES

B.G. ARMSTRONG

LitPrime
"Your story is our priority"

LitPrime Solutions
21250 Hawthorne Blvd
Suite 500, Torrance, CA 90503
www.litprime.com
Phone: 1-800-981-9893

Published by LitPrime Solutions   02/14/2023

ISBN: 979-8-88703-102-6(sc)
ISBN: 979-8-88703-103-3(hc)
ISBN: 979-8-88703-104-0(e)

Library of Congress Control Number: 2022922740

CONTENTS

PART I: WHEN I WAS YOUNG AND LIFE WAS LONG

PART II: GO BACK AND GET IT! SANKOFA
Gray - Hammond – Branch

PART III: MY JOURNEY HOME

INTRODUCTION

My Life in Pieces

I started writing a memoir in 2010, inspired by a book review of *The Help*, a novel by Katherine Stockett. The story was set in Jackson, Mississippi, in 1962. The reviewer Ann B. Jones, Ph.D., said she reluctantly read it, stating, "I didn't want to risk a plunge downward." Finally, however, she got over her initial response to the subject matter, took the plunge, and read the book. Her review was so interesting that it sent me to the bookstore immediately.

As I started reading the book, I was first repelled by Stockett's use of dialect. I thought, "How dare this white woman mock those black maids?" It seemed like mockery; I wanted to lay aside the book. I didn't. I took a deep breath and continued reading. The pages flew by, and I could not put it down.

After only a few pages, I realized that "I was "the help." I was inspired by this fictional tale of black maids and their relationships with the white women they worked for. So, I decided to write about my experience as a nanny and maid during that summer of 1962.

Once I started writing, memories flowed through situations I hadn't thought of in many years. After I finished that essay, I began to recollect forgotten pieces of my childhood and youth and record them for posterity. I wanted my children and grandchildren to come to know and understand me through my early years and through the family, friends, and people I knew. My youth was spent in Tennessee—Memphis, Somerville, Clarksville, Nashville, and Jackson.

I believe that we are who we are not just due to the circumstance of our birth—what we inherit from our parents and ancestors, but that our personalities and characters are developed through our interactions and experiences with others. A particular situation or circumstance may define some lives; however, most are probably the sum of all that they have experienced, the pieces they have collected and fashioned into a life.

Often the people with the most important and inspiring stories rise out of the muck and mire of adversity. Unfortunately, I am not one of those, yet I have an American story. I was born and reared in the Jim Crow South less than 100 years after slavery ended with the signing of the Emancipation Proclamation1863 and the 13th Amendment 1865. When I was born, black and white people lived parallel lives -- separate but unequal. Yet, black people struggled to rise from a legacy of Slavery and Reconstruction.

This book represents only a few pieces of my life and the lives of family members set in a momentous time in America. There are many more. Unfortunately, some will remain in the bin for lack of time and space. Others will be saved for another project. Still, others will be discarded.

I was young when black people were called colored or Nergo and endured much adversity, yet made gains and improved in some areas of life. Still, much more needed to be done before they could be fully empowered citizens.

I know how it is to live in a divided country with few rights when Black people living in the South were compelled to boycott, demonstrate, and march for the right to participate in the American way of life. As a result, many jobs, schools, and neighborhoods were off-limits. There were obstacles in every direction, and peaceful protests brought opposition from some white citizens. In contrast, some white people from the North came to join the demonstrations and assist in voter registration.

Students on college campuses took issue with how things were being done in America. Both black and white students revolted against the status quo. Many college uprisings took place, and some became violent. Amid the struggle for civil rights, young people were protesting the Vietnam War. Some didn't see sense in going to war and killing people, the Viet Kong, for no reason they knew of; they said "No" when invited by Uncle Sam. Some fought in court; others fled the country. They became known as draft dodgers. The government required 18-year-old males to register for the military. I remember going to court to support a young man who refused to join the Army based on his religion as one of Jehovah's Witnesses. He won his case and did not have to enlist.

Though I was the age of many protestors, I was involved in marriage, raising children, and attending school. I participated in the boycotts of the 1960s, yet I put my activism -- marching and protesting off for a much later date. I marched to protest the Iraq War and joined the Women's March of 2016 shortly after the presidential election.

Initially, I thought this book would be just for my children and family. Yet, after I began writing it, I felt that much of it was akin to the lives of other African Americans and maybe other Americans.

America is no longer black and white. It is all the shades of humanity. That diversity gives it richness. Immigrant cultures, traditions, cuisines, and celebrations have helped make this a great nation.

America has come a long way since the Jim Crow era, but as demonstrated recently, it has much further to go. People are losing their rights. Women have lost the right to safe and legal abortion, and marriage and LGBTQ+ rights are threatened, as are voting rights. Education is under attack as many books are being banned. American history, especially African American history, including slavery, is being attacked and rewritten.

Each of us has a story, and only we can tell it.

WHAT'S IN A NAME

What is in a name? Does it carry any real meaning? Does it identify the bearer's qualities, traits, or characteristics, suggesting an origin or destiny? For example, the darker skin brothers and sisters in America have had many names or designations, such as African, slave, enslaved person, Negro, mulatto, colored, black, Afro-American and African American, and more.

As I started this writing journey, I pondered what name I would use when writing about black American citizens of African heritage. My journey reaches back to slavery and before. Should I call the ancestors "slaves?" That was the designation given to them at that time. Using "African American" seemed strange since the owners considered slaves as property, not citizens, not even fully human.

This name game has been played for centuries and several times during my lifetime. My dilemma was which designation to use predominately. To me, "African American" is inaccurate when applied to black people before 1990. To use it would be tantamount to rewriting history. History should remain – the good, the bad, and the ugly.

In this book, I use all of the designations mentioned above for darker skin people in America. I don't particularly appreciate thinking of the people brought here from Africa as slaves, as they were not. The masters enslaved them, i.e., subjugated, dominated, and sometimes raped, beat, bound, and chained them. They were Africans made into slaves to serve and enrich the lives of white people. The United States of America kept the institution of slavery longer than any other country.

Portuguese and Spaniards also enslaved Africans. They called them "Negro," Spanish for black. After the Africans spent a few years in America, enslavers called the children whose black mothers they, the overseers, and other white men raped mulatto. After a few generations in America, more and more slaves were not black in skin color. Whites decided to call them "colored." However, as time passed, black people didn't like being called colored and returned to Negro. Somehow, Negro seemed stronger than colored. Yet, Negro did not last long.

In the 1960s, H. Rap Brown said, "You must begin to define yourself; you must begin to define your Black self." We called ourselves Black, especially after James Brown sang, "I'm Black and I'm Proud." We had slogans such as "Black is beautiful" and "Black Power." Black is only a color. Since our ancestors came from Africa, rich in history, culture, and resources, let us embrace the continent's riches. Afro-Americans? That was a good name for the hairstyle, but the people didn't embrace it. "Afri-Americans" would have been better.

Since our ancestors were African and we were born in America, that makes us African American. However, I am not sure what makes us American. Is it adhering to the American Creed? We have had to fight for our right to vote, for jobs and fair wages, fair housing, and all privileges that other Americans took for granted. Some of our ancestors came from Europe, and others from the Native American Indian nations.

Jesse Jackson suggested, in a speech in 1990, that we refer to ourselves with the more fitting name, African-American. Jackson had read the poem "I Can" in Dr. Johnny Duncan's Black History Calendar, published in 1986. Duncan saw a sign posted in a dark Georgia swamp while on an Army maneuver, which read, "The last four letters in American spell xxiii MY LIFE IN PIECES I Can." Duncan later noticed that the last four letters in the word African also spell I Can. He wrote, "The last four letters of my (African) heritage and my (American) Creed spell I Can!" Therefore, we should credit Johnny Duncan and his poem for our present designation, African American.

I WAS "THE HELP"

As far as I knew, White women were never lonely, except in books. White men adored them, Black men desired them, and Black women worked for them. -- Maya Angelou

I was not born to serve. However, no one told my mother that. That is why when she heard of a young woman who needed a nanny for her two-year-old daughter, she hurried and made sure I was first in line for the position. I had babysat a few times; I was good at it; therefore, Mommy was confident I could handle the job for three months.

When Mommy was a teen, Papa did not want her to do domestic work for whites; however, she didn't have any qualms about such work. She was not partial to black or white. Her favorite color was green. She painted her living and dining rooms a soft mint green and her bedroom avocado. Her first car was a light olive green 1969 Ford. I can still remember the nubby feel of her moss green coat. Mommy lived for the new and fresh greens that signaled spring.

In later years, as I was going through Mommy's things, I discovered a Gladiator composition book she used for a "Maid's Course in Home Economics." Her home economics teacher, Miss Fuqua, taught the twelfth grade girls how to work in white peoples' homes. Mommy was eager to learn domestic work then because that was all that was available to her; she wanted to earn her own money.

She worked on the family farm, but she received no money for that. Black women could work few places during the 1930s and 1940s. Domestic workers were always in great demand.

Mommy did not bother consulting me to see what my plans were for the summer. She decided the job was mine as soon as she heard about it. I had to pack away my summer plans as winter clothes. Mommy wanted me to earn money for clothing and things I would need for college. She was struggling just to pay household expenses. Therefore, I had to step up and grow up. That summer, Frankie Vali and The Four Seasons sang "Big Girls Don't Cry." I did not.

No matter Kennedy's promise, America did not win the race to the moon. However, John Glenn did orbit Earth three times that year in the spacecraft Friendship 7; Albert Sabin licensed the oral polio vaccine; Kmart, Wal-Mart and Target eased upon the American landscape to define a new way of shopping. My favorite writer William Faulkner died that year, and so did Norma Jean Mortenson, better known as cultural icon and sex symbol Marilyn Monroe. The Civil Rights Movement was evolving after 1955 when a group of white men beat a black boy, Emmett Till, to death and threw his body into the Tallahatchie River in Money, Mississippi. The movement gained momentum when they arrested Rosa Parks for refusing to give up her seat on the bus to a white man. The Civil Rights Act and the Voting Rights Act were yet to come; therefore, America remained greatly divided along the color line.

It was 1962. I was participating in a rite of passage designed to propel me into the adventures, challenges and joys of adulthood. I had been staying in Memphis and attending high school for two years, and I thought I had one more summer to spend in Somerville before I moved on. All I wanted to hear was my name called so I could quickly walk up and receive my diploma from those people I would not miss. Both Mommy and Daddy were there sitting together as if they were a couple; I was anxious to get the formalities over and collect my gifts. After everything ended, I hurried to the designated classroom and flung my gown onto the black pile, silently promising to never step foot inside that building again. With that, I closed the door on my carefree days and opened another to the uncertain, but desired future that lay ahead.

Once the opportunity for me to earn some money came across Mommy's radar, she contacted the right person; and before I had a chance to spend a few mornings sleeping late and a few lazy afternoons reading *True Confession*, I had joined the workforce. My mother believed in putting us to work when we were old enough to walk and pick up our toys. We worked in the house, the garden and later the fields. She wanted no one around who wasn't working. When there was a paycheck at the end of the week that made it even better. Our uncle, we called Brother, was a farmer and raised many different crops. Daily, Mommy ushered the boys off to Brother's fields to plow, chop or hoe cotton, okra, soybeans or some other crop. I had been responsible for the domestic chores including cooking; however, all that changed when Mommy realized there could be money if I did the same work for someone else. Sure, she would miss my free labor that summer, but she would make do as long as I was earning a paycheck.

I felt trapped, caught up in a plan I did not know was in the making. The summer of 1962 was supposed to be my last summer of freedom. However, I wouldn't get to spend hot summer nights sitting in the theater crunching popcorn, slurping orange soda and living vicariously through the actors who paraded across the silver screen.

My brother Malcolm and I had spent many nights at the Fair Theater in previous summers. It was my place to escape the heat of an un-air-conditioned house. We would sit in the balcony, the place designated for black patrons, and sometimes contemplate what would happened if we let a cup of soda pop flip over onto the patrons below. Malcolm was the mischievous sort who could have easily done that if given some encouragement. Both of us knew better.

In the theater, I could visit faraway places, like Egypt during the time of Moses, in the *Ten Commandments*. On the other hand, I could see other parts of the United States such as New York City, and imagine myself singing and dancing alongside Natalie Wood and Rita Moreno in *West Side Story*. For only twenty cents, I could see a world very different from mine. Nevertheless, my favorite summer activity would have to wait because the world of work was demanding my participation. It would be another year before I would enjoy the antics of Scout and Jem in Harper Lee's *To Kill a Mockingbird*. Although published in 1960 and already an academy award winning movie, I had not read the book. I had it on my reading list for the summer of 1962.

Spending summers in the country was difficult for me during my teen years. I would escape through reading any kind of romantic magazine and comics I could get at the Rexall Drug Store. I didn't know that my time reading such was about to end abruptly.

Off to Memphis I went to live in as the help for a young woman I will refer to as Miss Ann. She hired me to provide care for her two-year-old daughter "Missy." Miss Ann was not a professional or a single mother who needed to work, but like many southern white women during that time, she enjoyed the services of a maid, or a nanny, or both. She was not the typical Southern Belle or lady of leisure. She didn't lunch with the girls or shop. Neither did she do charity work. She did not read or have a hobby. Miss Ann simply was not into mothering or cleaning. Sometimes she would help "Mr. G" with his houses. He was a contractor and her lover who, much to my displeasure, also lived there. I didn't like the idea of living with him, but I only learned of that arrangement after I had accepted the job. I think if Mommy had known, she wouldn't have let me take the job.

Miss Ann hired me as a nanny, but I soon became victim of the old "bait and switch." In a short time, I was "chief cook and bottle washer." That is to say, I was the maid, cook, shopper, laundress, hairdresser, bartender and chauffer. It didn't take Miss Ann long to discover that I had skills, and that I was willing to learn others. All that cooking, cleaning and laundry I had done at home had prepared me well. Miss Ann showed me what I didn't know such as how to polish silver and clean carpet. We would get down on our knees with a soft brush and scrub the light beige carpet together. I was not fond of carpet cleaning or polishing silver, which I did every two weeks;

however, I enjoyed the gleam of the silver and looked forward to the day I would have my own.

Miss Ann was particular about how she wanted things done. It was no different with her laundry, especially her undergarments, which she wanted me to wash by hand. That was where I drew the line. I put those delicate items right into the washer with the rest of the clothes, and she was none the wiser. She sent me to the liquor store, which was in walking distance, to buy vodka, vermouth and Burgundy wine until the store manager looked at me on about the third trip and asked, "How old are you?"

I didn't know why he was asking, but I answered proudly, "I'm seventeen."

"Well, you *gonna* have to stop coming here *gitin'* liquor. *You* underage. What's your boss lady's telephone number?"

I gave him the number and he called Miss Ann while I waited.

"Ma'am, I'm the manager at the liquor store. You *gonna* have to stop *sendin'* this girl here to get liquor. I *cain't* be selling to nobody under twenty-one. I'm gonna let her have it this time, but I *cain't* do it again." With a quick phone call, my trips to the liquor store ended. I could strike that chore off my list.

Miss Ann was a little disappointed that I could no longer get liquor, but it was not long before she realized I could drive her to the store, and she could run in and get it.

At first, I felt like Milberry in Langston Hughes' short story "Berry," that I was being imposed upon "in that taken-for-granted way white folks do with Negro help."

Miss Ann was a perfectionist, which worked well for me. I liked the idea of order and beauty. She wanted everything in her environment to be in perfect order--her home, her clothing and appearance, as well as her daughter and her meals. Miss Ann's apartment looked like a spread from *House and Garden Magazine.* I got a sense of arranging a home attractively because of Miss Ann. I took much from her that I would later incorporate into my lifestyle. She was a good cook. I think she enjoyed the few times she joined me in the kitchen. I loved the taste of Italy in her use of garlic, oregano and olive oil.

One time we were making crab cakes and one of them fell apart. She said, "Throw that out. It's not right. Get rid of it." It wasn't shaped perfectly and didn't hold together right. I grabbed it and looked at her to see if she was serious. I reluctantly threw it in the trashcan thinking how Mommy would never throw away good food.

When Miss Ann sent me to Montesi's Supermarket to get steaks, she would say, "Tell the butcher to cut them exactly two inches thick." Her instructions on how to prepare them for the grill were, "Rub them with olive oil, split open a fresh garlic clove and rub it on the steaks, and then sprinkle salt and black pepper on them."

Mr. G would grill them so they were charred on the outside and bloody in the center. They smelled delicious, but that bloody meat was such a turnoff that on those nights Missy and I would eat tuna or chicken.

The twice-baked potatoes had to be perfect in shape and color. Miss Ann showed me how to rub olive oil and a fresh garlic clove inside the wooden salad bowl to season it before I filled it with lettuce, perfectly sliced green peppers, carrots, red onions and ripe tomatoes. With that fare, they would have Burgundy wine served at room temperature. I would have set the table with good china, crystal and cloth napkins. No matter the menu, the table setting would be exquisite, elegant and inviting.

Shortly after I arrived, Miss Ann told me to make two BLTs and bring them to the bedroom. I said, "Yes ma'am," and into the kitchen I went to look for a box or a bag with "BLT" on it. First, I looked in the cabinets, and then I looked in the refrigerator. I couldn't find anything with BLT on it. So after a long search, somewhat embarrassed, I knocked on her bedroom door and asked unapologetically, "Miss Ann, what is a BLT?"

She said, "Bacon, lettuce and tomato sandwich." She probably had wondered why she wasn't enjoying the aroma of bacon frying.

I should have known that, I thought. I felt stupid for a minute, but Miss Ann didn't respond with sarcasm or act as if I should have known. Therefore, I got over my embarrassment, went back to the kitchen and fried the bacon to the right crispness, sliced the tomatoes, washed and dried the lettuce and toasted the white bread to perfection. When I presented the sandwiches on a silver tray, Miss Ann smiled and offered a simple thank you. I left smiling because it was then that I knew I had the ability to do the job well. I felt obligated to do well to please Mommy, and I didn't want to let down the woman who was instrumental in my getting the job.

The first time Miss Ann told me to make a Bloody Mary and Martini, I had no idea what they were. Daddy drank whiskey, and I had seen homemade wine during Christmas at my grandparents' home. Beer was common enough. I knew nothing about cocktails. Miss Ann told me exactly how much gin and vermouth to pour for the Martini, how many olives to add and the proper glasses to use. The Bloody Mary was more complicated. It contained vodka, tomato juice, Worcestershire sauce, lemon, hot sauce, and a stalk of celery for garnish. Neither drink enticed me; therefore, I never tasted them. Miss Ann gave good instructions, and I followed them exactly. I enjoyed doing those tasks more than I enjoyed taking care of Missy because I felt more grownup.

Miss Ann paid me $25.00 each week. She would sign the check, and I would write it.

The average salary at that time was $5,500.00 a year, but I think this didn't include the salaries of African Americans. At any rate, I was way below average. I also wrote checks to the grocery, drug store, liquor store, the landlord, and for whatever else she needed. I learned fast. She would sign the checks and send me on my way. Her rent for the luxury apartment was $375.00 per month. The average rent in America in 1962 was $110.00 per month. Again, I don't think black people were included in that statistic.

Young professionals such as pilots, stewardesses, nurses and some older people with money lived in the complex, which encircled a courtyard with a pool as its centerpiece. It was exclusive.

One afternoon as I was going across the courtyard around the pool to the laundry room, I saw some high school girls laughing, talking, and slathering on suntan lotion. They looked at me as if I had drunk from the "white only" water fountain or entered the "whites only" waiting room. I was also curious about them. After all, I lived there and they didn't. They had come to visit someone in the complex so they could get some sun and swim. As I passed, one girl asked, "How old are you?"

"I'm seventeen."

"We thought you were older."

They were giddy girls who wore too much makeup and red lipstick and had nothing more to do than lounge around the pool laughing and talking and enjoying their leisure. I, on the other hand, was slaving from dawn until dark, enjoying no leisure, not even reading or watching television. I guessed that their maids were older women with husbands and children of their own who had decided to make caring for white people their vocation. So perhaps they thought it odd that someone near their age would be doing such work.

To add to my more mature status I said, "I'll be going to college in the fall."

That pronouncement caused them to look at me with a bit of awe and maybe a little respect and envy. I smiled as I hurried off with the laundry basket to the sounds of Chubby Checker singing "The Twist" on the transistor while leaving them to wonder why a Negro girl was even thinking about going to college. Marriage was the goal for many white girls after high school in the 1950s and early 1960s.

I have fond memories of the people who lived near Miss Ann. They were nice to me, not at all condescending. They didn't live or act like southerners and were to me avant-garde. I think they had come from California. I was glad to meet white people who didn't fit the stereotypical southern way of being where matters of color and race were concerned. They and Miss Ann are the reason I didn't lump all white people together and judge them as being prejudiced. My early interactions with them allowed me to relate well to other white people and to enjoy many good relationships over the years, from Nashville to Charleston, Louisville, Mobile and Atlanta.

I found it uplifting that white people who visited or lived in

Europe for a time had a broader worldview that made them more accepting of other groups. Many of those who remained stateside held onto their southern traditions, customs and ideals. Europeans were welcoming to many black people such as writers Langston Hughes and James Baldwin, and performers like Josephine Baker. White people in Europe were not living under the slave system and Jim Crow mentality of racial superiority, as were whites in America.

Along with cooking, cleaning, shopping, errands, I took care of Missy. Before

Miss Ann and Mr. G got out of bed I had already washed and dressed myself, washed and dressed Missy and cleaned the bathroom so it would be fresh and shiny when they rose. Missy and I would often be finished with breakfast, and I would be cleaning the kitchen before we would see either of them.

Not so cute, Missy was a strong willed, stoutly built child with pale skin and wispy blond hair. She was not sweet and cuddly. One evening Miss Ann and Mr. G were going out, and I had a difficult time controlling Missy as she threw a fit on the sidewalk. Her bulky frame slipped through my hands. I reached for her as she fell to the concrete. I had a difficult time getting her back into the apartment as all eyes around the pool turned to look at me. I felt a little inept, so I scooped her up and took her inside as quickly as I could.

Mommy tried to prepare me to live with white people as best she could never having had that experience herself. She gave me advice that I heeded: "Don't you spank that girl. It will leave red marks on her skin." I did not know about time-out then, and in my experience, if an adult caught you doing something wrong, you got a spanking or whipping with a switch, which you had to procure from one of the trees in the yard. We did not know if white people spanked their children. I followed Mommy's advice even when I wanted to tap Missy's hand to keep her out of something. I would respect her little temper tantrum, allow her to work it out, and then I would talk to her. I actually felt sorry for Missy. I knew she hungered for her mother's attention and was probably jealous of Mr. G. I could tell that she did not like him anymore than I did. He paid her less attention than he paid me, which was none. That was good for me, but not so good for her.

I will not say Miss Ann didn't love her daughter. She didn't pay her much attention, but she loved her enough to see that she was safe and had good care. Miss Ann was into her life with her man, but not with any zeal or passion that I at seventeen could see. However, what did I know about how lovers acted in a live-in relationship? I had observed aunts and uncles who were married and lived together; however, Mommy and Daddy separated when I was three or four, so what did I know about how a man and a woman were supposed to relate to one another?

Miss Ann was the glamorous type. She had lived and worked as a model in Europe for some years. Models were not so thin and tall then. It was before waif-like, British model Twiggy came on the scene. Miss Ann had pale skin, but was attractive enough and was the size of many young white woman of the time. She wore size six clothing and stood five feet seven inches tall. White women and most of the young black women I saw were slim. It was before fast foods and convenience foods became popular. People cooked and ate healthier meals at home. Miss Ann had married an Italian man, but they must have divorced. I never saw any trace of him, just his last name that she and Missy carried.

I knew nothing about Mr. G, but I don't think he grew up in the south. He was good-looking, medium height with brunette hair and olive skin that looked like it would darken with a good dose of sunshine. He and Miss Ann used to fight often, not just verbally, but physically. Sometimes there would be blood. The first time they fought, I was so scared. I didn't know what to do except get out of bed and lock the door. I listened through the wall until the noise subsided, and then I fell into an uneasy sleep. The next time they fought, I just turned over and went back to sleep believing it was just something they did, and I would have to become accustomed to it. I had not heard grown-ups fighting before, and it was very strange. I guessed that Mommy and Daddy decided to go their separate ways to keep from getting to that stage.

I went home on the weekends to gorge on field peas and turnip greens with sliced tomatoes and green onion that came from Mommy's garden. I watched some television. I liked Westerns like *Gunsmoke* and *Wagon Trail*. I enjoyed daydreaming in the tub where I could soak for an hour or until someone ran me out. I would shampoo my hair and Mommy would hot comb and curl it to last the week.

My hair was somewhat of a mystery to Miss Ann. She often commented on how nice it looked and what body it had. One day she asked, "How do you get your hair to look so full?" I did not know how to answer. I didn't think it took any effort. I thought it was just natural once Mommy curled it, and I combed and styled it. I didn't want to give her a primer on the care of black hair. I didn't want her to know how my hair curled or coiled tightly when I washed it, or how Mommy straightened it with a very hot, metal comb before she used the hot Marcel curling iron. I did not want to share with her the struggle black women had with their hair. Alternatively, should I tell her the *herstory* of Madam C.J. Walker who invented the straightening comb in 1905, so black women with kinks could have straight hair like white women? She knew I didn't wash my hair daily and fuss with it as she did with hers. Therefore, she was curious. Her hair was bleached blond, not silky and natural looking. She backcombed, teased and sprayed it daily to get it to look full and perfectly coiffured.

Therefore, I said, "I don't do anything special to maintain it each day. I just set it on rollers at night and comb it out in the morning."

One day Miss Ann decided to bleach her hair and she needed my help. Our efforts were disastrous. The color did not turn out right. She said, "You have to go to the drugstore and get me a toner." I didn't have a clue about a toner. All I had ever put on my hair was a henna rinse, but I could read, so off I went to search the shelves and to ask the clerk if necessary. I found what she needed and hurried back so we could put it in.

"It looks horrible," She said trying not to become hysterical. "Get the keys and drive me to the beauty shop so I can get my color fixed."

I said, "I don't have my driver's license yet." I didn't tell her that Mommy wanted me to wait until I was eighteen and could be responsible for myself.

"Can you drive?"

"Yes ma'am."

"Then drive me to the shop." She said as she threw me the car keys, and we were on our way.

I assumed she didn't like driving. I was willing and grateful for the opportunity. I had learned to drive when I was twelve, but that was only up and down the driveway at my grandparents' home or on a country road that had very little traffic. I had no real driving experience, but I didn't tell Miss Ann. I just jumped behind the wheel and took off.

That was one more chore I could add to the list. From that day forward, I drove whenever it was necessary. Sometimes I went alone. In my thinking, she was a wealthy, white woman accustomed to having her own way; therefore, I figured she knew what she was doing by allowing me to drive without a license. I am grateful I always returned safely. Again, reflecting on Langston Hughes' *The Ways of White Folk*, I was not sure I would have been able to count on her.

I decided to stay in Memphis and visit my cousin one weekend. Shortly after I got to my cousin's apartment, Miss Ann came looking for me. "I need you. Can you come back? I just can't deal with Missy right now." I wasn't happy, but I gave up the potential fun for the definite extra money. I never figured out how she found me. I learned then that white people had a way of getting whatever they wanted.

I had a couple of unpleasant and downright scary experiences while working for Miss Ann. She and Mr. G had a knock-down-drag-out one night that sounded more ferocious than the ones before. The next day he was moving out. Miss Ann told me to help him take his belongings to his car. I jumped at the task. I was smiling and almost floating down the sidewalk as I struggled with each armload. I couldn't stop smiling inside as he left in a hurry.

Mr. G was not an awful man, and he never said anything to offend me, but I didn't like his presence. I wondered why Miss Ann was with him. I did silently celebrate his hasty departure, and so did Missy. She grinned broadly and toddled to the window to look out as Mr. G bounded down the walkway wearing his angry face.

Our celebrating was a bit premature. The following day I had to lug all those belongs back and put them away. I was boiling inside. It puzzled me that Miss Ann and Mr. G could stay together when they fought so often. I chalked it up to the ways of white folk, which I was yet learning.

One afternoon Miss Ann wanted to inspect one of Mr. G's houses to make sure it was ready for market. Missy and I accompanied her to the subdivision on what was to be a short mission. Miss Ann left me at the house to clean up some paper while she and Missy went to the store. I was okay, but a little uncomfortable since I was there alone. I was rolling up the brown paper, which the workers had used to keep the carpet clean while they did their final touches. I went down the hallway and into the back bedroom where I came upon an old man. He was doing some wiping marks off the walls. I gasped when I saw him. He had been quiet while Miss Ann was telling me the plan.

My fear was no secret to him. He said, "I didn't mean to scare ya." He grinned, and I backed out of the room holding the paper I had collected. I went to the backyard where I placed it on the pile to burn. The old man followed, bringing the rest of the paper and throwing it onto the pile. I bent over to pick up some that had slipped off. As I rose, the old man said, "I hope you don't take this the wrong way, but you got the prettiest pair of tits I ever seen."

I was wearing a scoop neck dress. The dress was one that Daddy had given me for graduation. It must have gaped when I bent over.

I took what the old man considered a complement the only way I could as a seventeen-year-old black girl in the South when confronted by a white man. I was aware that white men could have their way with black girls and women without penalty. I knew the dynamics at work. I knew what happened to Emmitt Till when they accused him of making a pass at a white woman. A white man could say anything to a black woman and could even get away with raping her. Who would believe her even if she had the courage to report it? Most likely, she wouldn't.

I was scared. I didn't go back inside the house. I sat on the stoop and waited for Miss Ann to return. I never said anything to the old man, and neither did I say anything to Miss Ann or anyone else about the incident.

On another occasion, Missy and I were alone in the apartment when there was a knock at the door. I opened it thinking it was one of the neighbors, but there was a man I had not seen before. He didn't wait for an invitation; he just barged in and closed the door.

I said, "I'm sorry sir, but Mr. G is not in." I was so unnerved that I repeated, "Mr. G is not in." Then I added, "I don't know when he will be back." I wished I had said, "He will be back soon." However, I didn't think of that until afterwards.

He planted himself in the center of the living room. His pasty skin was sweating from the summer sun; he was breathing heavily, nostrils flaring like a bull about to charge a matador. No, not the matador. The *muleta*. I felt like the *muleta*, the red flag that attracts the bull, inhuman. I was an object to contemplate, not a thinking person who could choose for herself. I knew I had no choice.

There he was in a drab colored suit that hugged his rotund body. He surveyed me as a hungry man would a table full of delicious foods prepared for someone else. Should I grab some and run was the question I saw in his eyes.

All I could do was stand still while my mind scanned its inventory for something that would add immediacy to the situation. I had been in similar situations before with white and black men. This time seemed different.

One afternoon during my senior year, I came home from school and headed towards the steps to my cousin's apartment where I was staying during the week. Three neighbors, all black men, were talking and laughing until I approached. Then they got quiet and started watching me. I was going up the open stairs. They were sitting on a bench at ground level a few feet away. I started up, but I became incensed at the unwanted attention. I backed down, turned around and walked over to where they were sitting. I was wearing my favorite dress, a red shirtwaist with a full skirt and the red leather flats that I had bought at Bakers shoe store. It must have been the color red, which brought out the fire in me that day. I walked up just close enough, pointed my finger in their faces and shouted, "Why are you looking at me like that? How would you like for someone to look at your daughters that way?" They sat stunned, looked at each other, and didn't utter a word. I backed away, turned around and ran up the stairs as fast as I could.

I thought it perverse for old men to look at me the way a boy my age would. I considered them old men, but they were probably no more than late twenties. They were black men who I felt had no right looking at me that way. I felt free to express my feelings to them.

I didn't understand what was going on with white men. It was common for them to cruise black neighborhoods looking for women for sex. I don't think they were necessarily looking for women who worked as prostitutes. They viewed all black girls and women as available for their use. Being female was scary.

The telephone rang and brought both of us back from the place the mind goes to weigh all options and possible consequences. Since the telephone was located in Miss Ann's room on the far side of the bed, I was afraid to answer it. But I had to. It could have been Miss Ann checking on Missy, who I wished would wake from her nap and call out for me. I never feared for Missy's safety. I thought if she woke, then I would go to her and he would leave. I turned and walked to the bedroom. He followed. I was trapped. My fear was rising as the mercury in a thermometer on a feverish patient. I was imagining what was going on inside of that fat man's head. He stood there leering and assessing.

"They should be here soon," I blurted.

Some time passed--minutes, hours, days--I didn't hear either of us speak, I stood next to the bed waiting. All I could hear was the noise inside that man's head. He changed his mind or his heart, spun around and headed for the front door. As he rushed out, I locked the door and fell back against it to steady myself.

One day Miss Ann decided to visit her parents and her older daughter who lived with them. I drove an hour each way that day glad to get some driving practice on a longer assignment. When I pulled up to the antebellum mansion, its stately appearance was overpowering. At any moment, I expected Prissy to run out of the door saying, "Miss Scarlet, I don't know nuttin' bout' birthin' no babies." The mansion was, of course, on the white side of town, and I had never seen a house of such grandeur except in the movies. Only black people who worked as maids, nannies and gardeners went to that part of town.

Miss Ann gave me a tour of the house. She showed me the upstairs where she lived with her first husband. Her mother had decorated the house beautifully in rich brocades and antiques. There were crystal chandeliers and Persian rugs. Visions of upstairs maids, dressed in starched uniforms fussing with dust bunnies and ruffled curtains, appeared in my head. Miss Ann showed me her older daughter's bedroom room.

When I met the maid, Olivia, I was so caught up in my *Gone with the Wind* fantasy that I was disappointed when she looked and talked nothing like Mammy. She was the one who helped me get the job through some circuitous means. Olivia told a neighbor at church about the job; that person mentioned it to a friend who told my mother. Olivia made a wonderful lunch of chicken salad sandwiches with lettuce and sliced tomatoes, iced tea and apricot tarts. She and I ate in the big, open kitchen.

I didn't set out on a journey to learn the ways of white folks; I just wanted to earn some money for college. However, I came away with the understanding that they were very human. They had more money, which afforded better housing and material goods. They had better access to the American systems, and the American dream was within easier reach for them. Still, they were as flawed and as imperfect as people I already knew.

I looked at my assignment as an adventure. I had no expectations, just the eagerness of a young woman ready to experience. I did come to love gracious living; however, I wanted to be the one on the receiving end and not the one providing it.

Life was interesting from my station that summer. It was never a question as to whether I would spend any more than those three months working as a maid and nanny. Those were certainly honorable professions, but I knew I had a different future and so did Miss Ann.

The choices for black youth after high school were the military, factory, learn a trade or go to college. My parents chose college for me. I accepted their choice. At first, I threatened to enlist in the military because I didn't want to attend Lane College where so many of my relatives had gone. Daddy wanted me to go to Spelman, but he was not financially able to send me there. Neither Mommy nor Daddy listened to my idea about enlisting; therefore, I gave in and settled on Lane College.

I believe Miss Ann wanted to learn something about black people as was evident when she asked about my hair. After skin color, hair was the most visible sign of racial difference. The Civil Rights Movement was making inroads and Negroes were largely an enigma to the white community. They thought of Negroes in terms of stereotypes and as an inferior species.

Black people on television were rare. There was *Amos 'n Andy* in the 1950s, which perpetuated those stereotypes. The original actors in *Amos 'n Andy* were white men with their faces painted black.

Julia starring Diahann Carroll, a young, single, professional woman raising a son, didn't debut until 1968. However, black people were beginning to make appearances on television in a limited way. I remember how excited we would get when someone who looked like us was on television. "A colored person is on TV!" would be the rallying call for all within earshot to come running. We would sit grinning and feeling proud to see ourselves in the person of Sammy Davis, Jr., Leslie Uggams, Pearl Bailey, Nat King Cole, Sam Cook or some other black person who had talent that white people could enjoy and exploit.

I am grateful for the opportunity to have worked for Miss Ann the summer of 1962.

America was on the cusp of great change and it was a good way for me to get to know some of the ways of white folks firsthand. I was familiar with the whites in situation comedies of the 1950s such as *I Love Lucy, Father Knows Best, Ozzie and Harriet, Leave it to Beaver,* and a few others. Those shows, for the most part, presented an idyllic white America, which was foreign to my way of living. I couldn't identify with them, yet I could enjoy watching them as entertainment. The ways they talked, dressed and acted were not part of my experience, but I thought it was a true representation of many white people.

Miss Ann's life was different though, as were the lives of the white people who lived close to us in Fayette County. On our road there were several rental houses grouped together and inhabited by poor white people. They were not as well off as we were.

White people were as varied in their way of being as black people were. There were the very wealthy and the extremely poor in both races, and most people fell somewhere in between.

One thing I appreciated about Miss Ann was that she didn't talk down to me or speak in any manner to demean; however, I cannot say that about some who came around. I became invisible to them as they spoke disparagingly of black people, even using nigger on occasion. Of course, I pretended not to hear. I kept on serving drinks and sandwiches and taking care of other chores. Mommy had already told me that the word nigger did not apply to me and I was never to answer to it. She said, "If a white person calls you nigger, just ignore them and keep on walking." She taught me early the art of ignoring people who were unkind. Young whites hurled that word my way a few times during my youth, but I never looked at them. I always looked straight ahead and kept on walking. It was my mother's way of protecting me. She must have believed as Eleanor Roosevelt who said, "No one can make you feel inferior without your consent."

The fall of 1962 found the world on the brink of disaster with the Cuban Missile Crisis brining us close to nuclear war. Russia was building nuclear bases in Cuba with missiles aimed toward the United States of America. President John F. Kennedy and Soviet Premier Nikita Khrushchev were beating drums and doing their war dance; a black man named James Meredith entered the University of Mississippi on his third attempt; and I was at Lane College in Jackson, Tennessee stumbling through the beginnings of college life.

GLORIOUS GOOD HAIR AND LOVELY LIGHT SKIN

If you are white, you're all right. If you are brown, stick around. If you are black, get back. Author Unknown

O n the day Mommy gave birth to me, she took one look and said, "She's such a pretty little pink girl, but she has nappy hair! What am I going to do? I don't know what to do with this kind of hair."

Mommy had good hair, the kind that didn't kink too much when it was wet and could easily go without straightening if necessary; therefore, she was greatly disappointed that her little girl did not have good hair. Sonny and Charles had good hair, and it didn't seem right to her that her daughter had bad hair.

It didn't take Mommy long to figure out what she needed to do. Before I grew enough hair for her to plait, she was off to cosmetology school gaining the knowledge and skills to give her daughter and other black girls and women good hair. Good thing Mommy had a little girl with kinks because she learned a trade that would be a lifesaver. She had not completed college; therefore, she had no marketable skill. Even after she graduated and became a schoolteacher, Mommy relied on having a few heads to "fix" each week to make ends meet. Fix was how we termed the process as if black women's hair was in a state of disrepair from birth and someone needed to find the remedy for it. That process was long and arduous. As a child, I felt I was sitting for hours while Mommy seemed to carry on a dialogue with my head, occasionally yanking when it didn't stay where she placed it. I was a bobble head with big ears that often got in the way of the hot comb. "Hold your ear, or it will get burned. Those elephant ears are always in the way. And hold still."

If you were one of the fortunate few Americans of African ancestry you had light skin and good hair. Light skin alone was a plus; the good hair just moved you to a higher plane. For a woman with light skin and kinky hair, the hot comb along with some Bergamot, Royal Crown, Hair Rep or Lovers Moon hair oil or grease could create good hair.

The hot comb was made of metal and heated on a cook stove, a hotplate or in a little unit designed for it. It was important to heat the comb to the right temperature. If it were not hot enough, it would not straighten resistant kinky or nappy hair, and if it got too hot, it would burn the hair. Mommy used to test the temperature by wiping the comb on a white cloth. If it were too hot, it would scorch the cloth. She would let it cool a little before using it.

Whether we like to admit it or not, the underlying motive for wanting to eliminate kinks from our hair was to imitate white people and be more acceptable to them--anything to get a pass. Not to cross over the color line and pass for white, as did some light skin blacks in the early part of the twentieth century, but to have easier access to the American institutions. Black people had a better chance of getting into top colleges and universities if they looked more like white people.

College and job applications required you to submit a picture. Light skin blacks were more likely candidates for certain organizations, opportunities and privileges than those with dark skin. They were prone to get jobs that put them out front in the public eye since they were more acceptable to whites. The darker skin brothers and sisters had to be smarter and more talented to compete with them.

When I was nine, I wished I looked like a girl named Charlene who had chocolate brown skin and silky, wavy hair that did not require a hot comb or curling iron. I knew nothing about the politics of skin color and hair texture; I just thought she was pretty. In my teens when I became interested in boys, I was attracted to dark skinned and so were my light-skinned girlfriends. Maybe it was simply a matter of opposites attracting.

Mommy made sure I understood that looks were not as important as who I was and how I presented myself to the world. When someone would say to me, "You're a pretty girl," Mommy would look at me and say, "Pretty is as pretty does." That was a constant refrain during my childhood.

I became intimately acquainted with my hair when I was ten years of age and thus began my love/hate relationship with it. Mommy was in St. Louis that summer, and I was taking care of my own hair. One day I was trying to pull my medium length hair back into a ponytail, but the front was a little too short and kept resisting as I brushed it back. I became impatient and, in a fury, I grabbed Mommy's sewing scissors, which were right next to me on the dresser and whacked it off. Immediately, I knew I had made the wrong decision and trouble threatened like an impending storm.

Come the following Saturday evening, Mama announced that she was taking me to the beauty shop to get my hair washed and pressed. Mommy was coming home soon, and Mama wanted me to look nice for her. I told Mama, "I don't want to get my hair done."

Mama said, "It has to be washed."

"Well, can I wash my bangs?"

"Go ahead."

Mama did not do hair, not even her own. Mommy kept it looking good by shampooing, straightening and putting in a blue rinse sometimes to keep the yellow out of the gray. Mama simply combed and styled her hair each day. At night, she would part off small sections and twirl each around until it made a small ball, and then she would stick in a hairpin to keep it in place. Mama was very particular about her hair and her appearance.

I washed the uneven bangs, gathered some of the longer hair up to join them, twisted and pinned it towards the front. When we got to the beauty shop, and it was my turn to get in the chair, I said to the beautician, "I already washed my bangs. You can just wash the rest."

She called Mama over to the chair, and repeated what I had said. I was sitting quietly, hoping she would honor my request. I just held my breath as Mama reached over and took out the hairpin and revealed my raggedy bangs. Both Mama and the beautician gasped.

"What did you do to your hair?" Mama said, as she stood in front of me looking over her eyeglasses, arms folded across her chest. I knew that stance; she was not happy with me. She could plainly see what I had done, but what could she say. She was mortified.

"I got mad because this hair up front wouldn't go back into my ponytail." I touched the raggedy bangs as I spoke with the assurance that what I had done was supposed to have made matters better. I wanted Mama to empathize with my impatience and my anger. After all, sometimes she got upset with Malcolm and me if we didn't move quickly enough when she gave us a directive. "I didn't mean to mess it up," I continued.

Mama stood there looking at me for the longest time trying not to laugh at the spectacle I had made of myself. The other patrons in the shop stared with mouths agape while a few chuckled, and I felt the blood rush to my cheeks.

The beautician shampooed all of my hair, pressed it and tried to even out the bangs. After she finished, Mama said, "What are you going to say?"

"Thank you?" I asked wondering if Mama had something else in mind, by the way she looked at me.

The patron who was waiting to occupy the chair blurted, "Mo hair. Chile, tell her mo hair."

I looked at Mama wondering if I should repeat it.

Mama said, "Tell her more hair."

"More hair," I offered softly.

The beautician said, "Grow Hair."

When Mommy got home, she already knew what I had done, so she just shook her head in disbelief and told me in a not so gentle tone, "Don't you ever do that again. Your hair looks awful. There is nothing I can do. It'll just have to grow out."

There was another instance when Mommy and I had a disagreement about my hair. I was a freshman at Lane College, and I had taken to coloring my hair with Miss Clairol. The coloring was very harsh and required a good conditioner to prevent breakage. I could not afford a conditioner; therefore, my hair was badly damaged and very short. When I went home for a weekend visit, Mommy took one look at my hair and again I heard, "What have you done to your hair? Why is it so short?"

Mommy wanted me to have long hair. She always sought out potions to make my hair grow. She used smelly Sulphur 8 to help eliminate my dandruff and to promote growth. She would only trim my ends when the moon was in its growth phase because that was supposed to make the hair grow. Mommy knew many myths associated with hair, for example, we burned the hair we cleaned out of the comb and brush or that we cut so the birds would not get it to make their nest. If they got possession of it, that would cause you to have an awful headache. Worse, if a person who didn't like you got possession of it, they could use it to harm you.

While Mommy worked on my hair, she complained, "It's so short I can hardly curl it."

I was tired of her complaining. I said, "Just leave it alone. I will curl it myself." She continued to curl in silence, occasionally yanking my head to place it while she worked.

In the days when the hot comb was the main event, there would sometimes be occasions when we needed a touch-up. The hair around the edges would get wet from bathing or perspiration and would revert to its natural kinky state. The main culprit was the kitchen, which was the short hair at the nape of the neck that would be exposed if a woman wore her hair up in a ponytail, chignon, French roll or some other up do. I could not allow my nappy kitchens to show; therefore, I resorted to a little grease and a hot comb, which quickly remedied the condition.

My most embarrassing moments with my hair happened in front

of white people. The first time was when I was a teen. The Civil Rights Movement had spread to Fayette County, Tennessee. White landowners had evicted black farmers or sharecroppers because they had registered to vote. The farmers and their families moved into tents donated anonymously by a white Somerville merchant. Such blatant race discrimination was taking place that it became national news. White college students from the north came to Fayette County to help with voter registration.

Mommy was contributing to the movement by opening her home to the students for showers and sometimes a meal. There were few homes in the black community with indoor plumbing. Many white homes were without such amenities. There I was having my kinks straightened that Saturday afternoon when some of the students came for showers. I quickly rose and retreated to my room for fear I would reveal the secret of black women's hair.

In the midst of that pivotal moment in history when I was close to getting voting rights and becoming part of the American political process, I was too focused on my nappy hair to appreciate it. No self-loving, good-hair-loving black woman wanted to be seen with nappy hair. From when I was sixteen and continuing, I have undergone the weekly ritual of fixing my hair or having someone else fix it.

The second time a white person caught me with my hair in its natural state was when I was a young mother living in Nashville. Mommy was visiting me and of course, I took advantage of her skills and had her do my hair. My friend and neighbor Ann, a white woman, came to the back door and knocked. I jumped up to flee when I heard her voice, but it was too late. Ann had entered my kitchen, and I was sitting there with hair she could not understand. "My, what is going on?" she asked as if she really needed to know. I didn't want to respond, but Mommy was too happy to explain the whole process and answer all of Ann's questions.

Mommy thought I was being overly sensitive and silly for being embarrassed. However, how could Ann understand? She had not been around many black people before having recently moved to Nashville from a lifetime in Minnesota.

My love/hate relationship with my hair has caused me to try many colors, shampoos, conditioners and chemical processes to make it more manageable and beautiful, or in other words, to give me good hair. I have spent thousands of dollars since the 1960s trying so many products and processes. When I was young, product choices were limited. Actually, products for black hair care were as rare as sanity in the political arena. I bought Breck or Halo shampoo and Tame conditioner. They were for white hair care.

I skipped the afro hairstyle in the 1960s. I couldn't stand the idea of having all of that kinky hair loose on my head. The style was beautiful when done right, and I admired those who wore it well, like Angela Davis. My hair needed to be under control where I could take care of it and keep it clean and neat. Therefore, it took more than fifty years for me to allow my kinks to show. Even then, I could only abide them in small measure.

There were a few times after that when I came close to being without my glory. In the 1960s, it was because of using too much Miss Clairol hair coloring. In the 1970s, it was due to harsh permanent straighteners, and in the 1980s, it was the Jheri curl. I suppose I was determined to have good hair one way or another, or I would go bald trying

Light skin men with not-so-kinky hair could get a close cut or fade and fake it. From the 1920s-1960s, those with serious kinks could get the congolene--conkaline or conk-- a caustic concoction made with lye. It was dangerous and could easily burn the scalp; however, those desperate for good hair would suffer the process. Even Malcolm Little sported the conk during his early years as Detroit Red. The moniker described his red hair and his light skin. Later, he became Malcolm X and returned to his naturally kinky hair.

Black entertainers such as Jackie Wilson, Little Richard, Nat King Cole, Little Anthony, Smokey Robinson and many others conked their hair. I despised that straight hair on black men. Their music was so great, but their appearance was a big turnoff for me as a young girl. Unless it was natural, straight hair did not look like it belonged on black men. I was glad when Sam Cook quit the conk and returned to the natural look.

In the 1960s, the permanent chemical straightener we called "perm" came to deliver black women from the hot comb, and give easy wash and wear styles. Again, lye was used to straighten the hair, but it was a different formulation than the conk. The processed hair remained straight, but new growth needed a touch up about every six weeks to two months. After the chemical straightening process, the hair was set on rollers to give it curl. Now, it is blown dry and styled with an electric curling iron or a flat iron. Most, if not all, relaxers have eliminated lye from their product. Some men such as James Brown and his protégé Rev. Al Sharpton resorted to this process to get good hair.

Many black men shave their heads because they are balding or maybe it is because they are mostly associating with white women. They also eliminate their mustache. My theory is that black men know they can't match their white counterpart's silky hair; therefore, they shave it. Perhaps white women complain about the rough, scratchy feel of their black man's beard, and the hair must go.

The Jheri Curl, created by and named after Jheri Redding, ruled the 1970s-80s. Some insisted on carrying it into the 1990s. Commonly called the Jerry Curl, it eliminated the need for rollers or curling irons by giving a permanent curl, easily maintained with a spray activator. The Jheri curl took advantage of the natural kinks or naps and fashioned them into smooth, shiny curls. Many black men acquired good hair during the Jheri curl era. It was often wet and messy because of the spray activator needed to keep the moisture in and retain the curl. Even though people slept in a plastic cap, many sheets and pillows along with sofas and chairs were soiled and stained with that drippy solution. The Jheri curl juice could also be dangerous. Pop singer Michael Jackson's hair caught on fire from the hot lights while filming a Pepsi Cola commercial. That set him on a path of pain and suffering. Nevertheless, African Americans wore the Jheri Curl for two decades, and there may still be a few around today.

In the 1980s at the height of the Jheri curl era, Malcolm came to visit me flaunting the style. He wore it well. He had a head full of soft beautiful curls with lots of body and movement. I was surprised to see his new look. When I greeted him, I said, "Look at you. You have a Jheri curl," as if he didn't already know it.

Malcolm grinned and said, "Yep, I have wanted good hair all of my life. And I finally got it."

I laughed at the phrase "good hair" because I had refrained from saying it for many years by then. It was common to say about someone with straight or curly hair when we were children, "She has good hair." When a baby was born, folks would check out the hair and skin color. Mothers, aunts and grandmothers would check closely to see if the child was going to have good hair. They would look at the color of the ears to see if the child would have light skin or if it was going to darken as the child grew older. It's not unusual for African American children to have soft straight hair and light skin at birth. Sometimes they have soft curls, which remain, or the curls may become kinks. Grownups crossed their fingers and hoped that the skin would not darken too much, and the hair would not kink.

I looked at my baby brother and remembered the tight kinks he had when we were children. His hair was little naps, each set off from the other. Mommy used to say it looked like "ants on a meat skin." Mommy was always telling him, "Boy, brush your nappy hair." There was no denying it; Malcolm did not have good hair to go along with his light skin. He did not have the kind of hair you could cut close and get the straight look.

I didn't really know how important skin color was when I was young even when it confronted me directly. I shunned being out front and getting attention, but teachers and others often asked me to join organizations and activities. According to my peers, it was because of my look. When I became a majorette in high school, one of my fellow students said, "She chose you because you're light skinned. You're not that good. You don't even know how to march."

There were many terms used to describe the color of light-skinned black people—yellow, red, redbone, fair, light, bright, coffee with cream, white girl, white boy and perhaps a few others. I had a Caucasian girlfriend in adulthood who described my color as beige. Aunt Virginia called me "Red" until I was fifteen and decided I had had enough. My cousins and I were driving through a neighborhood in Somerville in the late 1980s where many black men were hanging out, and as we passed by them, they yelled, "High *yellas*!"

Some people were called by nicknames that used the word black if their skin was very dark such as Black Willie, Shine, Blackie, or Blue if their skin was so black that it looked blue.

Vera, one of my classmates, saw fit to identify me by skin color linked with an ugly term. One day I was a yellow bitch, and on another day, I was a red bitch.

She had a dark complexion and beautiful black hair that she wore in a short cut. She and I became friends after she realized I was not interested in her big yellow boyfriend Ronald. Several of my classmates and friends -- Vera, Andrew, Ella and A.J.--used to play the Dozens and talk about each other's black skin, engaging in name-calling and having fun. Playing the Dozens was a favorite pastime of some. It was a game where insults would pass between people and each would try to outdo the other. It was humorous, creative and done in a spirit of fun.

It was routine for young people to call one another "black," sometimes in play and other times to hurt. They would use "black" to introduce any number of offensive terms as if the word black compounded the effects of that term. Black did not become beautiful until 1968 when soul singer James Brown recorded, "Say It Loud—I'm Black and I'm Proud." We decided to embrace our blackness after being brainwashed for years believing that black was evil and ugly.

People used the term black in negative ways so often that we did not like being associated with it. Only in a few important ways was black a positive word. Most every woman either has or wants black lingerie and an LBD, a little black dress. "In the black" and "Black Friday" are used when referring to finances. Black Friday started in a negative way because the police in Philadelphia used it to refer to the traffic congestion on the Friday and Saturday after Thanksgiving;

however, its meaning became positive because those were and still are the biggest shopping days of the year. Merchants gain, and the economy is stimulated. The aim of business and financial institutions is to be in the black as opposed to being in the red.

Bishop, a classmate who was closer to his white roots than most of us, showed me around Lester High when I entered as a junior, and we became friends. When Mommy met him, she immediately chose him as a prototype of the man I should marry. He was smart, polite, funny and very charming, but Mommy only saw his light skin and good hair. She had visions of the little paleface grandbabies we would make, and she would parade around for all of her friends to see. Mommy did not hide the fact that she wanted me to marry an educated man with light skin. To her, that would be my ticket to a better lifestyle. Yes, Mommy was color struck, and it was no secret.

Daddy had dark skin, beautiful wavy hair courtesy of Royal Crown hairdressing for men. Daddy mixed it with water and slicked his hair back with a fine tooth, skinny barber comb. Daddy was dark and handsome, and if ever I were to marry, he too would be dark. Moreover, we would make little brown babies. I made a conscious decision, but whether it was in response to Mommy's preference or just because I was crazy about Daddy, I do not know.

Women such as Lena Horne, Dorothy Dandridge and Josephine Baker set the standard of beauty for black women. They were light-skinned women who wore their hair in the same styles as white women. Their look was very close to that of white women; therefore, people saw them as beautiful.

I think what drove Mommy and others of her generation to go towards the light skin, was subconscious, born out of past conditioning during slavery and beyond. However, it had become conscious, and it proved to be detrimental to the self-image and self-esteem of generations of black children.

Historically, they used skin color and hair texture to divide and conquer black people. There were two kinds of slaves, the house slaves and the field slaves. Those in the master's house had privilege. They were shielded from the heat of summer and the cold of winter.

They wore better clothing and ate better food than those in the field. Some house slaves were a lighter complexion, and they had different hair texture. They were often the product of miscegenation. That was the term used to describe sexual relations between master and slave that produced offspring. Privilege became associated with light skin and good hair.

In the early part of the twentieth century, upper class black people had the "brown paper bag test" to determine if a person's skin was light enough to gain admittance to certain soirées and organizations. The person's skin had to be lighter than a brown paper bag. It was a crude and cruel practice, but the brainwash was great, and some black people wanted to lighten the race. They did not want to mix with dark-skinned blacks. White brainwash was and is still pervasive, and colorism as the practice is called was a reality for African Americans.

Sonny, Malcolm, Jack, Melvin and Freddy were popular with the girls because they had light skin. I do not know how conscious they were of color, but others thought their light skin made them good looking. This led to jealousy and envy, and it may have given them an inflated sense of self, solely based on skin color.

When I was fifteen, I spent a few days with my paternal grandparents, Big Mama and Big Daddy. Big Mama called several of her friends and told them that I was visiting. One day, I heard her talking on the telephone to one of them, "My granddaughter is visiting," she said proudly. The woman must have asked her, which granddaughter, because Big Mama said, "It's the pretty one the light skinned one, Clinton's daughter."

In 1969 when I was a student at Tennessee State, there was an incident that illustrates the power of light skin on the black psyche. A woman and a little girl came into my American Literature class; some mumbled comments such as, "She's pretty." "She's so beautiful." "How cute." My professor said to me later that the class was really noticing the child's color and not her features. I had to agree because the child was not beautiful; she was just "light, bright and damn near white." In addition, she had very long, almost blond hair.

I didn't think much about skin color when I was young because

I was too busy fighting the losing battle with my nappy hair. I too wanted good hair. Many of us black women missed fun times because of our hair. We couldn't swim, wouldn't participate in sports, and why? Because before we had chemical straighteners, our hair when wet would revert to its natural kink, and it would become unmanageable. We didn't want to sweat or to get our hair wet in public.

When I was in my fifties and tired of being a slave to the chemicals I had used for so long, I started thinking about how unfair it all was when it came to men and women and hair. I felt a little envious of men so I decided to do something about it. I went to a neighborhood barbershop, walked to the nearest barber, and said, "Cut it off. I want it off." It was not as easy as it sounds. It took a few years for me to gather the courage to shed my glory. The Bible writer Paul said, "A woman's hair is her glory." I thought, to hell with glory. I want freedom. Not that I thought of my hair as glorious; however, it was sufficient, and had adorned me for over fifty years

Sigmund Freud came up with the inane notion that women suffer penis envy. Not! What I and many women envy is that men can shower every morning without wearing a cap. They can walk in the rain without worrying about their "do" going back. Men can roll around in bed, get up and answer the doorbell without reaching for the comb, and the visitor is none the wiser. Men can spend a short time at the barbershop, pay a few dollars and leave looking handsome and feeling lighter. Men can exercise or play their favorite sport then shower, shampoo and be on their way in a third of the time women would take. Men do not need flat irons, curling irons, blow dryers, hot combs, perms, straighteners, gels, mousses, conditioners, coloring and on and on. Of course, some men envy women.

"Cut it off," I repeated.

"Ma'am, are you sure you want it that short?"

"Yes."

I sat in the barber chair and watched my hair fall to the floor in colorful straight strands and nappy clumps. Knowing that there was no turning back, I closed my eyes and waited. I had told the barber to take it down close to the scalp but leave a couple of inches on top. After he finished, I stood straighter and taller. I felt lighter. I gained a sense of freedom that was tremendously empowering. All that chemical straightener, color and naps lay on the floor. I wondered why I had ever bothered with the chemicals in the first place. My natural kinks on top looked beautiful. The little hair that remained on the sides and in the back lay straight. I was amazed that I had naturally what I had been buying all those years. Sure, I had a little gray showing, but at fifty plus, I was okay with that. I gave the barber $10.00 including the tip, and I was on my way.

As soon as I stepped out of the shop, people noticed, and I felt proud and okay with the attention. Somehow, I felt more connected to my roots. I was proud to let Africa be my testament to the world. One young man turned as I passed and said, "Sister, you sure do look good. I like your hair."

I liked when people asked, "Why did you cut off your hair?"

I said I'm tired of chemical straighteners and coloring. I am tired of spending so much time and money on my hair. I like to exercise and play tennis, I like to shampoo often, but when blow drying and curling is part of the process, it becomes tedious, drudgery. I hate it. What I really wanted to say was I cut my hair because I envy men. I want freedom. Besides, I have always wanted good hair.

I visited Mommy in the hospital in Memphis shortly after I got that haircut. My son was with me. When we entered Mommy's room, she looked up at me and frowned. "What did you do to your hair?" She then turned to her grandson and asked, "Why did you let your mother cut off all of her hair?"

When I cut my hair short, there were times when I wanted it long. I often resorted to wigs to get the look I wanted at a particular time. I relied on wigs to get me through difficult periods such as when I had damaged my hair and it needed a good long rest. I never felt a need to pass off a wig as my own hair. For some reason whenever someone said, "I like your hair. That style is so becoming on you," I always smiled and said, "It's a wig."

I have preferred short cuts for most of my life. I have only had a close cut maybe six times. I have let it grow to neck and shoulder length a few times. I do not know what it is about my hair that caused me to want to put it through so many changes all these years I have been in charge of it, but I am constantly trying new products, styles, cuts, processes. I have had it twisted, cornrowed, put up in fancy braids and formal up-dos.

When I was getting ready to travel to Ghana, West Africa in 2002, I went to get my hair braided by a woman from Senegal. It took hours, but she gave me a fancy African style designed to free me from my hair struggles while traveling. There were several African women in the shop that day just talking with familiarity. One woman's husband came in and more talk about Senegal ensued. Somehow, the topic turned to skin color, and the man said, "I hate to see my African sisters bleaching their skin. It is so ugly. They have this beautiful black skin and they try to lighten it to look like European women."

I sat there stunned wondering if I should join the conversation uninvited. Could it really be true or why would he be saying it? I interrupted, "African women bleaching their skin?"

"That's right, so many of them are doing it. It just makes their skin look rough and unnatural. I don't like it."

I and other African American women had used bleach cream, but not to change our skin color, not to make our faces white. We used it on our knees and elbows to make to lighten that skin. We used it to lighten dark spots that remained after bursting a pimple.

Even though I had heard the young man in the braid shop lament the actions of his sisters disdain for their own skin color, I was unprepared for the billboards in Ghana that showed African women advertising bleach cream. I could not understand it. Did they reason that lightening their skin would be the magic trick that would get them a better life? What about their features? What about their kinky hair? Some did use chemical relaxers on their hair. The brainwash was great. "If you are white, you're all right. If you are brown, stick around. If you're black, get back!" These billboards of African women with bleach cream were juxtaposed with billboards of white Jesus, with long blond hair, showing the way to salvation.

I had thought African men and women had a certain pride associated with being part of a nation, connected to a land base. They were Nigerian, Ghanaian, Ashanti and so many more nations. Many African Americans felt homeless in a sense. There was no land to call ours; therefore, we attached ourselves to Africa, the land of our ancestors and felt a sense of pride associated with it.

The ubiquitous white Jesus has done more to destroy the esteem of Africans and African Americans than any other. When I saw white Jesus on those billboards, I understood why Africa was so undeveloped. The African learned to look for future blessings in another life, "pie in the sky" as Reverend Ike (Frederick Joseph Eikerenkoetter II) used to say. They are not encouraged and empowered to make this life the best it can be. Someone taught them to look for a savior to rescue them out of their misery. That savior has a white face.

I will admit the brainwash is insidious, often subliminal, yet powerful and difficult to escape unscathed. The people who hold the power set the standards for beauty and all else. In America, we have come a long way in our development as black people. We have come to accept that black is beautiful, or have we. When I turn on the news, watch a movie or a television show with African American women, I cannot help but notice the skin color and the hair, or should I say the weave that at first notice makes them look white?

Black women have made wealthy many Asians and others who have built thriving businesses on supplying good hair and hair care products. The weave has been around for many years dating back to ancient Egypt; however, it has become extremely popular in recent years with entertainers, professional women, students and all. Black women want good hair, and that often means long, straight hair that could not have come from their own scalps. So, grow it Indians. Bring it Asians. We black women will buy it.

What I like about hair is there are so many choices. We can wear our hair in many different styles, colors and lengths. We can wear wigs, weaves, braids, cornrows, afros and close cuts. We, black women can choose to have good hair in so many different ways or we can choose to have no hair at all.

It is the twenty-first century, and I am hearing that young black people still have problems around skin color. They still use terms like "good hair" and "fair skinned." There is often jealousy, envy and discrimination based on color. When will it end? When will we begin to see past the color of a person's skin and realize that color does not define who we are? It is at best a superficial way of identifying individuals and nothing more. I am not suggesting that we become a colorblind society. A person's ethnic group or upbringing is important to who they are. Color is not. However, just as the determination to have good hair continues for black women, so will the politics of skin color.

SCHOOL DAZE

I have never let my schooling interfere with my education.-
-Mark Twain

I hated school. I detested the smell. I despised know-it-all, know-nothing teachers. I disliked being in lines, teacher's pets, cafeteria workers and school food. I loathed principals who walked the halls barking orders as if they had real power. I abhorred leering male teachers. I found confinement stifling. Yet, my parents required me to attend school. Education was important to them. They saw it as the only way to improve our standards and improve the race. Unlike, my friends and even my brothers, I attended several schools in as many cities.

Fayette County Training School

Education for black students had a slow beginning in Fayette County. They started the first school for white students in 1826 while black people were still enslaved. It wasn't until 1873 that Fayette County included black children in education. In 1907, there were 68 schools and 74 teachers for black students. They were one and two-room schools scattered throughout the county for students in grades 1-8. There were many because the Board of Education did not want to provide busses for black children. Children had to walk to their neighborhood school. For some, the walk was long.

They organized the first black high school, Jones Hall, in 1912. It held classes in the old Masonic Hall in Somerville and Mt. Zion Baptist Church.

Prior to 1937, there were five, two-year high schools for white students in Fayette County. There was only one for black students. By 1937, they closed all five of the county high schools that served white students. White students were then bussed to Somerville to their beautiful new Fayette County High School.

In 1928, Fayette County Training School for black students became a four-year school. W.P. Ware was its first principal. In the 1940s, the county built a two-story brick building on ten acres of land south of Somerville. The initial frame structure was built with money and labor donated by local citizens and with funds from the Julius T. Rosenwald Fund. Rosenwald, part owner of Sears, Roebuck and Company in 1895, was interested in social issues and in educating black children. The Rosenwald Fund donated money to build many schools for black children in the rural south. The schools became known as Rosenwald Schools. (Tennessee County History Series: Fayette County, by Dorothy Rich Morton; Charles W. Crawford, editor; Memphis State Press, 1989)

By the time I started first grade in the summer of 1949, there were still many community schools; however, I attended Fayette County Training School. I don't remember my teacher, classmates or even learning to read. Sonny, Charles and I got on the yellow school bus each day and off we went. I know that much because when I was four and didn't go to school, I would run after my brothers crying and screaming, "I *wanna* go!" as they walked up the driveway to the road to catch the bus.

I was five years of age when I entered school that summer. FCTS taught grades one through eight in one building and the other building contained grades 9-12. It was the main school for colored students in Fayette County. All secondary black students in Fayette County attended that high school.

It must have been during first grade that I sat too close to the wood burning stove and my teacher had a fit. She tried to get me to move away for fear I would burn to a crisp. I was very hot, but for some unknown reason, I would not move. After a few minutes and lots of pleading, the teacher sent for my big brother to come and intercede. Sonny tried to talk me into moving. It is a wonder he didn't just snatch me up and move me. I guess he didn't want to do that in front of the teacher. After a while, I did move, but it was on my own terms. My teacher thought I didn't have sense enough to know when to move. I didn't like that. I watched her squirm, fearful that if I were burned she would be in trouble. Mommy said I was born with a stubborn streak. I really should have moved sooner.

Cobb Elementary School

When I was seven and had already started second grade at FCTS, Daddy decided that I should live with him. Daddy had gotten a job teaching social studies and coaching girls' basketball at Burt High School in Clarksville, Tennessee. He was also going to be an assistant football coach. He would be busy, but he and Mommy thought Burt was a much better school and that Sonny, Charles and I should be with him. Malcolm was only five; he stayed with Mommy.

Miss Allison, a petite woman who wore glasses and a bun that made her look like the old maid of the card game, was my teacher. She liked Daddy, but she didn't like me. The feeling was mutual. When she hit me in the palm of my hand with a ruler for some infraction, I returned the hit. Her already big eyes bulged more; she caught her breath in her throat and became speechless. I guess that was a first for her, too. She told Daddy. When he asked, "Why did you hit Miss Allison?"

I said, "I hit her because she hit me."

Actually, she startled me. I guess my first grade teacher never hit me. It was a natural reflex action for me to hit back. Daddy didn't question me or say anything because he had a short temper, and he understood.

I learned to tell time during second grade. A neighbor who lived across the street from us and used to look in on me when Daddy was away gave me a Cinderella watch for my seventh birthday. It was a real watch complete with the glass slipper. Actually, it was clear plastic. I was so happy to get it even though I couldn't tell time. There were no digital timepieces then; therefore, we had to learn to tell time the old-fashioned way. I asked Charles to teach me. He took a few minutes and taught me how to count the dots between each number to determine the minutes before or after the hour.

In third grade, I had a classmate whose mother had recently died. Sometimes she would see her mother in the classroom. On one occasion, Marie wanted Linda and me to see her. We went to the back of the classroom near the storage closet. Marie said, "See her. Look at my mother."

"Where," we chimed in unison.

She said, "Right there" as she pointed toward the closet door. We turned to look in that direction, but couldn't see anyone.

"She has on red lipstick, and she's wearing a long white dress." Marie said as if we needed a description. We strained and tried hard to see her, but we could not. After a few more tries, Marie gave up.

Early in life, I valued friendship. I liked having one or two girlfriends at a time. I didn't care for large groups. Being more introverted, I wasn't much of a joiner, but Daddy wanted me to get involved in activities. He wanted me to be a majorette. There were around ten or twelve little girls who performed at basketball and football games, and marched in parades. We wore gold blouses and black skirts with gold trim around them. We also wore gold Mary Jane shoes and black socks.

I joined the Brownie scouts at Daddy's insistence. We did crafts; I made a little leather wallet. Daddy showed his pride by giving me some money to put in it. I didn't get an allowance; therefore, I was happy to get some money whenever Daddy gave it to me. I remember a Brownie Christmas party where we brought our own lunch. Daddy had made a potted meat sandwich for. The meat came in a tin can. He mixed the mystery meat with mayonnaise and sweet pickle relish and spread it on white bread with the crusts trimmed off. The teacher gave us oranges and peppermint sticks. That made for a tasty treat when I stuck the peppermint into the orange to suck the juice.

Mrs. Walton made third grade interesting and fun. I was a good student. I learned cursive writing that year. The highlight for me was when Mrs. Walton chose me to dance during the end of school program. Each class participated. My partner was a boy whose last name was Fisher. Mrs. Walton's teenage daughter taught us a creative dance. He wore a tuxedo; I wore a short lavender organza dress trimmed in gold foil ribbon that smelled like castor oil. The dance was a big hit. Fisher and I looked like miniature adults, and we must have danced like professionals. We entered the stage from opposite sides in a very dramatic way. When he lifted me and spun me around, the audience applauded. Daddy grinned with pride afterwards, "Baby, I didn't know you could dance like that." I could have said, "I didn't either."

Though I was shy, when it was time to perform, I always did well. I had the ability to tune out everyone and everything and be present with what I was doing. I think my partner was shy also. Maybe that's why Mrs. Walton chose us. We were stars for a while. Our class had two other dance numbers. One group danced to "Sentimental Journey" and the other to "Louisiana Hayride." Our song was "The Tennessee Waltz."

I was in third grade when Daddy gave me my first whipping. It was picture day, and I don't know why, but I had an aversion to being photographed. I would do anything to dodge the camera. Before it was time for my class to take pictures, I escaped from the line and went home. Shortly after I arrived home, I heard Daddy open the door calling, "Barbara Jean, where are you?"

In a short time he had me by one hand, and flailed me with his belt with the other. "You must not ever leave school again. Do you understand me? Why did you leave?"

Through snot, tears and sniffles, I said, "cause I didn't want to take a picture."

Living with Daddy was an adventure. When we first went to Clarksville, we had a housekeeper. She didn't last. Daddy was not a good money manager. He was too free-spirited and impractical, the kind of person who didn't like to give much thought to plan except when it came to his work.

Women liked Daddy. I would say that he was a ladies man because he had female friends and lovers, and he was a good daddy for me. I consider myself a daddy's girl for sure. I did not vie for that title; it just came naturally. Being the only girl must have helped.

My brothers and I often had to fend for ourselves, cooking our own meals and caring for our needs. Charles was third grade and Sonny was sixth grade when we went to Clarksville. As big brother, Sonny was in charge when Daddy was coaching after school. Daddy wanted to do what was best for us, but he could have used some help. It must have been an overwhelming responsibility for him. It was more than disconcerting to go to the faucet for a glass of water and find that there was none. Or, to flip the light switch and darkness remained. Daddy often forgot to pay the bills or he had no money to pay. That was no fun, but I was too young at first for it to become an issue.

In the fourth grade, I had Miss S, a lazy teacher who ate all the time and didn't do much teaching. Thank God, Mommy taught me most of the fourth grade or all of Mrs. Walton's work would have been for nothing. How I got back to Somerville and to Mommy in fourth grade was exciting. What a trip!

Mommy and Malcolm came to visit one weekend as happened on occasion. When they left that Sunday, I threw a fit. I did not want Mommy to leave. When she drove away, I ran behind the car crying, screaming and yelling, "Take me with you. I want to go home with you Mommy!" She drove away with tears in her eyes. I quickly dried mine. I didn't want to leave Daddy even though life with him was still challenging for a nine year old. I enjoyed the freedom I had with Daddy, but with Mommy, there was more stability and structure. And even though I ate very little, I liked having regular meals.

The following Sunday Mommy came back with Brother. Daddy was not at home. Mommy instructed Charles and Sonny to help me get my clothes together. She kept an eye out for Daddy as we gathered my things and hurried out the front door before he returned. I don't know why Mommy felt the need to kidnap me. Both she and Daddy had agreed for me to live there in the first place; therefore, they could have discussed it.

I was happy to be with Mommy and Malcolm, so off I went. I thought Daddy would miss me, but I knew my brothers were probably happy for me to leave because they would no longer have to stay with me when Daddy was away. Sometimes I was home alone, which didn't seem to be a big deal then. Most of the time we didn't lock the doors and no one feared for their safety.

Mt. Lebanon Elementary School

Fourth and fifth grades with Mommy went well. Mommy was the only teacher at Mt. Lebanon Elementary School with grades 1-8. One, two or three room schools were common in rural areas serving black folks until the 1960s when districts began to consolidate them. Mt. Lebanon was a small primitive space with plank floors that we--teacher and students--kept dust free with a mixture of sawdust and oil. We would spread the mixture down before we swept the floors. In wintertime students gathered wood to keep a fire going in the stove. Students cleaned the outdoor toilets, as there was no custodian. Students were eager to help in all areas. Mommy made curtains for the windows and arranged the room in the best way so each grade could have their own space. She taught as many as eight grades at one time. There were only a few students in each grade, sometimes only one. Older, smart students often helped with the younger ones. Somehow, learning took place in that environment. Mommy had skills when it came to teaching.

Since the county did not provide buses for black elementary students in that part of the county, Mommy used her 1953 Ford truck to pick up many of the students whose houses she passed on her way to school. She had a cab put over the truck bed and put in seating. There was a bench on each side and one down the middle. Each morning, Mommy would pick up the children from several families and drop them off at their homes in the afternoon.

Mommy taught all subjects plus manners, values, and personal grooming. There was a song, scripture, prayer and Pledge of Allegiance to the Flag each morning. We called it "Devotion." Fourth grade was when I became very interested in my personal hygiene and how I looked each day. Mommy made a chart with everyone's name on it and hung it on the wall for all to see. Each day we would get a gold, blue, or red star according to how well groomed we were. Gold was the highest. My best friend Clementine and I always tried to earn gold. I would prepare my clothes and polish my black and white Saddle Oxfords at night. I would rise early each morning, bathe and dress neatly. Mommy combed my hair. Most days I would get a gold star.

Sometimes Mommy would bring treats for the students such as homemade soup or hot chocolate with marshmallows. She would prepare them on the stove. We got drinking water from a pump outside. A student would move the pump handle up and down several times to bring water up from the ground and collect in a tin bucket each morning and as needed. We used a dipper to pour water into each student's cup.

Field Day at Mt. Lebanon was an exciting time for students, parents and people in the community. It was a day of fun, games and good food. I can close my eyes and see, smell and taste the hot dogs on steamed buns with coleslaw. Some of the men in the community would dig a pit in the ground and barbecue a whole hog. They would stay up all night barbecuing and socializing with one another. The next day, the meat would be so tender they could pull it right off the bones. There were home-baked cakes and pies and everyone's favorite, homemade ice cream hand cranked on the school grounds. For just a few cents, we could buy a sandwich, cold drink and dessert.

Women from the community would bring handmade quilts and embroidered items they were proud to display. There would also be home-canned fruits, jellies and vegetables submitted for judging and prizes.

Every school had a Field Day. They would invite one or two other schools to compete in games like sack races, foot races, horseshoe and softball. It was a full day of fun. It took place in May when the weather was warm. Teachers and students would prepare for their visitors by cleaning the school grounds and whitewashing the bottom of the trees and toilets. Toilets were outhouses built over a hole in the ground. They had a raised seat built over the hole. Of course, they were not heated, and it was not a good place to be in the wintertime. There was a lid to close off the stench after use. It was not pleasant, but most black people in the country during that time had outdoor toilets and running water.

Besides church, school was the place where the community could go for a good time. Schools often had Socials, events centered on a theme where the community would pay a small fee to attend. When I was fifth grade, Aunt Penny took me to a social at Alexander Elementary School where she taught. It was a "Heaven and Hell Social." You could choose to go to heaven and eat ice cream, or go to hell and have spaghetti. It was all good clean fun; people enjoyed the opportunity to meet and socialize with their neighbors. I bought a ticket to hell so I could eat spaghetti, which I seldom had at home. I met a boy named A.D. Neal who must have also liked spaghetti. It seemed the grownups went to heaven and most of the youngsters went to hell. A.D. and I met again during our teens when he worked at the Fair Theater, collecting tickets from the black patrons.

When I was sixteen, Mommy allowed A.D. to come for Sunday visits. Since his sisters were Mommy's clients, she thought he was okay. Boys used to visit girls in their homes on Sundays. As far as I knew, there were no places to go on a date in Fayette County other than the movie. Parents were often overprotective of their daughters and thought they could keep a closer watch on them if they allowed them to have company at home. They called it courting or having company. Mommy had not bought living room furniture for her new house because she could not afford what she wanted; therefore, we had to sit in dining room chairs during the visits.

A Cakewalk was another community favorite. It started during slavery as a form of entertainment and continued into the 1950's with some tweaks. A cakewalk was like musical chairs where you strutted or walked with style in a circle as the music played. If you were in a certain spot when the music stopped, you would win. The prize was either a cake or a pie. Mommy had a cakewalk when she taught at Seymour School. The mother of one of her students had brought a pecan pie. I won it. We had never had pecan pie before. It was so delicious that Mommy got the recipe, and from that time throughout many years, she made those wonderful pecan pies.

Morrow's Grove Elementary School

When I was fifth grade, we moved to Morrows Grove School. They were starting to consolidate outlying one-room schools. Morrow's Grove had three rooms, three teachers. I was glad Mommy taught fifth grade because she would continue as my teacher.

Near the end of the school year, teachers presented programs so the students could perform for their parents and the community.

The community supported those events. There was very good parent involvement. The parents were concerned about their children's academic progress and their behavior. On Mommy's program that year, I acted in a play as a sassy character from Chicago. While my performance had been rather lackluster during practice, the night of the program I brought it. Mommy was especially pleased and relieved that I did not embarrass her. I also sang with a group of girls.

I received my worst whippings when I was fifth grade. One morning I was in charge of devotion. Mommy was going to say the prayer that day and for some reason unknown to me, she said, "Call me Mrs. Gray" as I asked for the prayer. I seldom had to call my mother anything while in school because I knew how to take direction and how to do the work. Therefore, when she said that, I became tongue-tied and nothing would come out. I thought *"Mrs. Gray."* It didn't sound natural in my mind. It wouldn't come out. I knew the boy whose mother taught there addressed her, as Mrs. I didn't care about that; she was Mommy to me at home and everywhere. I was not going to call her anything else.

Mrs. Gray whispered, "I'll get you when we get home." I thought she might forget about it during the day; nevertheless, I wanted that school day to go on forever. It flew by. When we got home, Mommy kept her promise. That was the only time I ever ran from her. I ran through the house out the front door and around the house into the back door a few times and all the while calling Mama, Papa, Brother, Aunt Penny and Malcolm. Mommy was right behind me all the way. I wanted someone to save me. It was as though everyone knew a tornado was coming and had evacuated the area. Obedience was required in those days, or you had to pay the price. I knew the deal.

I got into a near fight with a fifth grade classmate. All I remember is Sherry hitting at me in classic girl style and me holding out my hands to block. I had probably said something she didn't like.

My fighting history was odd. I had only had a few fights with Malcolm. Those fights were not serious. Malcolm and I would be friends again shortly after one of us passed the last lick. Sometimes it was important for me to have the last lick and other times for him. I don't know what instigated the quasi-fight

Fayette County Training School

I went back to FCTS, where I had spent first grade, for sixth and seventh grades. Mrs. Mayes and Mr. Bonds were my teachers. I liked starched and pristine Mrs. Mayes. She was a good teacher who also tried to help us become proper ladies. That was the first year of the "becoming young ladies talks" that I dreaded. There was more involved in teaching black children in those days than mere subject matter. Learning was fun and schoolwork was easy for me. I was carrying over my habits from fifth grade. Both teachers were strict. Mr. Bonds was an extremely tough teacher and principal. I didn't like him at all. When he hit me in the palm of my hand for missing a math problem, I thought I would hold it against him for the rest of my life. I didn't hold it against him, but he may have been the reason I never liked math.

What I liked about going to school in Fayette County was being out of school in the fall and going to the Fair. FCTS used to have what they called split-sessions where they would start school in hot July and get out of school to pick cotton in the fall. White and black farmers needed laborers. After cotton-picking season ended in November, the school year would resume. White schools did not operate on that schedule.

The Tri-State Fair took place around the end of September into October each year beginning in 1856. It started as the Mid-South Fair and changed its name to Tri-State Fair in 1908. In 1929, the fair changed its name back to Mid-South Fair. The Shelby County Agricultural Society, formed in 1854, started the fair to promote the interest of farmers and businessmen in the area. The fair was for white people. They didn't integrate it until 1962.

Since it's no fun knowing that others are enjoying such festivities and not being allowed to participate, black people started the Negro

Tri-State Fair in 1911. It operated until 1959. I went from fourth through seventh grades. It was great fun; I would enjoy staying all day and into the night riding the Ferris wheel, Caterpillar and Grand Carousel merry-go-round. I was fearful of riding the Zippin Pippin roller coaster. The smell of corn dogs and popcorn lured me, and I couldn't leave without a candy apples. There were exhibits of all sorts--agricultural, baked and canned foods, quilts, livestock shows, music and contests. The black fair was located in the same place as the white fair and used some of the same exhibits.

After 1969, FCTS operated on two campuses under the name Fayette-Ware Comprehensive High School. In 1984, the county constructed a new facility next to the Comprehensive Vocational School two miles north of Somerville on Highway 59.

Burt High School

Mommy wanted me to have a better life than she had. She wanted me to go to a city school where I would get a better education. Therefore, I went back to live with Daddy in eighth and ninth grades. By then, I had no real interest in school. Yet, I did okay in all but math. I was on the school drill team and marched at football games and in parades.

I had an incident with my math teacher that year. I didn't hit him. I wouldn't attempt to do my work one day, and he summoned Daddy from his classroom to come and talk to me. Daddy didn't chastise me as Mr. Q would have liked.

I didn't like much about life when I was a young teen. I liked boys but was too young to date. The only thing I looked forward to was watching Dick Clark's "American Bandstand" and going to an occasional Sock Hop. We called it a sock hop because we danced in our socks on the gym floor. I liked trying out the steps I had learned from Bandstand. I danced with boys and girls. Boys were often shy and clumsy on the dance floor leaving girls to dance with one another. I danced with girls through tenth grade. After that, I only danced with boys.

I loved science classes from eighth through twelfth grades. Each science teacher was knowledgeable and made the class interesting. I suppose I could have liked all subjects if I had had teachers who made learning interesting.

I got my last whipping from Daddy the night Wilma Rudolph graduated. Again, I was escaping from an unbearable situation. I had found a seat on the end of the bleachers not too high up so I could easily slip off and leave when I became bored. I was fond of Wilma, but I did not want to be at her graduation. Someone must have seen me drop from the bleacher onto the floor and tip out.

Evidently, Daddy left immediately after I did. When I heard him coming, I ran to the basement, which wasn't much more than a crawl space under the house. I bumped into old discards and walked into spider webs trying to find a hiding place. I was scared in that moldy cellar but, I knew I was in trouble; I must have flashed back to third grade and panicked. I came out.

Again, Daddy pulled the brown belt from his charcoal grey slacks and gave me a few whacks. I cried as if he were killing me or about to, not because it hurt but because my daddy, my ebony-colored, natty-dressing, woman-loving, daughter-loving-daddy was making me feel like an ordinary disobedient child who insisted on doing her own thing because she thought she had the right.

Daddy was afraid for me. He wanted to protect me, to see me graduate and go to college. Then into life, as though it were a door you entered after college, and not as you exited the womb and started on this wondrous journey, learning the foundation of everything you would ever need to know. I was living, learning, stumbling, running into roadblocks and trying to dodge the wrath of adults.

In a letter to Mommy the summer of 1959, Daddy wrote, "I would like for Bar to go to school in Memphis and stay with my mother. I will see Mother about it. She will have to do as Mother wants her to do. I would like you to be on Mother's side most of the time. I don't want Bar to come up with a baby."

Mommy and Daddy had a discussion, about me growing up and needing a woman's care. I was fifteen and both had fears that I would become pregnant and bring shame on them and a difficult life for us all. That was the furthest thing from my mind, but since they didn't trust me, they decided that I should go to Memphis to live with Big Mama, as if she could have kept up with me. Mommy believed I would get a better education in Memphis than I would in Somerville. Being teachers, both knew that schools for black children were inferior to white schools and that schools in the country were inferior to those in the city.

Off to Memphis I went, however, I could not enroll in any school because I had two able-bodied parents living somewhere else. Big Mama and Big Daddy were not my legal guardians. I was not heartbroken. Neither Mommy nor Daddy considered that their little girl couldn't care less about getting a quality education. She could read, write, observe others, and learn all she needed to know

Big Mama's House

Big Mama put her heart and might into her efforts to get me into Memphis City Schools. She took me from one school to another on the city bus. When that failed, she took me to a catholic school. All of her efforts were in vain.

While I was at Big Mama's house, I met Martin who lived down the street. He invited me to his Back to School Lawn Party. That would be my first party, and I was excited. I didn't like the idea of being a stranger and not knowing anyone there; however, I wanted to dance. I had known Big Mama all my life and had visited with some regularity throughout the years, but I had never stayed with her without Daddy being there. Big Mama and I were okay, but we were not friends. She and Anita were tight. I was apprehensive as I approached Big Mama. I tried to keep my expectations in check.

"Big Mama, may I go to the party at Martin's house? He's the boy who lives down the street." She knew him because he always spoke to her when she was on the front porch where she liked to sit in her glider on nice weather days.

"I don't know if your daddy would want you to go to a party."

I stood there with my fingers crossed behind my back, holding my breath and trying not to say anything more. Big Mama was folding the whitest sheets I had ever seen and mulling over what my daddy might think if he found out I was at a party with a boy. She paused from her work and stared out into the eternal distance, as if that was the place she went for council. I hoped the gods were on my side that day.

"Well, I guess I'll let you go for a little while, but don't you get into any trouble."

I walked down the street in daylight that Saturday evening. Martin greeted me with a smile, grabbed my hand, and led me to the dance area. I was having so much fun doing the Stroll to "I Hear You Knocking" by Fats Domino, bopping to "A Lover's Question" by the Platters, "Yakety Yak" by the Coasters and "What'd I Say" by Ray Charles. Just as I was settling into Martin's arms for a slow dance to "Tears on My Pillow," I heard, "Barbara. Barbara Jean." I jerked my head toward the ancient voice, and there stood Big Mama in hair rollers, housedress, and house shoes. I backed away from Martin as I mumbled without pause, "I'm sorry excuse me I have to go." I did not thank him for inviting me to his party. My cheeks were stinging and my eyes burning. Darkness was a friend that came just in time to shield my embarrassment. Big Mama shuffled back up the street with me trailing, rolling my eyes and making faces.

I got to spend an afternoon with my cousin Melvin while I was visiting Big Mama. She called her niece Maureen and implored her to send Melvin over to take me out for ice cream as though I were four instead of fourteen. Melvin was a nineteen-year- old college student, and his Sunday pleasure must have been pursuing girls. He came over, picked me up, and drove me from one girl's home to another's. I don't remember getting ice cream.

Pearl Sr. High School

Since Memphis city schools wouldn't have me, Daddy hustled me off to his sister's home in Nashville. With Mommy's reluctant blessing, I would spend tenth grade with Aunt Virginia, Uncle Fred, Anita and Freddy. The Westbrooks were well connected; therefore, I could get into Pearl High without any problem. Their home was beautiful and they dressed well. To me, it seemed that the Westbrooks were rich, among Nashville's black elite.

During that year, I decided to study and make good grades again. I became interested in English and Biology because I had great teachers in those subjects. My English teacher taught us on the college level. She had high expectations for all; therefore, I decided to live up to them. My big project for that year was "Silas Marner" by George Elliot. I had to read and analyze it, and write character analysis, themes and more. It was long and in depth. I took typing that year so I was able to do a good job on the presentation. It was my first project of that magnitude. I had nothing on the undergraduate level that surpassed it. I made an "A." Aunt Virginia, who taught ninth grade English, gave me some suggestions, but she didn't do my work.

The Westbrooks watched "The Huntley-Brinkley Report" each evening during dinner; therefore, I began to learn more about what was happening in the world, especially in civil rights. It was 1959, and some more "Strange Fruit" hung from a tree in Mississippi. His name was Mack Charles Parker. They had accused him of raping a pregnant white woman. I would hear Uncle Fred and Aunt Virginia talk about what was happening to black people in the South. They would donate money to the National Association for the Advancement of Colored People (NAACP) to fight racism. I listened, and I learned.

My cousin Anita and I were the same age and grade, but we had very different personalities and interests, which meant we were not the best of friends that year. Our friendship developed later. We shared a room though and got along well. Anita had a tendency to be unorganized and a bit messy in how she kept her things. I liked order and neatness having picked up those traits in my early years from both grandmothers. Aunt Virginia considered that I was more like her than her own daughter. She kept her beautifully decorated house neat and clean. Aunt Virginia often made comparisons between Anita and me, telling Anita that she should be more like me. That pronouncement dropped between us like a giant brick wall, which prevented us from having a deep friendship when we were teenagers. We were able to get past that in later years.

We participated in some of the same activities and attended the same parties, but I had my friends and I shared hers to some extent. Anita played classical piano and was a member of Jack and Jill, the elite organization created in 1938 for upper class black children to meet their civic, cultural and social needs. Anita was perfect for that organization. She was classy and sophisticated and loved socializing with the upper crust. She was proper and respectful to adults. Her social skills were impeccable. Freddy was not as interested in impressing the upper crust. His childhood friends were not members of the black upper class. He and I were more alike in the area.

Freddy was three years my junior, yet we had much in common. We bonded shortly after I moved in. When his neighbor friend was not around, he and I would play football or baseball. Both of us enjoyed being outside while Anita preferred the house. On more than one occasion, Freddy and I argued about what to watch on television, and it ended in a fight. We had a few fights that year always over something silly. Sometimes it would be over who was eating too much of the popcorn. I don't know why we ate popcorn from the same bowl. Our fights were not serious, and after they were over, we were friends again. We did have one fight that got somewhat serious. We tore each other's clothing and Aunt Virginia had to intervene. Of course, she jumped all over me, the older one who should have known better. Throughout the years, she often reminded us how we used to fight; she also reminded us how much we loved each other.

Aunt Virginia carried a youthful spirit into her classroom and used it to relate to her students. She loved her students and wanted to help them succeed. She had lots of energy and exuberance for life.

When Anita and I would be in the kitchen dancing to "American Bandstand" after school, she would sometimes join us.

There were certain people Anita could have as friends, and though she always tried to include me, I didn't see myself as one of them. I went to their parties, and I became friends with two girls. All of the children's parents were college professors, teachers, doctors, dentists, lawyers, entrepreneurs and other professionals.

During that year, Anita and I both had boyfriends who didn't meet the Westbrook standard. It didn't matter much because Aunt Virginia didn't allow us to have male company or go on dates. We were fourteen when we started tenth grade. We only saw the boys at school and at basement and lawn parties, which were always chaperoned.

Anita and I did disobey Aunt Virginia one time. We wanted to have some boys over for a visit one Sunday evening when Aunt Virginia and Uncle Fred were at church. The boys were from Clarksville, but were in town and called to see if they could stop by.

One was my brother Charles' friend. We liked each other when I lived in Clarksville the year before. Anita had answered the telephone and was standing there listening. I told Anita who it was on the phone and what he wanted. I was about to tell him that they couldn't come when Anita interrupted and said, "Tell them to come in thirty minutes." I looked at her questioningly, but I told him what she said.

Anita hatched a plan and either bribed or threatened Freddy so he would stay in the kitchen and watch television and wouldn't tell on us. I was a little leery but excited at the prospects of doing something so daring. Aunt Virginia could ground us for the rest of the year if she found out we were so brazen and common. "Common" was her word for what we were not to become.

Anita and I hurried to the bedroom and changed into our satin pajama sets we had modeled in a fashion show at Fisk University. Aunt Dorinda had gotten them from Japan. The pants were black satin; the quilted jackets were embroidered in Asian designs of red, gold, ivory and green. Harry Belafonte's first wife Marguerite was the special guest model in that show.

Anita and I were excited to have boys visiting, if only for a few minutes. We sat in the living room and talked. The evening went well. Freddy stayed in the kitchen with Mark, the golden collie. The boys left before Aunt Virginia and Uncle Fred returned. Anita and I had something to talk about for a while.

Daddy used to come over from Clarksville to visit me sometimes. On one of those visits, I told Daddy I wanted a portable record player. He promised to bring me one on his next visit. When I saw him coming a week later, I ran to greet him, excited to get my record player. I was disappointed when Daddy confessed, "I'm sorry baby, but I haven't gotten it yet."

I pouted and acted like a brat for a moment letting Daddy know how he had let me down. The next week Daddy came back bearing the portable record player and "Shimmy, Shimmy Ko Ko Bop" by Little Anthony and the Imperials. I loved doing the

Cha-cha to that record.

Anita and I had a scary moment in the neighborhood theater on Jefferson Street, just up from Tennessee State University. It was a scary movie. Anita and I were talking, saying things like, "What's he going to do next?" "I'm scared." The man sitting close to us said, "Shut up." We ignored him and continued wondering aloud what was going to happen. He told us again, "Shut up." Then he took out his pocketknife and flashed it in the light. Anita and I got up promptly and moved away from him without emitting another sound.

On another occasion, Anita and I outsmarted Aunt Virginia. We were in college then. I was in Nashville visiting during my spring break. I had met my future husband in Nashville, Thanksgiving 1963 when he was a student at Tennessee State University. He was dropping out of school and enlisting in the Air Force when we met. During my spring break Joel was on thirty-day leave before going to his assigned base; therefore, we were going to meet in Nashville. His home was about fifty miles from Nashville in a small town called Mt. Pleasant.

Joel and Anita's boyfriend who she called Butch came over that Sunday to visit us. We could finally have male company. They were dressed in their Sunday best and so were we. I was wearing a fuchsia pink shantung dress that I had gotten from Goldsmith's department store. I had charged it to Mommy's account without her permission. When the bill came and she saw what I had done, she was not amused. I had to earn the $15.00 to pay for it.

By then, Aunt Virginia and Uncle Fred had added on a family room with white leather sectional couch and plush white carpet. We were happy to be entertaining in that beautiful room. During the evening after it became dark, Anita turned on a lamp. As the evening progressed, Butch decided to reach over and turn off the lamp, which left the room rather dark. Right after he turned it off, Aunt Virginia stuck her head in and said, "Anita, turn that light back on."

Aunt Virginia wanted to believe that Joel was the one who had turned off the light. She knew Butch was the son of a college professor. Since she didn't know Joel, she thought maybe he did it. She later came to know the kind of person that he was.

The next day Joel came over while Aunt Virginia and Uncle Fred were at work, he said, "I want to take you home to meet my family."

"I don't know if Aunt Virginia will let me go. I'll have to ask her." When Anita came in that evening, I told her the situation. She thought for a moment and said, "Let's go ask Mother."

Cowardly, I went into the kitchen with Anita following. Right away, I said, "Aunt Virginia, Joel wants to take me to meet his family. They live in Mt. Pleasant, which is fifty miles on the other side of Columbia."

"We don't know him. We don't know his family. I don't know. He's a soldier."

"Who are his folks?" she added.

"You don't know them but his mother is a schoolteacher." I thought that would help.

"No, I don't think you should go."

Anita spoke up, "Mother, why can't she go? It's not that far."

"Barbara Jean, you can't go."

Anita and I retreated to her room where she came up with a plan. "Tomorrow, ask Mother if you can go to a movie with Joel. If she says yes, then you all can go to Mt. Pleasant. You just can't stay a long time."

"Anita, I don't know if we can do that."

"Yes, you can. You can do it."

The next day when Joel called, I told him the plan. He picked me up for the movie; however, he drove to Mt. Pleasant instead. He knocked out the fifty miles in record time. We rushed into the house where I met Mr. and Mrs. Armstrong and Joel's sisters, Cheryl who was fifteen and Floretta who was eight. Floretta's toothless grin captured my heart, and we immediately bonded. She and I remained friends all of her too short life.

Mrs. Armstrong had made dinner for us but we didn't have time to eat it. They were expecting us to come earlier in the day and to stay a while. Joel told them that we had to hurry back to Nashville. His mother rushed into the kitchen and cut slices of her cake for us to carry back. On our way out of town, Joel drove to the area where his brother Bradley hung out and introduced me to him. His older brother Raymond was in college. Later I would meet James and Walter (Walee).

We returned to Nashville in time to make my curfew. I was nineteen and a college sophomore, but that didn't matter to Aunt Virginia. I went to Anita's room where she was doing homework. We sat on the floor. I reached into my purse and pulled out the yellow layer cake with its thick, chocolate fudge frosting, which I was too excited to eat, and gave it to Anita. She savored every morsel while we talked. As far as I know, Aunt Virginia never found out about that escapade.

Aunt Virginia exposed me to many cultural events that year. I saw my first college play, "Our Town," and my first classical concert. At the beginning of the school year, Dr. Davis, president of Tennessee State University where Uncle Fred was an agronomy professor, had a picnic on his farm for the faculty and their families. It lasted into the night. There were games, live music, dancing and lots of food and soft drinks. The air filled with smells of hot dogs and hamburgers during the day, and frying fish scented the night. Aunt Virginia wore a starched cotton sundress, and Anita and I wore pedal pushers and tennis shoes. It seemed all of Nashville's black elite were there.

Living with Aunt Virginia was an important time in my development as a young woman. I learned things I would not have learned being with Mommy or Daddy. I was exposed to many black professionals and young people with great opportunities for achieving their American dreams. I became more motivated in school, made the honor roll and the principal's list, which was all "A's." I felt good about myself. I knew I could do whatever I desired.

Lester High School

My junior year found me at yet another school in another city, where I would make new friends and begin to feel that I was growing up and living on my own. I lived with Aunt Thelma, Dorothy, Jack and his wife Azater in a small duplex. It was not an ideal living situation; however, it sufficed for a while. Later that year, we moved to a larger apartment.

My first day at Lester High, a counselor assigned Bishop and Ester to take me on a tour of the school and introduce me to my teachers. Bishop and I became friends. Ester died from an asthma attack shortly after our meeting. Later that year, a female classmate was kidnapped and killed. They found her body under a house, miles away from the city; A boy was shot and killed at a football game; and one boy stabbed another in the hall at school. I was unaccustomed to such tragedy and violence. I had entered a different world.

Even though we had used textbooks, substandard equipment, inadequate supplies and an overall inferior system when compared to our white counterparts, we had some excellent teachers who cared about educating us. My favorite was my English teacher, who was a little scary in his teaching style. He would call a student "dumb" without hesitation. That was during a time when grownups thought shaming was going to make a person do better. It didn't seem to have the shock value then that it has today. I don't believe he ever referred to a girl that way. He often referred to a girl as "daughter."

In Mr. Spillers' class, I fell in love with poets and poetry. I learned to recite "Thanatopsis" by William Cullen Bryant; "Chicago" by Carl Sandburg; "The Road Not Taken" by Robert Frost; "The Raven" by Edgar Allen Poe: the 24th Psalm; "How do I Love Thee" by Elizabeth Barrett Browning. I had quite a repertoire of poetry that I committed to memory. Poetry interested me because I loved the way poets used language to present images, and evoke emotions.

On Fridays, we would have spelling. Since we had to do lots of writing, the teacher wanted us to spell correctly; therefore, he would have the class stand, and he would call out a word to each of us in turn. If a student spelled the word correctly, she would remain standing. If the student missed the word, she would sit. The first Friday he did that, I was the only one standing. The teacher took the rest of the period to chastise the class, excluding me. I could spell most words then; therefore, I looked forward to the quizzes each week. My English teacher held me on high as a model for the class to emulate. That did not make me a person any of the girls wanted to befriend. The boys were not bothered by that. They were still vying for my attention. It took a while, but I did get a couple of girlfriends.

Another teacher who I liked was my Spanish teacher. She was attractive, smart, and well dressed. Teachers had an unwritten dress code at that time that helped define their professionalism and set them apart. I took Spanish my junior and senior years.

Lester High was a small school and some teachers taught both juniors and seniors; therefore, I had the same English, Spanish, and chemistry/physics teachers both years.

Shortly after the year began, the physical education teacher asked me to try out for band majorette. I did, and she selected me. That caused lots of anger and criticism from some of my schoolmates who said about me, "She can't march." "She just has light skin and big legs." Someone always made sure that whatever negative thing anyone said about me got back to me.

I wasn't much of a joiner. I did not like to compete with anyone.

I didn't care that much about being a majorette; however, the teacher asked me to try out. Since she picked me, I accepted. I didn't realize that some of the girls had tried out before, and they really wanted to be selected.

I was the new girl at school, and many of the junior and senior boys wanted to talk to me. Some wanted to be friends and others wanted me to be their girlfriend. It was kind of fun and sometimes annoying, but I would talk to any of them for a minute between classes or after school. I had noticed a senior who was not pursuing me. He kept a respectable distance, but I could see him checking me out a few times. Around the second or third week of school, he made his move. It was the right move at the right time. He later confessed, "I waited because I wanted the other guys to have their chance." We became a couple, which caused me to incur the wrath of his former girlfriend Liz and her cohorts. In all fairness to Liz, I must say that the negativity came from her friends, Star being the ringleader. They were senior girls who would prove to be trouble for me before the year ended.

In one year, I had gone from living an upper middle class lifestyle to an in-the-'hood lifestyle. I didn't fit perfectly into either, yet I had more freedom and fun with my peers in the 'hood. My boyfriend Leon was a confident young man who had the respect and admiration of the teachers, students, the community and the guys who hung on the corner. He was smart, polite, tall, handsome and a gifted singer. He also played basketball. I was in awe of him, never felt equal to him; therefore, we had a very sophisticated relationship that entailed conversation at lunchtime and sitting on the sofa one night a week talking.

With my classmates, I could laugh and act silly and just hang out. Johnny was the only one who smoked cigarettes but not when we were together. I never saw any of them drink alcohol. Johnny drove his 1957 Ford Fairlane with all of us in it. There was E. J., Chuck, Dot, Mara, and I. We had lots of fun riding around Memphis listening to WDIA radio station. It was popular, the first station in the country programmed by and for black people. Nat D. Williams, the first black radio announcer in Memphis, and Rufus Thomas kept us entertained. My favorite song that year was "Soldier Boy" by the Shirelles.

The members of the Gracious Ladies Club invited me to join. The club was for junior and senior girls. My nemeses were members. In the spring of my junior year, my teachers selected me to represent Lester High and compete for Miss Bronze Queen. The contest was associated with the Cotton Makers Jubilee.

The white community started Cotton Carnival during the Depression in 1931 to pay tribute to cotton and to promote it as their city's lifeblood. Since the black community, due to segregation, could not participate in Cotton Carnival, Dr. R.Q. and Mrs. Ethyl H. Venson cofounded the Cotton Makers Jubilee in 1935 to acknowledge the contributions of black people to the cotton industry. The celebration had many activities and events associated—balls, parades and luncheons. They also had a King and Queen. Miss Bronze Queen was an event for high school junior girls.

I allowed Leon to talk me into competing. He helped me write the essay and wished me well. I think my essay got an honorable mention. All I remember from the essay are the words "formidable adversary" and "morass."

I competed with girls from all the Memphis black schools. We wore evening gowns and each of us answered a question just as they did in the Miss America Pageant. My question was, "What if you were asked to go on a blind date, how would you feel?" My answer was not intelligent or memorable. They didn't crown me Miss Bronze Queen.

I put a halfhearted effort into all of those activities that teachers selected me for because I simply was not interested. I went along with what they wanted. I am not proud of that. I believe young people should be completely invested in whatever endeavor they undertake. It doesn't matter whether they volunteered or were selected. I learned that later in life.

I still remember the incident that happened in January or February of my junior year that caused me to see teachers in a new light. I remember it so clearly because of its unfair outcome. My nemesis Liz and her girlfriends were still unhappy that I was with Leon. Even though girls were not as mean and as violent then as they are today, they still found ways to let you know they didn't like you or were jealous of you.

It was a cold winter day that started out like the day before. However, there was a rumor circulating about Liz's girlfriend Star and me. Star was all of four feet tall, with a mouth and personality to rival the Grand Canyon. All that fateful day, students eagerly passed on the rumor that Star and I were going to fight after school. The rumor seemed to have come from the ether; nevertheless, there we were, caught up in a whirlwind of confusion and excitement propelled by whispers and stares from the whole school.

When the day ended, I retrieved my coat from my locker and felt dread as I stuck each arm inside each sleeve. I headed for home as usual. Star and I traveled the same route, living a few houses from each other. So there we were with half the school following behind and alongside us. The bloodthirsty throng was egging us on, yelling, "Ya wanna fight? Ya wanna fight, huh?" They encircled us. They were hungry animals lusting for fresh kill. I kept walking as best as I could somewhat restricted by the throng. It closed in, forcing us close together. The crowd had a mind of its own. It acted as though it should decide our course. We had no say in what was happening. I didn't utter a word to anyone. I tried to walk home.

I heard Aunt Virginia's voice in my head, "Don't be common. You're not common." She never explained to me what things were common, but I had a strong inclination that street fighting would fall into that category. I didn't fight anyway. My fights with Malcolm ended when I was twelve, and my fights with Freddy ended when I moved away from Nashville.

The crowd pushed us close together, as close as they could. We did not fight. After a few minutes, the disappointed crowd split off to their separate homes. Mommy had always said, "If people are running towards a fight, you run in the opposite direction. You never know if they have a gun, a bullet has no eyes." She never told me what to do if I was supposed to be the one fighting. She didn't expect her daughter to fight.

The next day, the principal summoned Star and me to his office. I knew I had done nothing wrong, so I walked to the office with an open mind. I didn't know what to expect. The principal, my homeroom teacher, and another staff person were present. It was then that I knew it was serious. I walked into the nicely arranged office noticing the framed diplomas on the wall, the blond veneer desk with neatly stacked papers, a stapler. The office, though perfectly ordered, did not match the principal's appearance. He dressed sharply and wore good suits befitting his position, his greying hair was brushed back to reveal tight waves.

As soon as the meeting started, my open mind snapped shut as a mousetrap on its intended victim. They had known Star for many years, but I was the new kid. What did they know about me? I had been marked "villain" from the outset. I didn't stand a chance.

Miss Star embodied the meaning of her name. A star was born. Star made such a superb defense for herself that I wouldn't be surprised to learn that she became a lawyer or perhaps an actor. Star talked a mile a minute saying, "I didn't start any fight. I wouldn't fight because I will soon be eighteen and I will be grown. I am a lady. I will be graduating in May, and I wouldn't fight." She went on for a while stating all of her pluses and throwing herself on the mercy of the staff.

When it was my turn, I was a cold, hard marble statue, perched on a wooden pedestal, silent. I offered no dossier, vitae or resume, no defense. I did not start a fight. I did not fight. There was no fight. Why didn't Star say that? How do you make a defense when there is nothing to defend? It is like trying to prove a negative, impossible. There was nothing to defend. I was not going to entertain those people as Star had. I couldn't tap dance that fast. Neither was I going to let them see me sweat. I ignored everything the principal and my homeroom teacher said. I stared into a hopeless gloom, yet I made sure my tears were a hoped-for rainstorm that never quite developed.

My homeroom teacher liked to sit behind me sometimes and

touch my hair, neck or shoulders. Each time he would try to touch me I would quickly brush his hand away and move my head. Therefore, I believe he was trying to retaliate. Some male teachers gave some female students inappropriate and unwanted attention. Some tried to date their students, and some did date them. I wasn't one of them.

The principal handed me the Home Suspension Notice and said, "You are suspended until your parent or guardian comes for a meeting." Star thanked them for the meeting, and she went back to class. I took the slip of paper, and I went home. I didn't read it until I got home. "This certifies that Barbara Gray has this day been suspended for: Fighting in the streets – Inciting the fight and Insubordination."

I could agree with the insubordination. The inciting only took place in the mind of the person who started the rumor. I later found out that a boy who I, as a hall monitor, had not allowed to come down the upstairs probably started it. He promised me some "git back," and it seems he delivered either on this or another matter.

I told Aunt Thelma what happened and I stayed home from school only one day. Aunt Thelma accompanied me back to school for a meeting. They accepted me back. I learned that teachers could be cruel and unfair in how they handle student problems. They are often as petty as their students.

According to what one teacher told me, that incident kept me out of the Honor Society. Teachers didn't vote for me because of my attitude. It was a good thing they didn't hold my self-esteem in the palms of their hands.

Teachers were ordinary people who I respected, but I didn't see them as mythical figures. I didn't even look to them as role models. I knew they were not always fair. They had biases and jealousies. They didn't always do or even know what was right.

At Lester, I was an National Defense Cadet Course (NDCC) sponsor. On Mondays the boys who were in NDCC and their Sponsors dressed in uniform. The NDCC was the black equivalent of the ROTC in white schools. Only boys could be in the NDCC, but they had girl Sponsors to march with them in parades. The boys wore their military uniforms, and Sponsors wore black straight skirts, white button-down shirts with black ties and white blazers, black loafers and white bobby socks.

Clothing styles were changing in the 1960s. Girls had pointed breasts, small waistlines and thin bodies, yet they sometimes wore girdles to keep their behinds from shaking. They wore either girdles or garter belts to hold up their stockings. There were no panty hose then. Skirts were mostly knee length. They were straight, pleated and full worn with button-down shirts, blouses and sweaters. Twin sweater sets were popular. I liked jumper dresses, blouses with Peter Pan collars, and circle pins. Girls didn't wear pants to school, only around the house or on a picnic. Elementary school girls wore pants with dresses over them in winter months. Jeans weren't popular. Capri pants, Bermuda shorts and pedal pushers were popular choices for girls and women, just not at school or church. They were only for leisure, sports and around the house. Plaid was a fashionable pattern in pants, skirts and dresses. Jacqueline Kennedy was the epitome of 1960s style with her short A-line skirts and pillbox hats and flip hairdo.

In the 1950s, hemlines were past the knee and skirts were full. Girls wore petticoats or can-can slips, named after the can-can dancers of Paris, underneath to give them a voluminous look. Those petticoats required a lot of work washing, starching and ironing to keep them full. I didn't miss them when the A-line skirts made them obsolete.

The 1960s styles liberated women from much of the fussiness in dressing well. More clothing was easy care, wash and wear; there was less fabric to deal with and simpler styles.

Boys and young men were conscious of their style of dress. They wore close fitting suits and skinny ties when they were dressed up. Their casual dress was khaki or gabardine slacks with Banlon sweaters and button-down shirts. In the wintertime, they wore corduroy and wool slacks with crew neck sweaters. Cardigans and V-neck sweaters were also popular. Both boys and girls wore car coats and penny loafers. Boys and girls both were conscious of their clothing styles.

I went to my junior prom with Leon and his best friend Paul Morton whose date was one of Star's friends. We double dated. The juniors made the gym Shangri-La with papier-mâché palm trees and colorful paper flowers. Mommy bought me a yellow semiformal dress and satin shoes. Leon gave me a corsage to match the dress. Most girls wore short or semi-formal dresses. Our dresses were knee length or tea length. Boys wore suits or dark slacks with white coats and ties. It was a night to look your very best.

My junior prom was not especially memorable, not much fun. We had a custom where a senior would sing a song to the junior class and a junior would sing to the seniors. They chose Leon to sing to the juniors. He kept his eyes on me as he sang "Let Me Call You Sweetheart."

After the prom, we rode around Memphis and ended up at a club called the Gay Hawk. I tried alcohol in the form of mint gin. The syrupy drink did not titillate my pallet. I was not ready for alcohol. There must not have been carding then. I was sixteen. Paul was in college and was perhaps no stranger to alcohol. Leon was not accustomed to drinking and became ill from the sweet, green liquor.

We were not out for long. Paul drove Leon home first. Perhaps it was to make sure his car remained clean. Then he dropped Ann off. I took that to mean they were not close. He drove me home last. Paul and I spent the night together. We sat on the front lawn talking and laughing until the sun rose to greet us. Although it would be another year before I would go away to college, I wanted to learn as much about college life as Paul was willing to share. I had more fun listening and talking to Paul that night than I did at the prom.

Somehow, our conversation turned to homosexuality. I don't know if we used that term, but the conversation was about professors having sex with male students. Generally, we used the terms "punk" and "funny" to describe men who were homosexual. I was intrigued by how Paul spoke about the subject. I had many questions. That was my first discussion on homosexuality. There was no controversy around homosexuality then; therefore, I knew nothing about it. Paul held nothing back; I was wide-awake, hanging on to his every word

I appeared on the 1962 yearbook cover. That was the first year for them to put students on the cover. The senior teachers selected six of us from the graduating class to pose. All but I were in the Honor Society. I'm not sure why they selected me. I was not photogenic and never liked having my picture taken; however, I felt it was an honor so I agreed to appear on the cover with two of my good friends, Maurice and Bishop. The other students selected were Joyce, Edith and Terry. The teachers told us to wear something colorful. I realized I had dark, dreary clothing, so I borrowed a purple sweater and skirt from my cousin Dorothy. The picture turned out okay. As I look back, I'm glad I agreed to do it.

My senior prom was an adventure of sorts as was the week leading up to it. I didn't have a boyfriend at that time; therefore, I had no reliable date. I had designed a gorgeous gown, and Mommy had it made for me. It was long, fitted, white on white cotton brocade with a little flare at the bottom. It had spaghetti straps that crisscrossed in the back, and a white organza overskirt bordered with a gold and white ribbon that tied at the waist. Aunt Dorinda had taken me shopping for gold pumps, purse and white gloves. All I needed was a date.

The week of the prom, folks started pairing off and making plans. The first boy to ask me was Bishop. He didn't have a girlfriend. I thanked him, but turned him down because I was waiting for Maurice to ask me. Maurice and I had been a couple earlier in the year, and we were still friends. I just assumed he would ask me to the prom. Tuesday went by and Thomas asked. I had one other offer and finally, the day before the prom, Maurice asked me to be his date. I said, "No, you should have asked me sooner." My foolish pride kept me from having a date for my senior prom.

When Azater, Cousin Jack's wife who I was living with at the time, found out about my situation she said, "You better go to your prom or I'm going to tell your mother. She spent all that money having your dress made, and your aunt bought those shoes and things. You better go, or I will tell."

I didn't care. I was skipping the prom. That Friday evening, as it was near the time for the festivities to begin, Azater said, "Barbara Jean, the least you can do is put on your dress so we can see how it looks on you."

After she begged me a few times, I acquiesced and got ready as though I were going to the prom. After I dressed, Azater and some of the neighbor ladies "oohed" and "awed" over how beautiful I looked and how gorgeous my gown was.

Before I could take off the gown, two of my friends who were juniors, Thomas and Charles, came to the door dressed in their formalwear. I said, "What are you all doing here?"

Thomas said, "We came to get you. You're going to the prom."

I tried to beg off but Azater looked at me, rolled her eyes, and nodded her head a couple of times. I knew she would tell Mommy that I had wasted her money; therefore, I grabbed my purse and out of the door I went. Both Thomas and Charles had dates that were waiting for them, so there I was on my own, flitting from table to table visiting with different ones including Maurice and Bishop and their dates that were from other schools. I was having a good time. Earnest C. Withers, who photographed the brutally murdered Emmitt Till, was our photographer. I had no money for pictures, but he said, "Let me take a picture of you for your daddy." He knew my daddy and remembered meting me.

The night was long and interesting. I went home and changed into a black sheath dress my seamstress also made. I went out with Larry whose date had a curfew, then later I was with my friend and classmate Ralph whose date also had an early curfew and other friends. It was a fun night that ended at dawn.

We did not have after parties at anyone's home. We didn't have limousines and all that the young people have today. No fancy hotels would have us then. Everything was simple, but tasteful. Moreover, we knew how to have a good time without making mischief, just being with one another.

The most hurtful thing that happened to me my senior year was losing my best friend Dee. She became pregnant, and they expelled her from school a couple of months before graduation. That was how it was done then if you couldn't hide the pregnancy.

Again, the rumor mill was busy. Someone had told the teacher that Dee was pregnant. Everyone turned against me, the suspected fink, tattler, snitch, informant. At first, I didn't know why all of a sudden no one wanted to talk to me at lunchtime. I started sneaking off campus and going home because I couldn't stand the atmosphere. I would sneak back on campus after lunch was over. One day my English teacher caught me sneaking back on campus.

"Where are you coming from, Daughter?"

"I went home for lunch."

"Who gave you permission?"

"No one."

"Stick out your hand."

He gave me a perfunctory whack with a strap. There I was seventeen and about to graduate, yet I was subjected to such treatment. I knew Mr. Spillers didn't want to hit me. He thought highly of me, still he had to do what some silly rule required and set an example for onlookers. It was the idea of it that hurt, though not as much as I was already hurting inside. Being ostracized was a bitch and not knowing the reason why made it even worse. Some time passed before I heard that I was the reason the teachers kicked Dee out of school. I was shocked that Dee thought I had told on her. I thought she knew that I was a real friend.

I must have been the only one in the whole school who didn't know Dee was pregnant. We were together most of the time. We always double and triple dated, or so I thought.

I went home and told Azater what I had found out. She said, "I knew that girl was pregnant."

"You did? How?"

"I had three babies. Don't you think I know when a girl is pregnant?"

"But I didn't know."

I finished the year in a lonely and sad place. I never tried to see Dee and tell her that I didn't snitch on her, that I didn't even know anything. I was not the one to go to a teacher and tell him or her anything. Teachers were not my friends. They had their place and I had mine. I just let it go and suffered in silence until graduation was over.

In 1986 when I was in Memphis, I saw Dee working in a store where I had gone to buy a birthday gift. We talked for a few minutes, and it was as though the teen angst of 1962 was a too distant memory to relive.

I never wanted to return to Lester High not even to visit the teachers I liked and appreciated. I never wanted to go back for a reunion and reminisce about days that were not kind to me. I never longed for the good old teen years and high school days. I ran from them as I would run from a fight. I'm still running.

Lane College

Out of place, any place. That was I. Mommy and Daddy decided I would go to Lane College just forty miles away in Jackson. I had no say and could offer no alternative that suited them. That was it. Therefore, after a summer of working to help pay my way, I was Lane College bound. Daddy came to Somerville to collect me and my belongings and drive to Jackson. He took me on a tour of the campus and showed me the room where he and Mommy met in 1939. I was not impressed. It could have been romantic if they had still been together. I didn't care. *Why am I here?* I'm thinking, *I'm going to flunk out and embarrass you.* Deep down I knew I wouldn't do that because I didn't want to embarrass myself.

Daddy arranged to pay, deposited me in my room on Cleaves Hall with strangers, and exited quickly. I was a boat on a country road. Lena was a junior, and a freshman counselor or whatever they called them. How convenient. She was okay, attractive, dark skinned, beautiful long hair and outgoing. Lena loved to bathe, dress and redress throughout the day. She loved beautiful clothes. My other roommate Martha was from Memphis. Both were nice girls; nevertheless, I didn't become friends with either.

I wasn't outgoing, but I was friendly when someone approached me. One day as I was standing in the cafeteria line, I heard a girl behind me talking. She was petite and very loquacious. Each time I saw her, I thought she needed to stop talking so much and rest.

We had English and some other classes together. She started talking to me and we became friends. Her name was Gloria Watson. Gloria shared a room with Betty Madison from Birmingham and Dianne from Denver. They had become close friends by the time I joined the group. Later editions were Joy from Detroit, Yvonne from Chicago and Margie from Millington, Tennessee. Yvonne and I learned that our parents had been at Lane together, and they had known each other.

Gloria was brilliant. She had gone to integrated schools in Toledo and had come to Lane on academic scholarship. She was majoring in sociology, but when she saw how much I loved literature, she changed her major to English.

Gloria kept me in school. When it was time to register for the second quarter, I decided I wasn't going to register. I was dropping out because I didn't like it there. I failed math, but that wasn't the reason I wanted to leave. That was rather expected since I graduated from high school without the required math. I absolutely hated math. Daddy had called in a favor from someone in Memphis city schools who allowed me to graduate without the required math. I wonder if it was the principal, perhaps to redeem himself for kicking me out of school unfairly. I never questioned Daddy; I was too glad to graduate.

Gloria grabbed my hand and pulled me towards the lines, "Girl, come on, I'll walk with you through the process. You're not dropping out." Gloria was very persuasive, and she wouldn't listen to anything I had to say. She repeated the process the third quarter.

Not only did I fail math my first year, I also failed humanities. No one failed humanities. It was a music and art appreciation class. We learned about the great masters and composers. The test was simple, besides I enjoyed art and music, so why did I sit there and not take the test?

After Daddy died, I didn't care about much. I remember sitting in class, on exam day, with my mind as far away from school as Mars is from Earth starring into the hall remembering the past and designing the future. Finally, a figure caught my attention. It was a young man I had not seen on campus. We locked eyes for a moment; he smiled and moved on. I still sat there doing nothing.

When I went back for summer school, that young man looked me up and we became friends for that summer, bonding over books and poetry. He was a beautiful writer, a person with so much talent unrealized. In later years, he became a victim of the drug culture.

My friend Betty was proper and sophisticated, the daughter of a schoolteacher and a steel industry worker. On the one hand, she and I had more in common being from the South and having mothers who were teachers. On the other hand, Betty wanted to be at Lane and she was about business. Betty was the level headed one in the group. She tried to keep everyone straight. She stood for no nonsense and always had a smile and a good spirit. When I met Betty's mother many years later, I understood why. Mrs. Madison was ninety-six years of age when I met her. She remembered me, and the things Betty had shared with her about me and the other girls, when we were in college. She has such a lovely smile, a sweet spirit.

Diane was the odd girl out. Her nickname was "The Blond." She had very pale skin, lighter than Gloria's or mine and blond hair. When she tried a different hair color, it didn't work. Diane was born to be blond whether it grew out of her scalp or came from Miss Clairol. Though all of us had lived sheltered lives, Diane's was the most extreme. We often talked to her about proper behavior as if we were her big sisters. We would have rap sessions some Sundays and talk about all sorts of things, sharing honestly with one another. We must have talked about boys. I didn't have a particular boyfriend my freshman year, only a junior in hot pursuit.

Joy was the biggest sister. She was nineteen. She taught all of us a few things about relationships, sex and life. One Sunday as we gathered in our favorite place -- Gloria, Betty and Diane's room, Joy announced in a matter of fact way, "My mother is my sister." Each of our mouths dropped open, eyes bugged out. It sounded like a riddle, and we were waiting for the rest of it. "My sister is really my mother." We were still stunned and speechless. "My mother gave birth to me when she was young, and her mother raised me as her own. My sister is my mother but my grandmother is my real mother." Okay, next subject.

We borrowed each other's clothes, shared whatever we had with one another and learned to cheat at bid whist, which we sometimes played until the wee hours. We played with other girls on the hall also. One was blue-eyed Grace from Mississippi, known for cheating and smoking. I fanned while the girls smoked. I couldn't tolerate cigarette smoke. My fanning was annoying to the others, especially to Gloria who insisted that I start smoking so the smoke wouldn't bother me. I tried. I didn't inhale. I didn't learn how to inhale that whole year.

In October, I received a telegram for my birthday from a young man named Clarence. I didn't know him. Although I wondered how he knew it was my birthday, I still wanted to thank him for thinking of me. I went to the campus grill, where we got bologna sandwiches, potato chips, pop, and asked if anyone could tell me who he was. I said, "He sent me a telegram for my birthday, and I just want to thank him." Someone finally pointed out Clarence, and I thanked him. The guys teased him. I didn't think it was more than a kind gesture. He was a junior and was always kind to me.

During the spring of my first year at Lane, I got into big trouble. I was in a foul mood one afternoon when the dorm mother hauled her ample frame up to the third floor to do room inspections. I was in my room ironing when she dared to enter without knocking. I became incensed. I opened my mouth and a barrage of cuss words flew out and smacked her in both ears. She almost fell over. She was too stunned to say anything; she spun on her heels and headed back towards the stairs.

The next day the dorm mother summoned the freshman girls

to the living room for a meeting with the Dean of Women. We sat there listening to a lecture on behavior for a while. After it was over, the Dean asked, "Who is Barbara Gray? Who is she? Where is she?" It seemed she asked those questions repeatedly for hours.

Each girl sat mute not wanting to snitch on me. I cut my eyes to those close around me, and they were staring straight ahead not looking my way. After eons it seemed, I realized no one was going to point me out; therefore, after Dean Penn did a final callout, "Who is Barbara Gray? Barbara Gray, stand up."

Dreading my fate, I slowly rose from my seat. How could I ignore a direct order? I had had no dealings with her before and I didn't know her. I knew the other dean, Dr. Stone. He never would have exposed me that way. He and Daddy had been classmates and were brothers of Alpha Phi Alpha fraternity. He looked out for me. I figured I would have been okay with him. I wasn't sure about her.

Would she put me out of the dormitory, out of school? Would she tell my mother? I admit I was scared and worried. She said, "Go to my office." Everyone looked at me as if I had committed a cardinal sin. They were relieved that I had owned up to what I had done. I didn't know what to expect from this fast-talking, fast walking, short, round, butter-colored woman whose reputation of toughness had preceded her.

I knew I was guilty as charged. I think the charge was "She was cussing like a sailor." That was my first attempt at cussing that way; it felt good, a wonderful release. I went to the Dean's office at the appointed time and waited for her to return. She arrived in a whirl, looked at me and said, "Who are you?"

"You told me to report to your office. I'm Barbara Gray."

"I want you to dust my desk and tidy up my office every day until I release you."

"Yes ma'am."

I could do that. It was no big deal. I had feared the worst, but the Dean was just placating the dorm mother. She didn't think what I had done was so horrible. I won't say she and I became bosom buddies, but we got along, and everything was okay.

I think I may have had that blowout shortly after Daddy died. In which case, the dean understood what I was going through; therefore, she let me get away with such insignificant punishment. I didn't talk ugly to the dorm mother or any other adult again. At least not that I recall.

I was glad I didn't take part in the Cleaves Hall Riot that year. I went to sleep early that night. I heard loud noise and got out of bed to see what was going on. When I opened the door and stuck my head out to look down the hall, a shoe went sailing by. Other items followed. That was when I decided to close the door and go back to bed. I think some girls got in trouble for that.

I looked forward to watching the fraternities and sororities perform. I was planning to pledge after I made up for those two "Fs" I had gotten. I knew I would pledge Alpha Kappa Alpha because of Aunt Virginia. Mommy didn't pledge, but if she had, she would have pledged Delta Sigma Theta. Aunt Virginia had already told me that she would pay my pledge fee. I pledged just before I left school in 1965.

During my first year, Kappa Alpha Psi Fraternity chose me as one of the attendants to their sweetheart Miss Kappa. They also chose another girl who left school before the years ended. Joy became the replacement. I didn't know why they chose me; nevertheless, I felt honored. They were a sophisticated group of young men. When they serenaded their sweetheart, I was included. It was nice when the fraternities serenaded their sweethearts or sang their hymns. I knew young men in each fraternity -- Alpha Phi Alpha, Omega Psi Phi and Phi Beta Sigma. During those years, they were men of character, mostly.

The day President John F. Kennedy was assassinated I was in front of the Administration building watching one of the fraternities perform their step show when someone sent the message through the crowd. A quiet shock was the general response. I wasn't overwhelmingly saddened by the tragedy because I didn't know what it meant for me. His world was so far from mine yet I had good feelings about him. President Eisenhower was the first one I took note of, but I remember President Truman. Kennedy was an exciting new breed of politician; someone we hoped would see the plight of the Negro and do something to remedy some of the wrongs.

On November 22, 1963, President Kennedy was shot and killed. He never had a chance to become truly great. I took the opportunity to see him when he visited Memphis shortly before the shooting.

College was better than high school. We had more freedom, maybe too much at seventeen. Not long after we got to Lane, Gloria and I went to some little joint and drank beer with an alumnus who was visiting. It was my first beer, and I quickly discovered that I liked it. Good thing I didn't know that when I was in high school. It was also a good thing I didn't have money to buy beer often.

I didn't do much partying because I went home on the weekends. I would get a ride home with a friend and fellow student named Lee who also lived in Fayette County. I had to do laundry, bathe in a bathtub, get my hair done and eat some real food. I especially looked forward to the chicken and dumplings Mommy would sometimes make for me.

One evening Gloria and I went to Papa Charlie's, the hole-in-the wall where we would go when we wanted to drink beer and feel grown-up. They shouldn't have let us in, but who cared about age in 1962? They wanted to sell beer; we wanted to drink it.

The place was packed with old men full of beer and fading memories. We spotted a booth hardly accommodating four students we recognized from campus. They were older, but they let us in. Gloria sat between Tex and a senior. I sat between Tex's girlfriend and a girl from Alabama. We ordered.

The six of us chatted about mid-terms and civil rights. Conversation was easy amidst a cloud of smoke, Muddy Waters and BB King on the jukebox and laughter of old men. I hated the Blues, and I didn't like old men.

Just as the effect of the beer was reaching its zenith, Tex was reaching for his. He put his hand under the old wooden table, grabbed my thigh and squeezed. I made a startled move and tried to shift in my seat; it was too close. His fingers began to caress slowly, deliberately as if they were not strangers to that region. Suddenly, the Blues died; the old men were sleeping babies, and I felt the blood rush to my cheeks with fervor.

I thought I heard myself scream, "You have the wrong thigh!" I didn't know how he could think that mine was the thigh of an Amazon. His girl was six-feet tall with gangly limbs and beauty that had taken flight at birth. She dressed well though, like a northerner whose daddy had a bank balance and a savings account.

My eyes searched fervently across the narrow table for Tex, but he was at that place where men go when they think they are about to get the prize. I couldn't breathe. A wave of heat and disgust washed over me like the foaming tide rushing ashore. Moments passed before Tex tried to connect with his love and share her pleasure. However, the senior had her deeply engrossed in conversation, and it seemed she had forgotten Tex was there.

Wake up you ninny! Tex must have heard my thoughts, he looked my way. My eyes caught his and held them long enough. He was already red; therefore, he blushed, deep crimson and withdrew as a cheating husband caught in the act.

We didn't drink beer often. Sometimes we went to Carol's for a barbecue sandwich. They costs twenty-five cents and were oh so good. Uncle Joe's was another barbecue restaurant. Both were places white people would bring pork shoulders and chickens for them to barbecue, especially for holidays. They only charged twenty-five cents to barbecue a chicken. Maybe it was a little more for a shoulder. White people could walk into any black business, sit wherever they desired, and it never became an issue.

One time we got some *splo*, which was corn liquor, white lightening, bootleg whisky. I don't know if we named it or it came named, but we called it splo. It was strong, and burned going down. I only remember drinking it once.

Gloria and I loved dancing. We would attend school dances together. I never wanted to go with a guy because I wanted to dance with many guys. We danced with Timmy Thomas who later became an R&B singer/musician, Nina Simone's brother Sam Waymon another singer/musician, and Cyrus my friend from Louisiana and others.

We had gotten away from the bop where you held hands with your partner. Most of the dances didn't require touching or a partner. There was the Twist, Watusi, Monkey, Swim, Mashed Potato, and the Jerk. The music was rhythmic and fast such as Dee Dee Sharp's "Mashed Potato Time," "Twisting the Night Away" by Sam Cooke, "The Locomotion" by Little Eva and so many more.

After my freshman year ended, I went home until summer school started. When I returned, I lived with Rev. and Mrs. Green on Farris Street. I remained there until I left school in January 1965. I had been going to school year around and was preparing to graduate in three years instead of four. Lane was a small school; therefore, it didn't offer some of the classes during both semesters. By then we were on semesters.

The summer of 1963, I roomed with Claudette and Barbara Morrow who I had known since elementary school. Mommy taught them. Barbara and my brother Sonny were good friends as children. All the Morrow girls who attended Lane -- Ophelia, Claudette, Barbara and Clementine -- stayed with the Greens.

Claudette and Barbara shared their resources and big sister wisdom with me. If I were not home on laundry day, either Claudette or Barbara would wash my clothes. We washed our clothes by hand using a tin tub and washboard. We hung them on the clothesline to dry.

After the Morrow girls graduated and moved on to their teaching jobs, they would come back to visit. It was routine for them to go through our dresser drawers and see if we were keeping things in order, making sure our bras were ironed and folded neatly. Our bras were made of cotton, which wrinkle when washed. They checked our clothes and our room. They were very particular in such matters. I listened and obeyed as if they were my big sisters.

I was in summer school to retake math and a couple of other classes as I was trying to graduate in three years. Ray, a friend who had left school to join the Air Force happened to be home on a thirty-day leave. I saw him on campus and asked him to tutor me. He had been a math major and readily agreed. I passed the class with a "C." In math, that was like an "A" to me.

I became friends with Will that summer. We went to movies and baseball games in the park. Will was smart, good looking, and an All-American basketball player. I learned the saying "Don't take any wooden nickels" from him. I took it to mean, "Don't fall for just any smooth talking guy."

When I came back to college for the fall semester, I found the Greens a little strict. I tried to smoke in the bathroom one time using the wet washrag twirl. I had learned that trick from Gloria. It didn't work. When I heard Rev. Green say, "I smell smoke. Who is that smoking in this house?" I quickly extinguished the cigarette, never to light up in his house again. I had to shape up.

Their youngest sister Clementine came to live there in the fall. She and I picked up our relationship from fifth grade and once again, we were good friends. Clem was low key, respectful, obedient, studious, and a loyal friend. She didn't drink, smoke or curse, yet we managed to enjoy each other's company and get along well.

During my sophomore year, I had a boyfriend for a short time. We sat together in class and talked while he drew beautiful images. He also played the saxophone. Sometimes he would walk me home from school, and he visited a time or two. Gloria used to tease me about him. He was quiet, not at all like the other guys. He was a great guy from a beautiful family there in Jackson.

My classmate and friend Buster took me to a Jerry Butler concert that year, the first R&B concert I ever attended. Buster was a local disc jockey and musician who had a refined, classy voice. In fact, it took him into a career of voice acting. It was nice to hear him on the radio sending out a request to me. He would say, "This song goes out to Venus."

He hosted a television show in 1973, "Soul Unlimited," a dance show for black youths. Dick Clark created the show to compete against Soul Train. I saw another classmate and dance partner Timmy Thomas on that show singing, "Why Can't We Live Together."

I met smart, talented and interesting people when I attended Lane College. I made some lasting friendships. Margie came to Lane our sophomore year and fell right in with Gloria, Betty and Diane. I was around her only a few times in college since I no longer lived on campus; however, our friendship developed in later years and continues.

During the Christmas holidays of 1963, I spent some time in Memphis visiting relatives. I stayed with my cousin Melvin and his wife one night. I was wearing a red pleated skirt, red mohair sweater, black patterned hose and black pumps. Melvin questioned my choice of stockings suggesting they looked like what "ladies of the evening" wore. I told him they were fashion.

He and his wife took me to a real nightclub called the Roaring Twenties to welcome in the New Year. Melvin introduced me to one of his fraternity brothers who introduced me to his younger brother. He was my age and a student at Southern Illinois University. He was a good dancer; therefore, we danced with each other all night. When it was time to leave, he asked if he could take me home. I told him to ask Melvin. Melvin gave his reluctant okay, and off we went. Actually, we rode with his brother and sister-in-law to their house for coffee and conversation. I must have arrived back at Melvin's house around three or four in the morning. Melvin was not happy. He was wide-awake, sitting up in his bed, waiting. He lectured me a bit on nice young ladies and decorum. I thought, what a hypocrite. There he was all married and respectable then and expecting his first child. I said, "I hope you don't have a daughter." And with that, I went to bed.

Melvin was being part of the village, trying to take care of me in the absence of my father or my brothers. Being a popular young man in his youth, he understood what was happening in the undercurrent of men's minds. I appreciated his concern, as I grew older.

For me, Lane College was a wonderful place to learn, develop and grow. It was a time when life was challenging though not overly complicated. I met strong and determined people who wanted to make good and successful lives for themselves. Most of the students were planning lives and careers where they could help change the world. They became teachers, ministers and social workers. Others studied business administration, science, history and math. It was easier to find jobs then; most went on to start their careers right after graduating.

Tennessee State University

Marriage interrupted my college career. I married in 1965, lived in Charleston, South Carolina until 1968, and then I moved to Nashville once again. I transferred to Tennessee A &I (Agricultural and Industrial) State University. They renamed it Tennessee State University. I had two children by then, and I was a motivated student. There was no campus life for me. No dances. No beer drinking. Only classes, homework and being a wife and mother.

I had a good neighbor who kept my children while I attended classes. She and her family had just moved to Nashville that summer for her husband to attend Fisk University. They were from Minnesota and had taken advantage of a program for teachers to attend school fulltime and earn a master's degree in a year. We became good friends. Because I had good help with my children, I was able to attend school fulltime and graduate with a BA in English in 1969.

University of South Alabama

Attending the University South Alabama was an interesting journey. It was my first experience attending school with white people. As a youngster, I grew up hearing how I, as a black person would, have a hard time making it in America. They told us we had to work twice as hard as white children; nothing would be easy for us. Some teachers gave the impression that white students were smarter than we were. I never thought much about white students until I entered graduate school. I certainly never thought they were smarter even though they had better schools and better resources than we had.

The University of South Alabama had regular students and many non-traditional students. I was in classes with both. I was usually one of two or three black students in my classes as the school was predominately white. There were very few black professors. I didn't have one. I must say that I was nervous going back to school after so many years. My nerves almost got the better of me when I was about to take my first test in a counseling class. I received the test, read the first question and immediately my mind went blank. Nothing was familiar to me. I sat staring at the paper with pen in hand, blinking back tears. It had been so long since I was in school that my fear was seizing me, gripping me, overwhelming me.

After what seemed the whole class period, I started writing. When the professor called time, I put my pen down and handed in my paper. I made an "A." All the information came back to me once I took a few deep breaths and relaxed.

It took me a moment to begin the test. I had had a recurring dream over many years that I was in a classroom staring at my test paper, and I couldn't remember anything I had studied. I would wake up in a panic thankful that it was only a dream.

In two of my counseling classes, I had some rather involved projects where research and organizational skills were required. I had fun doing those assignments, and I did such an excellent job that one professor wrote on my project, "This is the best work I have ever seen on this assignment." The other professor singled me out in class. He held up my paper and told the class, "This is the way this project should be done." He went on to chastise the class, talking to them as if they were high school students. Some were young students, but many were teachers and other non-traditional students. I was embarrassed but glad that I fully understood and executed the assignment.

What I noticed was that many students turned in handwritten work on notebook paper without any regard for following the American Psychological Association (APA) Style of writing. I noticed the same thing when I took graduate classes in English. In those classes, we were required to follow the Modern Language Association (MLA)

Style. Both styles of writing papers have very specific guidelines for their respective fields of study.

My American Literature professor assigned *The Adventures of Huckleberry Finn.* We were to read it and choose a theme on which to write a paper. When we got our papers back, I asked a young man in the class to let me see his paper. I wanted to see how an "A" paper looked. He handed it over gladly. I read a bit, examined the presentation, and gave it back.

His theme had to do with Huck as a fourteen-year-old boy. It was handwritten on notebook paper, far from the MLA Style, and wasn't especially substantive. My theme was "Nigger Jim: Should the African American Student be Offended?"

I followed the MLA style religiously as I carefully examined Jim's character and noticed how Mark Twain had skillfully taken each stereotype attributed to black people and ascribed them to white people. In spite of being called nigger, Jim was a positive character, and I wanted to present him that way as had Twain. I got a "B+" on the paper.

I only had maybe three professors who I thought were a little biased. I liked the few I had who were very exacting. I liked knowing what they expected. I found most of them fair. The white students were not as smart, and neither were the professors as tough as I had heard during my youth. I didn't feel I could simply get by as some did. I worked at least twice as hard as they.

I earned my Master of Science degree in counseling from the University of South Alabama in 1989.

WHERE ARE YOU GOD AND WHAT ARE YOU?

Losing My Religion and Finding My Spirit

God made so many different kinds of people. Why would
He allow only one way to serve Him? Martin Buber

The mystery of all mysteries is how I have seen God in different ways throughout my life. When I was a young child, Malcolm and I used to lie on the grass, look up at the sky, and try to imagine what God looked like and what he was doing. I knew God had to be male because folks always said he when referring to God. I accepted that, but I couldn't understand how something we referred to as he could create everything, know everything, and have everything under his control. None of it made sense to me.

"I bet he's a white man with a long white beard," Malcolm said, as we lay on our backs under the azure sky dotted with puffy white clouds. We wanted so much to see God appear in the sky as a rainbow did after a summer shower. I wanted to find his face in one of the marshmallow clouds.

Of course, that made sense. God must be a man, a white man. White men owned everything and ran the world. Both of us knew that. I was wondering though if Malcolm had God confused with Santa Claus. I knew Santa was white and had a long white beard, but he wore a red suit. Santa was a benevolent sort; however, both of us found him a little scary when Mommy took us to see him at Goldsmith's Department Store. God would not wear red, yet they told us to fear him. I wondered.

I said, "God could be a woman; women have babies."

Having babies was the biggest feat I could think of when I was nine, and our cousin Jean gave birth to her baby boy. Mama went to Aunt Thelma's house where Jean and her husband Henry lived and delivered the baby. I wasn't sure how she got him out, but I knew he came from Jean's stomach. That was my first real acquaintance with a miracle. I knew God made miracles. I didn't know how the baby got inside Jean, but I thought God must have put it in there.

Malcolm agreed, "Yeah, God could be a woman."

I had already gotten to know a little about the devil a few years earlier when I was five. The family knew I didn't like cats; therefore, when I stepped on a kitten and it died, everyone was suspicious. Mommy, who loved cats and all animals, was shocked. When she discovered what I had done, she said, "The cat devil is going to get you for killing that kitten."

I screamed and cried, but she just repeated, "The cat devil is going to get you, little girl, for killing that kitten" I lived in fear for days imagining that horned creature coming to get me. I believed the cat devil was the same as the regular devil. I knew more about the devil than I did about God. I knew that Satan had horns for ears and a pointy tail. He wore a red suit, carried a pitchfork, lived in a fiery place called hell, and he beat his wife every time it rained while the sun was shining.

On one rainy day, Malcolm and I put our ears to the ground to hear Mrs. Satan crying while she got her beating. Since we didn't hear her, we reasoned that hell must be too far down in the ground. It must have been somewhere near China, which we had heard was on the other side of the earth. If we could dig right through the ground, we would see China.

I used to say, my folks were heathens or pagans. The terms simply refer to people who are not Christian, or people who have a reverence for the land and nature in all its forms. Papa was the only one in my maternal family who I would call a bona fide Christian, yet he didn't go to church. He went to Sunday school and read the Bible regularly. Mama, Mommy and Brother made infrequent visits to Mt. Zion Baptist Church or to Pulliam Chapel. Attending church was not a thing that we did. Jesus' name wasn't that familiar to us. Easter found me learning a speech and getting a new dress a few times. When I was fifth grade, I had a long speech, the longest in my Sunday school class. It was about Jesus praying in the garden the night before they crucified him. The adults were impressed at how I could pronounce Gethsemane and recite such a long speech. Christmas meant wonderful food, fruits and nuts to eat and a few toys, not necessarily under a tree. We didn't believe it was Jesus' birthday.

We did give thanks for our food. It was customary for an adult to give a general blessing over the food, and then each individual would recite a Bible verse. We had learned the Beatitudes.

The summer we moved into our new house, Mommy's cousin Beatrice from Raleigh, North Carolina came for a two- or-three week visit. She was very particular about living gracefully and graciously. Cousin Beatrice enforced manners and etiquette. She insisted that we set the table properly and all sit and eat together each day. She would always offer the blessing, which could go on for some duration. Cousin Beatrice was a good cook, and she made some wonderful fried apple and peach pies. She was from Mama's side of the family, the Howells. Mommy was glad to have her for a visit, but we were glad to see her go.

I grew up mostly unceremoniously but nonetheless groomed with a sense of morality and a bit of civility. I had good manners, and I understood that I was to be respectful, obedient, and responsible. I made up my mind early in life that I would have a minister perform my ceremony when the time came for marriage. I always figured I would go to church when I grew up. It would be the thing to do then. I reckoned I would need help in raising good, moral children who would be responsible citizens.

Truthfully, I did not like church. I couldn't focus on what the minister was saying. I would daydream or write notes to a girlfriend on the few occasions that found me there. I could probably count on one hand the times I attended church before I reached the age of fourteen.

When I was fourteen, I lived with the Westbrooks in Nashville. They were dedicated churchgoers, which meant that I had to accompany the family to First Baptist Church, Capitol Hill every Sunday without exception for that whole year. I saw no value in church attendance then. If I couldn't pay attention at First Baptist, church wasn't for me. Kelly Miller Smith, a social gospel minister, president of Nashville's chapter of the NAACP and co-founder of Nashville Christian Leadership Council (NCLC), was the minister. He was smart and so good to look at. I could look forward to seeing him each Sunday, but that was all.

Still, I used to pray. Prayer was my therapy whenever I needed something to get me through a situation or a circumstance. I was a crying and a praying child, but only in private. Publicly I was stubborn and tough, a façade I wore well. My stubbornness often choked out my humility and caused me to seem hard as granite when in fact I was as soft and resilient as the cakes Mommy would bake. When Mommy made a cake, she would test its doneness by lightly pressing the top with her finger. When the cake wasn't quite done, it would be too soft and her finger would leave an impression; however, when the cake was done and ready to come out of the oven, it would bounce back to its perfect form. My prayer life kept me like that cake, soft in the center, but done, and when pressed by various circumstances, I would yield somewhat, but I would always bounce back.

I did not know if God was masculine, but I knew God was real. Mama and Mommy said Sonny, Charles and I survived living with Daddy only because they prayed for us constantly. They knew Daddy loved us, but they were not completely sure he knew what he was taking on when he decided that we three should live with him.

We probably did survive a few potential house fires and car crashes thanks to their prayers.

Even when I suffered a few times due to my choices, I prayed to God for deliverance, and though God didn't come through as I desired, I didn't stop believing or praying. I believed that I deserved the consequence due to some transgression on my part. I wasn't familiar with karma then. However, "You reap what you sow" was a Bible reference I had heard a few times.

I had to have a reason for all that existed, and I couldn't think of any other explanation than God, the Mystery among mysteries. I wanted to know more, but I didn't know where to go or to whom. Church was a place to wear pretty clothes, enjoy singing and listening to lots of talk of future times. It was either heavenly bliss or hell and damnation at some churches. Neither held my interest. I couldn't imagine either being as I had heard them described. I didn't feel like I was bound for either place. Heaven appeared unbelievably boring, and hell sounded painfully impossible. I did not want to "walk around heaven all day" on "streets paved with gold," or to play a harp. Moreover, how could someone burn forever? And why? I learned "God is love," yet, God would torture his creation. What was a child to believe?

My peers joined either Baptist or Methodist churches and were baptized by age twelve. I joined when I was sixteen and about to enter my senior year of high school. I needed to fill in the religion blank on my college application. Not a good reason to choose a religion or church, but that was what I did. I told Mommy what I was going to do. She and I went to church one Sunday, and I walked through when the minister announced, "The doors of the church are open." That was the invitation for all heathens who wanted to change their ways and accept the "blood of the Lamb" as their saving grace to come forth and declare that publicly.

The Reverend finished his sermon on a high note, took a few breaths, wiped his brow, and in a serious tone he said, "The doors of the church are open." The choir sang a solemn song. The minister beseeched all those who were not yet "saved" to come forth and accept salvation through Jesus. I used to hate that time when I attended church with Aunt Virginia. She would always glance over at me, the only teenage heathen in the whole church, with a look that said, "Shouldn't you be on your way to the altar?"

"The doors of the church are open," Reverend said for the second time as he called upon the sinners to give up their sinful ways. One more time he said, "The doors of the church are open." When he opened them that time, I rose from my seat and walked through. That meant I would sit on the mourner's bench until the spirit hit me, then I would become a convert to Christianity and a candidate for baptism. I was not looking forward to the mourning process, but I had made the commitment and had to follow through with bowed head and humble heart.

That summer during Revival week, I took my seat on the mourner's bench, a literal bench, with the rest of the heathens who were younger and perhaps had few or no sins to repent. I tried to mourn my past deeds and get the spirit but it was challenging. On about the third night of revival, Sonny talked to me, and I tried to look sad and repentant enough that I could move from the mourners' bench to the converts' bench. I was glad to move over even though I didn't feel any different inside.

Next was the baptism. That ritual took place at a nearby pond where cows and other livestock went to drink and bathe. That didn't frighten me since I was used to frolicking in Brother's pond while my brothers and cousin were swimming and living dangerously.

The water was brown, not at all transparent. It was easy to imagine all sorts of creatures living beneath its surface. I wasn't afraid. I went willingly, dressed in old clothes, holding my nose tightly against the microscopic pond life as the minister proclaimed to all within earshot, "I now baptize you in the name of the Father, the Son and the Holy Ghost." Amen. Amen. Amen.

Though we were not big churchgoers, we still remembered the Sabbath day and tried to keep it holy. In Papa's house, we honored that day by playing only gospel music. Our favorite radio station was WDIA out of Memphis, and they played gospel all day on Sunday.

We never danced, played cards or did any other enjoyable activities. Sunday dinners were nice, and we would visit relatives or friends, or sometimes we would have visitors. I never liked Sunday. I never knew why other than that it was a day of little or no activity. Later, I came to believe it was because I was born on Sunday, and I had come here with some reluctance.

I knew Lane College was a church supported school, and they expected students to attend mid-week services on campus and Sunday services at St. Paul CME Church. I attended each a couple of times. Sunday was for sleeping late and socializing in the afternoon when I didn't go home for the weekend. On one occasion when I did go to Sunday school, the teacher asked, "Why do we attend church?" Everybody looked around, not wanting to say something stupid. I don't know why, but I raised my hand and offered, "Because it's our tradition." Not mine, I could have added, but the collective "our." I just couldn't think of another reason. I could have answered that it makes us better people, but I didn't believe that. I was beginning to identify the hypocrites in my midst. I hadn't read the scripture that says, "Judge not that you be not judged." I was discovering that church attendance or membership was no deterrent to wrongdoing. The fires of hell were not real or hot enough to keep humankind from participating in certain sins. Maybe I was looking at church in the wrong way and expecting too much from those who professed Christianity; however, I wanted to see them living a "perfect" life. No sin. No fun.

Reverend Blake of Charleston performed my marriage ceremony in 1965. Just as I had planned, a minister joined me to my husband in holy wedlock. It was time to grow up and make a decent life for my future children. When I moved to Charleston, I looked up the reverend's church and started attending. I went a few times, but found nothing to captivate me and hold me there. It would be a few more years before I would try that again.

In 1970, Malcolm came to visit me in Nashville with a message about Jehovah God and paradise earth. I had heard that my youngest brother had found a religion that held out hope of salvation for believers to live forever in paradise right here on earth. Of course, God would clean up the earth and rid it of all evil and wrongdoing first. This great worldwide destruction would take place during the battle of Armageddon as written in the Bible book of Revelation. It was an exciting message, frightening yet filled with promise. I thought I needed something to teach my children and set them on a good path so they could develop into moral and productive people. I immediately started studying the Bible with Jehovah's Witnesses. I did this because I was impressed with how Malcolm had changed his life. He appeared more focused than before he went into the military. I thought he was showing some maturity; I was glad to see that.

I had some memory of being associated with Jehovah's Witnesses when I was a child. For a little while, Mommy studied the Bible with them, and we attended an assembly and a meeting or two. That was when we learned that the holidays had their roots in paganism. They had nothing to do with Christianity. From that time forth, we didn't celebrate the holidays. That proved to be a money-saver.

I spent the next twelve years of my life in worldly darkness. I closed out all things that were not associated with the Bible and Jehovah's Witnesses. I spent time studying the Bible, attending Book Study on Tuesday night where we studied various books written by members of the Watch Tower Bible and Tract Society (WTBTS) that dealt with Bible prophesies. I attended Ministerial School on Friday nights where I learned to be more effective in door-to-door and informal witnessing. I attended the Sunday meeting where there was a talk or lecture given by one of the elders. Afterwards there was a discussion of a Watchtower article. The religion required much time and study, but I was able to do it and not neglect my duties associated with being wife, mother and homemaker. In fact, being a capable wife, mother and homemaker were highly valued and were encouraged. They stressed raising godly children. My life was full and somewhat satisfying. My children were young and had no choice except to accompany me to meetings and take part in field service some Saturday mornings. Field service was the door-to-door witnessing activity that all members were encouraged to do. Everyone was required to witness. Those not able to go door-to-door could witness to their family members who were not Witnesses. They could witness on their jobs or with neighbors. Disabled members could witness via telephone or through letter writing.

It was the 1971, and Jehovah's Witnesses were teaching that we were living in the "last days" of this "wicked system." Everything centered on the last days. One had to be ready because "No one knows the day or hour." Only the righteous, the meek, would be saved. They searched the Bible looking for scriptures that pointed to the last days or end times. They did calculations from the beginning of creation as recorded in Genesis and considered the prophesies of Daniel and others to determine that we were living in the last days, and that soon Jehovah God would destroy the wicked, and cleanse the earth for the meek. If you were not one of Jehovah's Witnesses, you belonged to "Babylon the Great." All other religions and pagans were included. According to some Bible scholars in the early twentieth century, the end time was to culminate in 1975. Some Witnesses prepared for that end by giving up many of the ordinary and normal human pursuits such as going to college, starting a career, getting married or having children. They figured they would delay such until the "New Order" was in place. After all, they had an eternity on earth to do whatever their hearts desired and their minds could conceive.

The thought of no death sounded appealing for a time. There were so many things to try that it could take an eternity. I think that was the draw for many. Others were thrilled that the Witnesses extinguished the fires of hell. They taught that hell, *hades* or *Sheol* was merely the grave, a place of concealment. There was no eternal torment. It was impossible. They taught that only a hundred forty-four thousand were going to heaven to rule over the New Earth with Jesus. From the look of the Watchtower Society, it appeared they were white and male. Most had already made the journey by then.

I was a dedicated and faithful servant of Jehovah God, or was it of the Watchtower Bible and Tract Society, until I began to grow tired of condemning others for their choice of religion and lifestyle. I grew tired of the family disunity it promoted and the separateness it preached—"Be not of the world. Do not become unevenly yoked." I only read publications written by the WTBTS. I seldom saw a movie or watched a television show with any substance. My world was very narrow. My involvement with people outside my family and the kingdom hall was nil. I wanted more.

Along came Malcolm again with new teachings, ideas, and revelations. He had had his differences with the elders. He was seeing scripture differently from what they were teaching. He dared to study the Bible in depth and to think for himself. I became concerned that he had become too involved in studying prophecy. I didn't think it was necessary or healthy. On the other hand, I had become disillusioned with the Witnesses teaching, and I was ready for change. I wanted nothing to do with Bible study any longer.

Being associated with Jehovah's Witnesses all those years had many positives and some negatives. My children and I enjoyed wholesome relationships with people of different races during those years. The Witnesses erased the color line early in their history. They knew that God was no "respecter of persons," and neither were they, except at the top perhaps. They made more of an effort to practice what they preached than most others. They taught moral values. If you did not honor those values, they would excommunicate you. Their word for it was "disfellowship."

Some people thought the religion was a cult. Members mostly associated with one another and only family members who were Witnesses. Their allegiance appeared to be to the WTBTS instead of God. There was a powerful figure at the top, the president of the WTBTS, and a body of elders who were in charge of the worldwide membership. All, throughout the world, spoke with one accord. The WTBTS was a smooth running machine. I was in awe. I felt that God's spirit had to be upon any group that could function in such a way with very little discord.

The downside was that the religion didn't promote critical thinking, curiosity, questioning. Outside reading was discouraged. The WTBTS published its own translation of the Bible. It published tracts, books to aid in understanding Bible prophecy; the *Watchtower* magazine, and the *Awake* magazine, which contained human-interest articles, personal experiences, and gave advice on living. Their literature was to be sufficient to inform and educate the membership. They frowned on any worldly literature and movies that showed violence or sex. They taught against participation in worldly or pagan holidays such as Christmas, Halloween, Easter, and all others. Since those holidays did not originate from Bible teaching, they were pagan and had no place in the Witnesses lives. There were no Christmas trees and gifts for the children and no Easter egg hunt, not even a tooth fairy, Mother Goose or make-believe. No birthday parties. The children grew up in a world void of fantasy. That didn't work well for many families since their children were exposed to all of those fun activities through their association with other children at school.

The Witnesses did have social events for their children where they invited others. They participated in some sports with other Witnesses, traveled to convention sites around the country and did things of that nature. They were not against good, clean fun with family and Witness friends.

They were against patriotic practices such as celebrating the Fourth of July, saying the Pledge of Allegiance to the flag, singing the national anthem. Witnesses did not vote. Jehovah's Witnesses were to keep themselves from nationalism and patriotism, and the corruptive influences of the world. They were to give their allegiance only to God's kingdom. It was a good way for a person to live if they were afraid of life or jaded by their life's experiences. It was a safe place to hide from life. It worked for me for a time.

There was no focus on achieving, acquiring, accomplishing, competing. What would be the purpose? All worldly pursuits were going to be destroyed during the "great tribulation and Armageddon," so what would be the use. Their focus was on preparing to live in the "New Earth" under the rule of the "New Heavens." Paradise on earth was the destination.

I didn't leave the organization under good terms; therefore, I lost all of my "friends." They allowed none of the members to speak to me if they saw me on the street or in the marketplace. To them I was an apostate. "Get the wicked one from among you" was the command. They believed "one rotten apple will spoil the whole bushel." Though I left willingly, I felt they treated me unfairly by disfellowshipping me. There was no way of explaining to my friends my reason for leaving. They could imagine whatever they desired. Each member lived in fear of doing something that would get him or her expelled from the congregation. They were fearful of losing Jehovah's favor or at least the WTBTS's favor.

I left that religion as an innocent where worldly matters were concerned. I had no knowledge of many normal human behaviors exhibited by people who were not Witnesses, so there was much for me to learn. I had been living a narrow way where so much was condemned. They judged worldly people as wicked and deserving of destruction by God.

The Witnesses did not consider themselves fundamentalist, but simply people who lived by the Bible. They took the Bible as the literal word of God. Though they took much of it literally, they knew some things were symbolic, spiritual, or allegorical. They believed the scriptures were for instruction and living by as the inspired word of God.

In 1982, I became an outcast from the Witnesses. I started thinking and planning for myself. I started by doing the one thing I missed most, reading materials other that those written and published by the WTBTS.

I always had a spiritual deficit. I longed to understand life from a spiritual point of view. Witnesses were grounded and earthbound. I found myself drawn to Metaphysical and New Thought books and pop psychology, authors such as Wayne Dyer, Joseph Murphy, Louise Hay, and others. I couldn't get enough. The message was so simple, loving, and supportive of humanity. There was nothing condemning, derogatory or punitive. It was okay to be human. God was bigger than I had known. I was learning that God was not male or female or created in the image of man. I liked that about this Mystery, Creator, Source or Spirit. I learned that this Spirit lived in, through and as all of us and all things. It is all there is. I was on my way. I did not have to forget all I had and learned; however, I did have to put that knowledge into proper perspective. I had to learn that there was more than one way to discover God, that it was okay to explore other religions, philosophies, and ideologies. Jesus was the right and perfect way for those who wanted to follow him. There were teachers for those who wanted to discover God in a different way. It would be extremely difficult to get all humans to agree on one way of seeing and doing anything.

Every book I read and every lecture I heard led me right back to my own being. I learned that I was already perfect, whole, and complete. Nothing about me needed fixing as though I were broken. I just needed to step into my own being, and allow God in me to express. It is a journey.

Learning is easy, but learning must only be a prelude to being. I did not say "doing;" I said "being." I came here trying to find out what I should be doing. I often asked the questions: "What am I supposed to do? Why am I here?" Too much focus on doing and not enough on being. It is in being that I learned what I should be doing. Deepak Chopra said in a meditation, "As an enlightened being I engage in all sorts of activities, yet I do nothing. All happens. Living happens. There is nothing to cling to or grasp. Nothing to run away from."

As Pierre Teilhard de Chardin wrote and many New Thought teachers say, "We are spiritual beings having a human experience." Some say God is in the stillness, which means we get our inspiration from the spirit within us. All things come from within. "Be still and know."

I learned that I am responsible for my life as its manifestations are the result of my thinking. That knowledge was a harsh revelation to me. It compelled me to review the major experiences in my life and ponder my part in their occurrence. There were times when I didn't like what I learned. I didn't want to be responsible for the awful occurrences in my life. I wanted to believe in fate and chance, maybe even in luck or predestination. I am not saying that I consciously thought about and planned all that I experienced in life. It is not always conscious. In fact, it is mostly subconscious.

It was after trying to shift the blame that I decided to start taking responsibility for my own actions and my own life. I felt greatly empowered when the meaning of all that entailed slowly unfolded before me. I no longer had to fear life and to be afraid of what I may have to face. I could have some control based on my thinking. However, there were things already set in motion by years of thinking that would not change overnight.

New Thought teaching opened up a world of possibility before me. It meant seeing in a different light all that I had learned. Jesus the Christ said, "Worship in spirit and truth." It is not about following the letter of some law or about the physical manifestation of a thing. It is about seeing from Spirit, with Spirit, as Spirit.

The Dali Lama stated, "By maintaining sharp awareness of the function of religion as expressed in the actuality of all teachings, we can escape the ruinous error of sectarian discrimination and partisanship, and we can avoid the grave sin of casting aside any religious teaching."

GET A JOB!

...when you work you fulfill a part of earth's furthest dream, assigned to you when that dream was born, and in keeping yourself with labour you are in truth loving life, And to love life through labour is to be intimate with life's inmost secret.

Kahlil Gibran, *The Prophet*

"Get a Job, Sha na na na, Sha na na na na Get a Job"—Those lyrics by the Silhouettes used to resound in my head at various times in my life when Aunt Virginia or Mommy would say to me, "When are you going to get a job? Why don't you get a job?"

At some stage in my life, I must have wanted a career. I must have wanted to earn my own money and the independence that came along with it. There were times during my childhood when I was eight or nine that I thought of becoming a movie star, a dancer, secretary, nurse or teacher. Mostly, I thought of becoming a wife and mother. When I was in my thirties, I had a secret desire to become a racecar driver. In my forties and fifties, I thought of joining the Peace Corp or some other group and traveling to some faraway place where I would live among the people and teach.

My parents wanted me to attend college and prepare to follow their examples and become a teacher, or to work in some other profession and be equipped to support myself. I enjoyed working for Miss Ann and earning money for college the summer of 1962. It was a natural progression in my development as a young woman. That summer, I came to appreciate money, and learned to use it so it would serve me well. I did not develop a love relationship with it. I didn't need it to give me a sense of self-worth or to make me feel independent. My sense of self-worth came from Daddy who adored me; my independence came from Mommy's example of a determined woman who knew it was up to her to make her own way in the world. Her fierceness grew out of the depression era mentality of scarcity and struggle. I did not share that, but I understood the importance of being able to make my own way. I watched as she struggled and worked more than one job at a time just to make ends meet, to get by, but never to get ahead. I didn't like that. I didn't want that.

Yet, I was going to college to prepare to enter the world of work in some capacity. I knew when I was in college that I didn't want to teach children. It was fun playing school when I was ten and eleven, but to place myself in a classroom with twenty or more children of different temperaments and learning styles year after year for twenty, thirty or forty years, was a future I couldn't picture. Nothing about that prospect appealed to me. Certainly not the meager salaries teachers received. I won't say "earned" because schoolteachers were and still are underpaid and underappreciated. They deserve much more in the way of money, respect and appreciation.

I imagine all of the professionals in America have had a teacher or many teachers who helped them develop and become who they are. Teachers have influenced so many people to become productive citizens, laborers, doctors, lawyers, engineers, scientists, entrepreneurs, politicians and even presidents. They taught those who made their fortunes in sports and entertainment. Yet they have to demonstrate and protest for a decent wage.

Some people go to college and learn how to teach; however, I think real teachers are born knowing how to reach inside their students and facilitate learning. I was not born to teach, but I did try my hand at substitute teaching beginning in February of 1965. Although I had just gotten married, I was staying with Mommy until summer school started. I needed to stay in Tennessee to complete my last few hours before I could get my degree, and then I would move to Charleston. I soon learned that I didn't like working with behavioral problems. I felt that students should come to school with a good attitude and a desire to learn the lessons for the day. They should be on their best behavior, be obedient, and be cooperative. Of course, that didn't happen. Besides, teaching was about more than just subject matter. It involved giving more of me than I was prepared to give. It involved too much disciplining. I was in a classroom only one or two days at a time as a substitute teacher. The time I spent with a class did not allow me to affect much change in the students.

Before I could enroll in summer school, Joel was in a car accident in Charleston; therefore, I left Tennessee immediately. Joel's parents drove me to Charleston. I didn't go back to Lane College that summer or ever again. My degree was on hold for a couple of years. When my son Alex was eight months old and needed such things as a highchair, playpen, and the like. I needed a part time job. I didn't want to work fulltime and leave my baby for someone else to raise, yet I wanted him to have some things that did not fit into our budget.

Again, I turned to substitute teaching. This time, it was Mary Ford Elementary School in Charleston, South Carolina. Patience was not one of my virtues, and I found it much needed to persevere as a substitute teacher. Charleston was unique to me—the food, culture and traditions and the language. Sometimes it was difficult for me to understand the students who spoke English with their Gullah-Geechi accent. Usually there was one child who could translate for me. The one thing on the lunch menu each day was rice, the mainstay of the low country diet. Hoppin John, which was black-eyed peas with rice, was a favorite. Once I started subbing at Mary Ford, the principal called me often. He would come to my house and pick me up when I needed a ride.

In April of that year, the principal asked me to replace a second grade teacher who was on extended leave. I was glad to get the job; however, I soon understood why the teacher was out. It was the last two months of the school year, and I had a heavy task ahead. I'm not putting it all on the students. I wasn't sure I was qualified to teach small children en masse. Two or three at a time I could handle.

In every class, there was always one child who would make me question my motive for being there. That time it was Lavon. He was a busy boy who liked to meddle with the other children and question everything. One day I turned from the blackboard and saw Lavon two rows over where he was thumping Jimmy on the head. I just looked at him without speaking. The class turned and stared. Jimmy recoiled from the thump and rubbed his head.

"I told him not to look at me like that," Lavon said.

"What?"

"Jimmy was looking at me, and it made me mad."

"You don't have a right to thump his head simply because he looked at you. I want you to write one hundred times, 'I'm sorry I thumped Jimmy's head' and give it to me before you leave today."

"I wish Miss Jones was here. She wouldn't make me write that. You're mean."

"Just sit down and do what I said. I understand now why Mrs. Jones is not here."

For the next school year, I decided to take my name off the substitute list and apply for a teacher's aide position. The principal was sorry to lose me as a substitute, but he was glad to have me as an aide. Working with Mrs. D and Mrs. J, two first grade teachers, was satisfying and fun. Mrs. D was in her late forties; Mrs. J was late fifties. Both depended on me to handle many tasks, mostly those of the nonteaching kind such as taking students to the bathroom, putting up bulletin boards, helping with lunch and play time. I would assist individual students who needed extra help. Most students had no preschool or kindergarten; therefore, were ill prepared for school. Some didn't know their names as their families had called them by nicknames all of their lives. I was twenty-two and pregnant with my second child, yet I had lots of energy and more patience in that position. Work was enjoyable; I looked forward to each day. The greater responsibility was on the teachers; I was happy to assist where necessary.

Both teachers cried when I told them I was moving back to Tennessee.

I was sad that I had to leave them in the middle of the school year; however, I was so glad to be going back home. Charleston was not the best place for black people in the 1960s, but since Joel was in the Air Force, I was somewhat shielded from some of the racial prejudice of that time. We went shopping, to movies, doctors and sporting events on the Air Force Base and Naval Station. We lived in George Legare housing and before we got our first car, we walked to Charleston Naval Station where we would shop at the commissary, then take a cab back home.

In January of 1968, Joel completed his four years in the Air Force and received his honorable discharge. We left immediately for Tennessee. Home, family and school were calling. It would be many years before I would again join the workforce. My work from 1968-86 was raising my children. I was a fulltime mama; I loved it. I'm the only woman I know who loved staying home doing laundry, cooking, cleaning and all the rest. I didn't bore with the mundane, necessary chores. I enjoyed order and cleanliness, meal planning and such. I enjoyed reading, sewing, taking exercise classes such as jazzercise, aerobics, ballet and skating over the years. I always felt a need to keep fit and to take part in enriching activities. Besides, it allowed me to spend much time in field service when I was one of Jehovah's Witnesses from 1970-82. I spent much of my time after 1982 doing volunteer work and going to school fulltime to earn my graduate degree in counseling.

In 1984, I decided to try substitute teaching in Mobile. I must have thought I had developed some patience by then. I had not. I quit and never attempted substituting again. A fourth-grade class helped me make up my mind that time.

I gave teaching children one more try. It was in 1986-87 when I moved to Memphis without my husband for what turned out to be a short break from marriage complete with divorce papers. The only thing I knew to do was teach. Mommy had suggested that I apply in Fayette County. They hired me.

Being the teacher, I could set the standard for expectations at the outset, which gave me some advantage. Of course, there is always one, who will try you. During that year, only one young man challenged me to the degree that we almost became physical. His name was

Jerry. He worked and probably helped to support his family. Jerry reminded me of James Dean, the rebellious movie star from the 1950s. He didn't want to follow instructions. We came to a meeting of the minds when I took him into the hall and talked with him about our expectations.

A couple of incidents saddened me that year. One of my students was compelled to withdraw from school so he could go to work and help support his family. I couldn't believe that was happening in the late 1980s. It was common for boys to drop out and work when I was young, but I thought that era had passed. He was a good student with good behavior; I didn't want him to leave. I thought he had so much promise.

Near the end of the school year, two students died in a car wreck. Students, Teachers and the community were shocked. After the memorial service in the school gymnasium, I went back to my classroom unable to shake off the gloom and sadness. I wrote the following poem:

Dying Young

Dry rotted youth what waste!
Daydreams end in dust
Scattered on marble walls
Clouding eternity from yesterday.
Melodies///// serenading plugged ears
Unplugged by sobs of frightened babies,
Mothers regretting labor pains,
Fathers holding back sorrow
Swallowing pain in lumps.
Cherry blossoms lose their fragrance.
Dogwoods wither from time.
Sun shines brightly on early morning dew
Aging from dawn,
Disappearing into day's journey,
Ending in darkest night,
Darker still in death.

In the late 1980s in Mobile, I attended a real estate seminar on buying property with no money down. The course was very interesting and informative. After I completed it, I went right out and purchased my first property. During that time, many people were losing their homes to foreclosure; therefore, buying a property before it foreclosed was a help to the homeowner. It was to be a win/win for both buyer and seller. However, was it? I suppose it helped the sellers in that they didn't lose their homes to the banks and mess up their credit, but they had to give up their homes along with the equity for very little cash in return. That was the way it was done. I bought the homes. Joel and I put much sweat equity into those properties. They were nice houses that had not received loving care. We scrubbed walls, kitchens and bathrooms, tiled floors, painted rooms and cleaned yards. The work was hard but very satisfying. After renting the houses for a while, I refinanced them, took out the equity, and then sold them.

One evening when Joel and I were working on one of the properties, a police officer drove up and asked, "What are you all doing?"

"We own this house" I said, "Why are you asking?" I felt it was none of his business why we were there. It was in a nice white neighborhood not far from where we lived. Our neighborhood was still predominately white but that one was all white. One of the neighbors had called because we looked suspicious. What made us look suspicious?

The business was profitable, but I felt after a time that I had exploited the homeowners; I wasn't proud. It didn't matter that acquiring real estate with no money down and very little paid to the owner was legal, it just didn't seem moral or ethical. I wanted to earn money, but I wanted to do it with a clear conscious.

At that time, I wanted to be in the stream of life. Money was not my motivation. My association with Jehovah's Witnesses had removed the materialistic quest from me before it fully developed. As a child, I always wanted to buy things. Every time I would go to the store with Mommy, I would beg for something--candy, a toy, anything. I knew she had no money to spend frivolously, yet I would ask anyway. I had the potential to be a black belt shopper, but the lack of money in those formative years curtailed that somewhat. However, it was being associated with Jehovah's Witnesses that gave me a different perspective on how I felt about acquiring material things. I knew I didn't want to work just to amass and accumulate material possessions. I wasn't interested in keeping up with the Joneses. I was willing and ready to work to try to make a difference in someone's life. I agree with this statement by Tom Brokaw, "It's easy to make a buck, it's a lot tougher to make a difference."

What would I do to contribute to the cosmic good, to help someone, to make a difference? I knew I owed something to life for my very existence, and that I would have to find a way to pay. Muhammad Ali, who had much to say on many subjects, said, "Service is the rent you pay for your room here on earth." I started looking for something interesting that I could put my heart and soul in. There was so much to do, so many in need of help.

Not knowing where to start, I turned to volunteer work and found it so satisfying that I joined several organizations over the years. Sometimes I worked with two or three organizations at one time. I worked with Contact Mobile Helpline, Rape Crisis Center, Greater Gulf Literacy Council, Adopt-A-Friend, American Red Cross and Hospice. Each organization had in-depth training conducted by professionals and dedicated volunteers. Being part of those organizations made me feel part of something bigger than myself, something that could help people, change lives and even save lives. After a while, I wanted to do more. I had found my calling in volunteer work.

Contact Mobile Helpline was the first organization I joined. The helpline was the number that people called when they were in some kind of trouble and needed a referral to a service, or they needed help in paying a utility bill. There were calls from people who were lonely and needed someone to talk with. Sometimes there were crank callers. There were callers with very personal and private situations; I learned how to respond to them. I learned to communicate with deaf callers via a TTY machine. Once, I passed on the news of a death to a deaf person via the TTY machine. My most critical call was from a person threatening suicide. With that call, I patched in the crisis center right away. Working with Contact Mobile taught me about the base desires and behaviors of humans. I learned that there were many people in need of help.

I chose the Adopt-A-Friend program even though I wasn't sure I would be comfortable with elderly people. Years later, I came to understand why I selected that organization. The program connected volunteers with local nursing homes. It paired a volunteer with a nursing home resident for weekly visits. The volunteer could take the resident out of the home on outings, the park or a restaurant. The Adopt-A-Friend program filled an important need for some nursing home residents who did not have relatives or friends to visit them. It helped ease some of the loneliness they experienced. It was a real stretch for me, but it was, I think, part of my effort to move out of my comfort zone and experience. I was uncomfortable with the idea of being in such a setting.

I thought back on the day Mama said to me, "Barbara Jean, go to Pat's house and sit with her a while. She's not feeling well today." I was nine and was deathly afraid of sick, old people. I knew death was next.

"I don't want to go. I'm scared."

"Scared of what? You and Malcolm go to Pat's house all the time."

That was true. Malcolm and I did go to Aunt Pat and Uncle Alf's house often to sit, talk, and partake of the delicious goodies they had such as lemonade, teacakes or a slice of pie. I didn't tell Mama I thought Aunt Pat might die and I was afraid of dead people.

"Go on," Mama said.

Reluctantly, I went down the path and sat with Aunt Pat. She recovered just fine and lived for another thirty years.

In short time, I became acquainted with my assigned friend at the nursing home and with many others. When I got to the nursing home for my first visit, the recreation director who was in charge said, "I thought you were white when we talked on the phone, so I assigned Mrs. H to you. She's white."

I said, "That's okay." It didn't matter with me whether my friend was black or white. When I met her, she didn't seem bothered that I was black. Nursing homes could be lonely places and the patients and staff always welcomed visitors.

Whenever I visited, I would make the rounds and spend a few minutes talking to several residents and greeting all. That experience was not only a portent; it also helped to allay many of my fears about growing old.

My eyes opened wide to the gravity of illiteracy in Alabama and throughout the country when I trained with the Greater Gulf Literacy Council. The most interesting thing I discovered about illiterate people was how well they coped. They often succeeded in life without knowing how to read. Many illiterate adults raised successful children who often did not know mama or daddy couldn't read. They would find ways of getting people to read for them using the excuse that they forgot their glasses, or the lighting was bad.

We were always in need of tutors and used local media to recruit. The program director asked me to appear on WBLX radio talk show to discuss the pervasiveness of illiteracy in Mobile. That was a new experience for me, and it wasn't as scary as I had imagined. Each time the host asked a question, she would say "tutorer" instead of "tutor." I kept correcting her. We both had a good laugh about that. I spoke to community groups and held workshops to inform the public on the problems and challenges of not being able to read. We had exercises that literate people could attempt to solve to give them some idea of how it was for an illiterate person when they look at the written. The exercises were fun and challenging. Teaching adults was not an easy task. They were busy making a living and taking care of families. They had little time for study. It was hard for some to concentrate, and oftentimes they had undiagnosed learning disabilities. Therefore, recruiting tutors was difficult. I had one student who was a high school graduate, yet could not read. Another was a middle age man who had raised a family. The oldest student I know learned to read at eighty-nine years of age.

I wanted to volunteer with Mercy Medical Hospice Program to observe the dying process. As a child, I feared death and dying. As a young woman, I started to become interested in death and the dying process. I imagined it. I wrote poetry about it. I believed I could help someone as I faced my own fears.

When I joined the Hospice program, I thought it would be scary, but I found the training very enlightening. I learned about palliative care, which is providing comfort and pain-free end of life experience. I discovered that some patients go through an obvious transition where they effectively separate from this material existence. By that, I mean the person loses interest in everyday matters and seems to be connecting with another realm. Sometimes they "see" or "talk" to relatives who have already passed. Later, when I witnessed the transitioning process with my relatives, I was glad I understood what was happening. During home visits, I sat and talked with patients and their caregivers. At times, I sat with the patient while their caregiver ran errands. We usually engaged in small talk. One thing I learned is that people don't want to talk about their impending death or speculate about what is beyond.

The work was only sad if the client lived alone and had only an occasional visit from a health aide. It seemed lonely and empty coming to the end of life alone. Of course, I didn't know that for sure. It was the way I felt whenever I visited one of my clients who had no wife or children to care for him.

Orson Wells wrote, "We're born alone, we live alone, we die alone. Only through our love and friendship can we create the illusion for the moment that we're not alone."

I came to understand that dying is truly a solo act. It doesn't matter who is present when someone dies; they have effectively separated from them and this life.

It was after serving on jury duty in 1985 that I became interested in volunteering with the Rape Crisis Center. The case involved the sexual molestation of an eight-year-old boy by a twenty-three year-old man. The boy's mother had left him in the young man's care when the incident occurred. The case was very interesting. It was my first time to serve on a jury. Unlike most, I wanted the lawyers to select me.

The defense attorney was a gruff, intimidating, greasy, rotund man who reminded me of Frank Cannon, a 1970's television private investigator. He employed the art of smoke screens in an effort to deflect the blame away from his client and place it on the mother. Since she was young and attractive, the defense attorney tried to make it seem that she was out partying and having fun while her son was in the young man's care. He tried day after day to make her responsible for what happened. His tactic worked on most of the jurors. When it came time for us to deliberate at least three of us could see the truth. We were not willing to let the mother be the scapegoat. Even though we thought she used poor judgment in the situation, the young man was responsible for his actions. He needed to pay for his crime. After much deliberation, we three had convinced the other jurors that the young man was guilty. It took a while, but they could see that the lawyer was playing the old blame game to throw us off track. He was blaming the mother of the victim instead of the perpetrator.

During the trial, I became aware that rape crisis counselors had accompanied the mother and her son to court. Shortly after the trial ended, I heard a PSA on television for rape crisis volunteers. I applied for the next training session and soon became a volunteer. There was an interview process prior to the weekend training session. They didn't accept everyone who applied or everyone who went through the training. The process was very selective due to the nature of the work. After a few years of working as a volunteer, I became one of the trainers and taught potential volunteers how to work with clients from different cultural backgrounds.

Counselors were on call for twenty-four hour shifts. Sometimes I worked two shifts during the month. When a victim reported to the hospital, my beeper would go off, and I would call the hospital and get basic information about the victim. I would then go to the hospital no matter the time of day or night, sometimes spending as many as eight hours at the emergency room. Unless it was a "violent" assault, it was not an emergency; therefore, the survivor would have to wait her turn as the nurse triaged patients. Rape victims didn't sit in the waiting room with other patients. They were taken into a private examining room upon arrived.

I emphasized violent because all rapes, sexual assaults, and abuse are violent in their very nature. Anything that happens that negatively affects your body, mind and spirit is violent. My job as counselor was to listen with empathy and understanding. Counselors were to be nonjudgmental.

I had many interesting cases over the years. It was not always easy being with the survivor, but I put aside my emotions such as anger, rage and sadness. It was about the victim. I was there to attend to the victim's needs and prepare her or him for the medical examination and rape kit collection. I also informed the victim of the next step in the process and answered any questions. Most times counselors worked in pairs. The primary counselor would spend time with the survivor while the backup counselor would meet with the individual who accompanied the person to the hospital. If the victim came alone or the police brought her to the hospital, the secondary counselor would contact a support person and apprise her/him of the situation, if appropriate. Sometimes a survivor would not want any relative or friend to know about their experience. As counselor, I took my cues from the victim.

As a court advocate, I informed survivors of the legal process and accompanied them to court. Cases the district attorney believed were winnable went to trial. Very few cases made it to trial for various reasons. Most were *nol pros*.

I worked in many positions during my ten years with Rape Crisis. Another volunteer and I staffed the Follow-Up Clinic each Wednesday for survivors who had presented at the hospital the week prior. We would assess the survivor's functioning in the aftermath of the rape. Sometimes a survivor would need further counseling. For that reason, the program director, two other volunteers and I started the Rape Survivors Support Group. It was during that time that we replaced the word "victim" with "survivor." Survivor was empowering and more aptly described those who had come through such an ordeal. We met once a week in a local church, had coffee and snacks, listened to the concerns and issues our group members expressed. One of our group members was so determined to catch the man who broke into her apartment while she was asleep and attacked her that she had her story enacted on "America's Most Wanted" television show.

The Rape Crisis Center was a nonprofit, housed in the Mobile Mental Health Center with one paid employee. It was dependent on donations. I often helped with fundraising.

As a member of the Speakers Bureau, I presented information on rape and sexual assault to women's groups, colleges, churches and other organizations. I wrote a monthly column for our newsletter *The Grapevine*. My articles contained advice and tips on coping in the aftermath of rape and rape prevention. I took a self-defense course and wrote an article on it as a preventative for sexual assault.

When the Rape Crisis Director, asked me to appear on the WALA television show "New Vision" and discuss "Date Rape" I tried to beg off. I had no desire to be on television but she persuaded me to do it. I accepted the assignment. Another volunteer appeared with me. After our appearance, the female host decided to become a volunteer. Later that year I made another appearance, and appeared on WBLX 660 AM talk radio to discuss "Date Rape."

Volunteer work was satisfying and fulfilling. I knew I was directly helping someone. The downside was the paperwork involved. It wasn't enjoyable, but good record keeping was required in all of my activities associated with Rape Crisis and with all the other organization.

Volunteering with Rape Crisis and Contact Mobile inspired me to go back to college for my graduate degree in counseling. I wanted to understand more about human behavior.

In his inaugural address, President George H.W. Bush invoked the vision of a "thousand points of light." He believed that there were many areas in life where individuals and organizations could make a difference in people's lives when government could not. In 1989, he established the Daily Point of Light Award for individuals and organizations making a difference. I worked with two organizations that were designated Points of Light for outstanding service—Rape Crisis and Greater Gulf Literacy Council.

After I received my Master's degree in 1989, I wanted to continue with some volunteer work along with paid employment. I went to work with the Mobile Community Action Agency, the umbrella organization for a number of programs that President Lyndon Baines Johnson initiated in his War on Poverty in 1965. Head Start was adding a Literacy Coordinator that year to work with the students' parents. Head Start was the premier early childhood program for income-eligible children and their parents. My position was part of the Parent Involvement Component, which served to inform and educate the parents of Head Start children. Since my position was new, the Director had no idea what it entailed; therefore, I was free to define my duties and to write my own job description.

In a short time, I moved to Staff Development Coordinator. I became acquainted with the staff in all ten Head Start centers. My job included designing two mandatory training programs for the entire staff twice each year. I hired national and local trainers and did some training myself. I also planned and conducted other training throughout the year.

When I worked as a volunteer, I felt I was providing a needed service. I took pride in what I was doing. I started out wanting to help others, but ended up being the one helped. Doing such work allowed me to step outside my comfort zone many times. It propelled me onto the literal stage many times. I always thought I was too shy to speak publicly. The nature of my volunteer work compelled me to speak about things that had previously made me uncomfortable. I learned to confront and to deal with my own demons as I helped others work through theirs.

The African American Summit, a group of men and women from different backgrounds --Muslims, Christians and others with an interest to improve the community, came to my attention. I attended one of their meetings and joined the group. We planned workshops and summits and brought in educators, politicians and other professionals to inform the community on matters that directly affected them. The Summit took positions on issues such as school uniforms, multicultural education, youth curfew, crime and violence. Before I became a member, the Summit had written a booklet entitled *Solutions*, which detailed their views on education, religion, economic development, the family and crime and violence. It gave doable solutions to these problems. Believing that positive images are important to the healthy self-development of young people, the Summit had a campaign to encourage local churches to remove pictures of white Jesus and other images that negatively effect black people. The historical Jesus did not come from Europe, therefore, did not have blue eyes and blond hair, yet this was the image black people had grown up with and accepted. The Summit took the position that positive images the children can identify with would help them improve their own self-esteem. Many churches agreed and changed the images.

Before I got the job with Mobile Community Action, Mommy and Aunt Virginia often asked, "Why don't you get a job and work to help your husband?" I would say, "I am working, my husband doesn't need any help." Neither of them could see the value in what I was doing as a community volunteer. If there was no paycheck, they didn't think it counted as work. After all, both of them were from that era of struggle. Besides, they wondered why I didn't use the two degrees that I had earned. Both my degrees served me well when I worked as a volunteer, a schoolteacher, a literacy teacher and a staff development coordinator. After a while, I didn't try to justify my lifestyle to them or to anyone. I had chosen a lifestyle that was satisfying for me.

There are many reasons why people work: to provide necessities, to gain the satisfaction that work brings, to acquire the luxuries of life; vacations and nice toys and maybe some other reasons. Many people define themselves by their jobs or careers: "I am an entrepreneur." "I am a teacher." "I am an electrician." When a person loses his job, he often suffers a loss of identity. Sometimes it can be detrimental to his self-esteem. A job gives that person worth not only in others eyes but in his own.

I didn't live my life based on the opinions of others. I never thought anyone was superior to me in any way or that I had to live up to anyone's expectations. I chose a lifestyle that one salary could sustain. It was never about acquiring stuff or competing with someone else. I didn't realize that parents wanted to brag on the accomplishments of their children to impress their friends. Perhaps Mommy wanted that, as did Aunt Virginia.

I was selected as Rape Crisis Center Volunteer of the Year in 1990. I received the JCPenney Golden Rule Award for exceptional volunteer service. Mobile United presented Citizens' Service Awards yearly to people who had made outstanding contributions through volunteer service. In 1992, Mobile United named me an "Unsung Hero" and presented me with the M.O. Beale Scroll of Merit. My picture appeared in the Mobile Press Register along with the other honorees. I got lots of kudos and accolades from fellow volunteers, coworkers and others. My greatest honor came from my sisters of Alpha Kappa Alpha Sorority, Inc. who invited me to the Sixtieth Southeastern Regional Conference to present me with a plaque for outstanding community service. To me the words of Winston Churchill "You make a living by what you get, but you make a life by what you give" ring true.

I had no idea that when I decided to dedicate some of my time to community service that they would honor me with dinners, gifts, certificates and plaques. I wanted to make a difference in someone's life, mostly mine. I did that. I felt better about myself and about life as a result. I support women who want, need or have to work for a living, doing just that. I expected to work outside the home when I was young and had many material desires; however, when my interests changed, I started to look towards a different lifestyle. I realized that I didn't need to work for any other reason than that I wanted to. Therefore, I chose to stay home, take care of my children, and live life as a wife and mother. I found much satisfaction in that.

During the 1960s and 70s as the Women's Liberation Movement

was underway throughout the United States, I was happy being a wife, mother and student. As a black woman I felt no need to be liberated, not from an oppressive husband or an unfulfilling lifestyle. Black women have always had a certain freedom to seek employment even though it was often substandard. I know the movement was unnecessarily necessary. By that, I mean women should have had the same rights as men all along. I supported women's efforts and was hopeful that the movement would bring needed change.

The busier I was the happier and more fulfilled I was. I have felt truly blessed to have a choice in whether to stay home and work or to go into the workplace. I am grateful for the opportunity to do both.

PART 11
Sankofa - Go Back and Get It

Family

Gray – Hammond – Branch

*In every conceivable manner, the family is the
link to our past, bridge to our future.*
Alex Haley

FROM YOUNG SLAVE
TO OLDEST MINISTER
IN AMERICA

William Harrison Hammond, 1843-1939
Polly Daniels Branch Hammond

Excerpted from newspaper article, "Oldest Pastor
In America Tells Of Long Career" 1936

Born a slave in Marshall County, Mississippi in 1843, William Harrison Hammond died a distinguished minister and community leader in 1939. In 1936, a Memphis newspaper wrote an article honoring him as the "oldest acting pastor, black or white, in the United States." He spent sixty-six years as minister of the church he founded and built with his own hands, Oak Springs Baptist Church. Reverend Hammond named it for its location beside an oak tree that hung over a spring of cool, fresh water. With the growth of families and communities, Reverend Hammond was asked to organize another church nearly ten miles from Oak Spring. He was to preach the gospel the first and third Sundays at one church and the second and fourth Sundays at the other. Since the new church was located near a grove of trees, the members agreed to name it

Hammond Grove. Both churches still function in the twenty first century as thriving congregations in Arlington, Tennessee.

He may have had three weeks of schooling when he was young and could read a few Bible verses, but William felt unprepared to answer his calling to the ministry. He was twenty-six years of age when he asked one of his employers to teach him to read. The employer taught him to read and to write. William expanded on what the man taught him and went on to educate himself. The interviewer wrote, "Today, he does the unusual for a colored man of pre-Civil War antecedents—he uses almost flawless English talking and preaching in the measured tones and balanced accents of a university graduate."

Reverend Hammond went on to collect many books and had one of the largest religious libraries in the area.

My aunt, Virginia Gray Westbrook, wrote a story to teach her children, nieces and nephews about her grandfather. What follows is an excerpt.

"The nearby creek served as the baptistery. The fourth Sunday in July 1889 was the first annual baptizing day. Eleven new converts would be added to the nearly eighty members.

Parson Hammond led the procession from the church to the creek singing "Take Me to The Water to Be Baptized." Two by two, they marched receiving motivation either from the Holy Ghost or from the imposing sun whose rays seemed focused on the Tennessee community.

The deacons were behind Pastor, the choir followed, their melodic voices sounding like angels. Lucinda's lyric soprano voice, divinely propelled, lifted spirits as a tornado lifts a mighty oak, removing its roots to reveal its secret hiding place. Other choir members sang according to the Spirit's command. Mother Robinson whose feet were slowed from daily toil led five other Mothers, each carrying freshly washed bath towels to comfort and dry the newborn Christians."

Great Grandpa Hammond believed that Christians should be readers and thinkers, not relying on emotionalism, which he said, were "often taken as acceptable religious expressions by colored people."

Aunt Virginia said her grandfather was sold away from his mother when he was nine and brought to Covington, Tennessee. He was a slave of Dr. Purnell Hammond in Covington, thus the name Hammond. Yet I saw in the 1860 Census a family that could have been his. It listed William H. Hammond as eighteen years of age along with four siblings ages six through sixteen and a J. Hodge who was fifty. One daughter was named Mary Jo Hammond; the other children had initials before their last name. The father was listed as James Hammond and the mother as O.S. Hammond. They lived in District 13 in West Tennessee. Whether or not Reverend Hammond came from an intact family who lived and worked on Dr. Hammond's property as slaves, I do not know.

One thing for certain, Reverend Hammond worked to improve his life and the lives of his family, and his neighbors. Parson Hammond, as his congregation called him, was a man interested in the goings on in the community, an activist of sorts, and the man to see if you needed help with the local authorities. He supported education and was interested in politics. Parson wanted to see his people advance as a race. Parson was also a prophet. The congregation feared when he prophesied because it would happen.

In her story, Aunt Virginia wrote about Parson Hammond meeting Polly Daniels as though she were an innocent maiden, but Polly had been married had three children with Branch as their last name. Parson outlived at least two wives. I do not know what year he married great-grandmother Polly or if she was the mother of all seventeen of his children. I believe Parson counted the Branch children as his. Did his other wives have a child or two that he counted as his? Perhaps two died during infancy. Florence Hammond and Richmond Hammond are listed in my grandmother's obituary as her siblings; however, they are not listed as Polly's children. I think their mother was Parson's first wife.

The newspaper stated, "The Parson is now living quietly with his third wife on his well-ordered and well-stocked farm near Barrett's Chapel school on the eastern edge of Shelby County." I do not know the names of the other two wives. Polly was already dead when the article was written; therefore, I think she must have been his second wife.

The children of Polly Daniels Branch were Cedric, Lafayette and Heiskell. Cedric Branch had two daughters, Marjorie and Catherine. Heiskell is the only Branch ancestor I ever met.

Aunt Virginia wrote, "Those were the golden years for Parson Hammond. He had seen his ten children; their children and grandchildren fulfill their goals. His many prayers for their success had been answered. His beautiful wife Polly had long been laid to rest, having died of blood poisoning developed after she cut her finger.

The sixty-three years Parson had spent at Oak Spring Baptist Church had taken a toll, and he was now focused on the great beyond. When Parson was bedridden and barely conscious, church members gathered on his five acres and picked his cotton. Mother Robinson directed the chores. Younger members had chores inside the house. Mrs. Lucinda directed the singing of Parson's favorite song "Amazing Grace." Her melodious voice softly led the singing. Parson must have heard because his hands began to wave as though he knew the time was near. His youngest daughter, who sat at his bedside, noticed that his feeble lips began to move. The singing softened to humming while they studied his lips. Parson asked for his Bible and in a faint voice, directed the reading of no other than St. John 14, "Christ's Farewell Sermon."

Brother Wilburn who once slept during Parson's preaching of this very sermon read forcefully with his aged, yet determined voice, "Let not your hearts be troubled; ye believe in God, believe also in me. In my father's house are many mansions; if it were not so, I would have told you, I go to prepare a place for you..."

Steadily, Parson's arms were moving as the scripture was being read. His lips were moving to the sound of the reading. Parson Hammond was preaching his own farewell sermon as the Angel of Death ushered him home with a final "Amen, Amen."

William Heiskell Branch was born April 22, 1872. He graduated from LeMoyne-Owen in 1892. In 1970, at ninety-eight years of age,

Heiskell was honored as the school's oldest living graduate. I always thought LeMoyne was a college back then and Uncle Heiskell was a college graduate; however, it was called LeMoyne Normal and Commercial School. It got its start in 1862 as a school for freedmen and runaway slaves; LeMoyne had its official opening in 1871. The school was named for Francis J. LeMoyne, a Pennsylvania doctor who donated $20,000.00 to the American Missionary Association to build an elementary and secondary school for prospective teachers. LeMoyne became a junior college in 1924 and a four-year college in 1930.

Owens College began in 1947, and had its official opening in 1954 as S.A. Owen Junior College. It later became Owen Junior College. LeMoyne and Owen merged in 1968. Therefore, I would say that William Heiskell Branch was the first high school graduate in the Branch family. His brother Lafayette was a member of the Lemoyne class of 1896. He was a letter carrier until his death July 4, 1964.

He married Betty Curry December 25, 1900, and remained single after she died in 1969. Heiskell and Betty had four beautiful and fashionable daughters-- Evelyn, Odessa, Veola Betty, and Leona Polly. Polly drove a convertible. Heiskell fathered another daughter, Isabelle, out of wedlock. When the girls met Isabell, perhaps as young adults, they embraced her as their sister and remained close throughout their lives.

I met Uncle Heiskell in 1963 when my daddy died. He and I sat on Big Mama's porch and talked. I learned that he liked to read. I was surprised to learn that he walked a mile a day and showered afterwards. Uncle Heiskell may have been trying to influence me when he confessed that he didn't smoke or drink alcohol. He was slim and tall, and stood rather straight at ninety. I was eighteen and not many adults captured my attention, yet I was impressed with him. I thought he was intelligent, sophisticated and elegant.

I read a letter he wrote to his great-granddaughter Genwyl dated November 15, 1969. Genwyl, the daughter of Viva and granddaughter of Veola, is the oldest in her family, and the first to attend college. He told her that what she was doing "will inspire the others to do it too." Heiskell further stated that he should have become a doctor, but perhaps he needed some encouragement. He also wrote, "I am 97 years and 7 months, and this morning I am afraid to walk a mile alone." In the same letter he wrote, "I can walk more than a mile." Genwyl's siblings did follow her example by becoming college graduates and going on to have wonderful careers.

Heiskell farmed in Mississippi in his early year, but moved back to Memphis where he gardened, worked in his church and made a living as a carpenter. Some of the houses he built are not only still standing, but have tenants.

Together, Parson and Polly had ten children: Harry, Cyrene, George Frederick, Ivory, Bostic, Nannie, Cassie, Willie Mae, and twins Minnie May belle, and my grandmother Lula Martell. Neither, Harry, Cyrene nor Ivory had children. Minnie may have become pregnant before she married and had a daughter, Vernon, who was adopted by the Ellis family. Minnie later married a man named Smith, and gave birth to Ludi Bell and Bernice.

Willie Mae Hammond Hall lived in Buffalo, New York and had a son named Joe who became a boxer. Joe fought under the alias "Buffalo Bison." He started fighting in 1924 at the Broadway Auditorium in Buffalo. He also fought in San Jose, California, Manila, Shanghai, China and Sidney, Australia where he went to live in 1925. Joe did not have an illustrious career. In fact, he lost more fights than he won; nevertheless, he must have been able to support his family. He had a daughter whose name was Dorothy. Aunt Virginia kept in contact with her throughout the years. She and Uncle Fred visited her during their trip to Australia. Aunt Willie also had two other sons Marvin and Parker.

Bostic Hammond worked as a furniture repairman. His wife Fannie died when their only child Maureen was a teen. After graduating from Woodstock High School, Maureen attended Lane College where she met Colonel Shaw of Stephenson-Shaw Funeral Home in Jackson. They had a son they named Melvin. Since Colonel was working in New York, Maureen raised Melvin in Woodstock with her father's help. Melvin described his grandfather Bostic as a quiet and gentle man, a loving father and grandfather, and a good cook. At age twelve, Melvin reconnected with his birth father Colonel, and the two enjoyed a wonderful relationship until Colonel passed away at age ninety-six.

George Frederick Hammond, called Fred, was the only one who followed his father's example and became a minister. His daughter Leona Hammond Irons died of tuberculosis at age twenty-two years. Leona had wanted her aunt, her mother's sister, Emma Hillhouse Green to raise both girls; however, Fred insisted on raising two-month-old Mary Jo. Emma raised eighteen-month old Freddie Mae. Their father Dan Irons was living, but Emma did not care for him, and thought she could do a better job of bringing up a girl. Freddie and Mary Jo had an older sister named Vivian Jean who died in infancy.

Fred and his second wife Susie Anna Searcy raised Mary Jo. For a while, they lived in Woodstock with Maureen and Melvin. Freddie grew up in Memphis. The girls saw each other on weekends mostly in Woodstock. Mary Jo would cry if she had to go to Memphis. When she was a teenager, Mary Jo would gladly escape Grandpa Fred to have a little fun in the city with her sister. Fred didn't allow any WDIA Rhythm & Blues played on the radio, only gospel. Dancing and movies were completely out of the question. Once while Freddie was visiting Mary Jo, they were listening to the radio until they heard "that old man," as they sometimes called him. Though they quickly turned off the radio, he said, in a humorous way, "I know you were listening to WDIA."

Although Reverend Fred was strict, organized, and capable, a get up and go kind of man, he was kind to the girls. He dressed his six-foot frame well, especially on Sundays when he wore his three-piece suits. When the girls would hear him preach at Beulah Baptist Church, they would always find something humorous in his sermon and get uncontrollable giggles.

Fred had no prohibitions against a little alcohol on occasion. He made wonderful grape wine that Freddie and Mary Jo would sometimes sneak into just for a little taste. He also liked to hunt rabbits in the nearby woods when they lived in Woodstock. One time he took his namesake, Freddie hunting; she was ten or eleven then, and one kick from the gun was enough for her.

Reverend Fred and his half-brother Heiskell had some kind of disagreement over matters that caused a faction or schism in the church. It may have been at Mt. Nebo Baptist Church. Not even their religion could prevent the brothers from holding ill feelings against one another for the rest of their lives.

Another of Big Mama's brothers was Cyrene Hammond, an entrepreneur who was a graduate of Howard University, and lived in Asbury Park, New Jersey. In the 1930s, Cyrene, called Uncle Cy, owned an ice and coal business in New Jersey. He sold coal in the winter and ice in the summer. According to my first cousin Robert "Bob" Gray of New Jersey, Uncle Cy also had a secondhand store and a rooming house. Bob's parents Herbert and Eartha lived in the rooming house that had a dance hall and Speakeasy upstairs. Each of Uncle Cy's businesses was on Springwood Avenue in Asbury Park. Every city had a street bustling with black owned businesses before desegregation, for example, Beale Street in Memphis, Mobile's Davis Avenue and Atlanta's Auburn Avenue. Springwood was that street located on the west side in Asbury Park, New Jersey.

William "Will" Gray 1888-1963
Lula Martel Hammond Gray 1890-1984

When I knew them, Daddy's parents lived at 1240 Race Street in Memphis. I called my grandmother Big Mama and my grandfather was Big Daddy. They were an odd couple to my young self. It's hard to know what brings two people together in marriage, but sometimes I wondered.

Big Mama seemed always in charge. She was short, thick but not fat, and focused. She was often busy washing, ironing, cooking and cleaning. When Daddy and his siblings were growing up, she sewed for people in the community, and for well-to-do white people. She was an excellent seamstress. She passed on her talent to three of her sons, yet all of her children had a knack for dressing. Big Mama also worked in white homes doing laundry for one dollar a day in the early days.

Big Daddy and Big Mama had six sons: Hammond, Herbert, Robert "Bob," Clinton, O.D. and Frank. They had two daughters: Virgie Mae, who died in infancy, and Virginia.

Big Daddy worked for Sears Roebuck and Company as a maintenance man after they escaped from the farm. Sears paid him $7.50 a week in the early years. He retired with a pension in the late 1940s or early 1950s. He must have gotten that job after the 1920 Census which lists him as a yardman. He probably worked as a yardman immediately after their escape.

I adored big Daddy with his mild, laid-back manner. He was tall and lanky with light skin, light colored eyes and reddish hair turning grey. I always thought he resembled Native American Indians with his high cheekbones. Big Daddy was nice to me and to all of his grandchildren. He never yelled at us when we climbed the tree in the front yard or picked figs from the trees that grew along the fence.

Once when I was young I cut the grass with Big Daddy's old push lawnmower, and he gave me a dollar. I didn't want the money; I just cut the grass so he wouldn't have to. When I was going to high school in Memphis, Daddy picked me up from Aunt Thelma's house and took me to spend the weekend with him at Big Mama and Big Daddy's house. I was thrilled to spend that time with my daddy.

Big Daddy's health was starting to decline, and Daddy wanted to do something to change the mood in the house. He said, "Baby, make a banana pudding and a lemon meringue pie for Big Daddy."

I said, "Daddy, I can't do that."

He disagreed, "Yes, you can."

Did he think I had inherited Mommy's talent for cooking? He must have remembered how I used to try to cook for him when I was very young, but perhaps he thought I had learned a bit more by then. Not wanting to disappoint Daddy or Big Daddy, I said, "I'll try." I had seen Mommy make both desserts several times. I knew the ingredients, so why couldn't I make them?

Daddy and I went to the store and bought the ingredients, and I made my first banana pudding and lemon meringue pie. Everyone enjoyed both. Big Mama seldom had desserts other than ice cream she bought at the corner store or the cobblers she made from the peaches growing in her backyard. I was proud of myself that Saturday.

I was closer to my maternal grandparents since I lived in their house after Mommy and Daddy separated. I visited my paternal grandparents often during my childhood and my teen years. As a young child, I spent time climbing the tree in the front yard and swinging in the glider on the big wraparound porch. In the back yard, I would visit through the wire fence with Jo, a white girl who lived next door. She and I were the same age. We never played together, only talked through the fence.

Big Daddy and Big Mama had bought their house in a previously white neighborhood in the late 1940s for $4,000.00. The money came from the death of their son, O.D. who was serving in the Army during World War II. He died in a military hospital in Biloxi, Mississippi. Aunt Virginia told me that her brother died from untreated syphilis as part of the Tuskegee Experiment. I questioned her about that since he was stationed in Biloxi while the experiment was taking place among black sharecroppers in Alabama. Aunt Virginia stuck by her assertion. O.D. was her favorite big brother and her best dance partner. She added, "The government covered it up."

In 1932, the U.S. Public Health Service wanted to learn what would happen if syphilis went untreated. They used Tuskegee Institute to target poor black men for their experiment. When the men presented for treatment, they told them they had "bad blood." Yet, the men were not treated for the bad blood. They were only of value in the experiment when they died, and their autopsies revealed the effects of the disease. In 1947, penicillin became the drug to cure syphilis. However, doctors did not use it on the surviving men.

Since Big Mama's brother Cyrene had no children, he wanted her sons to come live with him so he could help them get their start in life. Hammond was the first to live with his uncle. He wasn't interested in the ice and coal business. He worked in a dry cleaner and apprenticed with a Jewish tailor who made fur coats. Neither of the brothers was interested in the ice and coal business. Each of the three--Hammond, Herbert and Robert--went North wanting to become tailors.

During that time, men and women paid attention to how they dressed. Even the average earner was often impeccably dressed. Whether they were going to church, work, downtown to shop, or college, they dressed appropriately for the occasion. Going to a park on a picnic required a style of dress far different from the jeans and tee shirts of today.

Black people had no real power in society and only limited power within their community. Their style of dress was one way they made a statement about who they were. It was an outward expression of how they felt about themselves. It may have grown out of a need to be noticed or a desire to be admired. It gave them a sense of importance.

While he was in high school, Hammond worked for a dry cleaners and made deliveries. He met a man at the Peabody Hotel while making a delivery. Hammond said to the man, "I am going to make you a coat, a sports coat."

The man said, "Can you do it?"

"Yes sir, I can do it."

Hammond made the coat and took it to the man. The man was pleased with it. That man must have been influential in helping Hammond go to Columbus, Ohio where he worked for a cleaner. The company moved to Asbury Park where Rudolph Valentino and many stars and millionaires were. They were his clientele for alterations and remodeling furs.

Hammond wanted to learn how to cut fur to make coats because there was good money in it. He asked his boss to teach him the trade, but his boss said, "You don't need to learn that, boy. You go on back there and finish your pressing." Hammond was determined to learn. He came up with a way to spy on his boss while he was cutting fur. Cutting fur required more skill than cutting fabric.

Hammond bored a hole in the wall behind a picture. When the man would cut the fur, Hammond would push the picture out of the way and spy on him. Hammond never formally studied tailoring or fur making, yet he became an expert. Uncle Hammond met and married Carolyn, and together they had six children: Carolyn Ann, Frederick, Ronald, Paulette, Dwight, and Mark.

Like Hammond, Herbert and Robert left Memphis after high school and headed north as many black people did during the Great Migration that began in 1915 and continued into the 1970s. It was during the time when conditions for black people in the South were very poor. Jim Crow laws prevented blacks from equal access to the American systems; therefore, many went north for jobs and better opportunities. The Gray boys were ambitious and ready to escape the oppression of the South when they were young.

William Robert "Bob" Gray, June 10, 1912-February 8, 2007, made his home in Detroit where he moved after serving as a Military Policeman in the U.S. Army. He received an honorable discharge in 1945. Bob married Alice Carlow.

Bob learned tailoring while working for Kimbrough Cleaners at 1500 Van Dyke. In 1958 when the owner wanted to retire, Bob bought the business with his savings and a small business loan. He and his wife Alice made Kimbrough Valet Service one of the most outstanding cleaners in Detroit. Bob was a fine tailor, even making suits for R&B singer Jackie Wilson.

Bob always dressed in a manner befitting his profession. He, like his brothers and many black men of his time, was sophisticated, elegant, suave and debonair. They were of the generation of black people who were trying to uplift the race by improving their own lives and trying to help others. Uncle Bob not only improved his life financially, he also helped Clinton, Virginia and Frank pay college expenses. He was generous to his family. He hired Malcolm to work in his cleaners one summer, and he even wanted Malcolm to move to Detroit and take over the business one day.

Uncle Herbert headed to New Jersey to take Uncle Cy up on his offer. Herbert worked in dry cleaning. He met Eartha Mae Caples, a beautiful young girl from Connecticut. They married in 1929, but divorced in 1934. They had only one child, a son they named after Herbert's brother Robert. Eartha Mae remarried soon after the divorce while their son was very young; therefore, they let him grow up with his stepfather's last name Coleman. Bob, as they called him, went to enlist in the Air Force in 1950 when he was only seventeen accompanied by his mother and stepfather. When Bob presented his birth certificate, the name on it was Robert Gray. His stepfather had not adopted him; therefore, his legal last name had remained Gray. The Air Force required Bob to enlist under the name Gray. He kept the name.

He knew his dad all those years and sometimes spoke with him. In 1952, he visited his dad in New York. Herbert Gray lived in Harlem, New York just at the tip of Manhattan. He and his second wife Vie lived there until his death.

Uncle Herbert wrote to me and sent me clothing when I was in college. I didn't meet my uncles until 1963 during my first year at Lane College. The occasion was their father's funeral. I visited Uncle Bob in Detroit in 1972. I saw them again in 1984 at their mother's funeral. I was at Uncle Frank's house in Memphis on that occasion and was enthralled by my handsome, well-dressed, intelligent uncles and wished I had known them all my life. They made me think of Daddy and wish he were there. The three of them came back to the South only a few times once they had escaped. They kept in touch with their family and helped them financially, yet they chose not to come back. I always knew about them, yet I did not know them or my first cousins only meeting a cousin when she came south to attend Tennessee State University.

I visited Uncle Frank and Aunt Virginia often over the years. They were my main source of Gray family history. I wish I had become interested early in life. I only started thinking of my elders and ancestors when I got older and more aware of how short life is and how quickly it ends.

When Uncle Frank and Aunt Virginia felt that Big Mama should no longer live alone, they decided to sell her house. She would then live with Uncle Frank. She preferred staying in Memphis and remained with Uncle Frank for two years until he found himself needing immediate medical attention.

He went for a checkup and his doctor said, "You need to go to the hospital now."

Uncle Frank said, "I can't go right now. I'm taking care of my mother." The doctor repeated, "You need to go to the hospital right now."

Uncle Frank didn't know what he was going to do because he thought Aunt Virginia was in Chicago with Uncle Fred who was attending a conference; therefore, he didn't know how to get in touch with them. He took a chance and called the house. Aunt Virginia answered, he was so relieved.

He said, "Sister got on a plane that night and came to Memphis. Mother didn't want to leave me or Memphis, but she knew I couldn't take care of her anymore."

Even though Big Mama was still able to take care of herself, Uncle Frank did not want to leave her in the house alone.

I visited Big Mama in the early 1980s while she was living with Uncle Frank. One day I was in her room when she opened a dresser drawer. I noticed how messy the drawer was so and I told her it needed straightening.

Big Mama said, "You leave me alone. You don't smell no old lady smells, do you?"

I had to admit that I didn't. I wasn't even sure what old lady smells were. I flashed back to the deep, claw foot bathtub in Big Mama's house and the smell of Cashmere Bouquet. Big Mama let me know she got in the tub every day. I used to love sitting in that tub when I visited. When I buy Cashmere Bouquet soap, I think of Big Mama.

Uncle Frank recovered from his illness met and married his second wife, Carolyn. He spent the last twenty-four years of his life with her. Aunt Virginia and Uncle Fred brought Big Mama back to Memphis for the wedding, but she returned with them to D.C. to live out her life.

Uncle Frank and Aunt Carolyn went to visit Big Mama when

she was hospitalized in Washington. Big Mama had taken a fall on the stairs and from that time forward, she had experienced health problems.

Uncle Frank said, "I've never said this before, but Sister, Fred and Carolyn went out of the room to get something to eat, and I stayed in the room beside Mother's bed. She was in a coma, couldn't talk. I was crying. Mother must have heard me because she woke up, turned to me and said, 'Why are you crying?'"

He said, "Because you're sick. She didn't say another word."

Uncle Frank became emotional and I waited a minute before I asked, why do you think she asked that? He looked out to that place where Big Mama used to go for answers. None came.

Maybe she wanted to know why you were sad since she was okay, and she didn't want you to be sad. Big Mama, a member of the Church of God in Christ, was a woman of faith. She was ninety-four, not able to live as she had since her fall, and probably wasn't asking God for any more time on earth.

"What do you want to know Barbara Jean?"

"Just anything," I say, "Just talk."

Uncle Frank was the baby of the family, a near perfect child. He observed the antics of his brothers Clinton and O.D. and saw how they got in trouble. He refrained from doing the things they did. He never got a spanking. Uncle Frank seemed the serious type, but he had a sense of humor. I think he would have loved being a father since he enjoyed family. He loved my visits. I believe it made him feel his brother's spirit.

Uncle Frank, tell me anything about the family and what my daddy and the other brothers did when they were young. He laughed and launched into a few stories. He confessed that he did not know the three older brothers—Hammond, Herbert, and Robert—during their youth since he was the baby of the family.

He began, "Daddy's grandfather was Washington "Wash" Gray who was born in 1826. Wash had two brothers, Lewis and Louie. The three of them came to Tennessee as slaves from North Carolina accompanied by an old woman. They settled in Gray's Creek. Later they went to Brunswick or Arlington. Wash fathered two sons, my daddy Will and his brother Grover. Grover had no children. Lewis Gray married FreeJoe's granddaughter, but they had no children.

"Oh, that's right," I said. "I remember FreeJoe from that black history tour we took during our Family Reunion in 1997. Aunt Virginia also told me that we were related to FreeJoe through marriage."

"Yes. That's right. Lewis Gray married Alice Harris who was the daughter of FreeJoe's son Peter." I later learned that they were married in 1852 and that Alice died September 2, 1939.

Uncle Frank thought they named Gray's Creek after the Gray family since there were so many Grays in the area at that time. I wanted to know for sure so I did some research and found the FreeJoe website set up by Earnest Lacey who wrote *The Search for FreeJoe*. The book chronicles Lacey's search for information on Joseph "FreeJoe" Harris, his great-great grandfather. I contacted Earnest via email and asked him who the area and church were named after. He said, "As far as I know, Gray's Creek Church was named after one or both of the white plantation owners who were brothers named Gray."

That bit of information left me wondering. Did my great-grandfather and great-great uncles come to Tennessee with Gray as their last name? Did the plantation owner name them Gray?

FreeJoe Harris was the man to know during his time. Born a slave in 1795, he became free in 1832. What I found remarkable about FreeJoe were his many skills and abilities. He was a landowner and a master carpenter; he owned a stagecoach line; and was an innkeeper. FreeJoe founded Gray's Creek Missionary Baptist Church in February 1843, and served as its first minister. I was glad to learn about my connection to FreeJoe no matter that it was through marriage and too far back to consider.

I visited FreeJoe's church in the summer of 2012. Gray's Creek is the oldest black church in Shelby County. I had passed by it on every trip I made to Memphis from Somerville over the years and wondered if it had any connection to my family.

I sat there that hot Sunday in July listening for echoes from the past. It had been many years since I had attended a Baptist church service. Reverend took his sermon from Luke 23:32 showing the necessity of the cross and Calvary. He preached about both Noah and Jesus obeying God and bringing salvation. He prayed about the ordinary things that we often take for granted such as being able to see and to walk.

The minister started in a slow easy manner, and then he shifted into a sing-*songy* tone accompanied by the organist who matched his occasional long-held syllables, and helped him build to a crescendo. He spoke from his gut in a call and response manner about the cross as a way of bringing us back to God. Deacons in dark suits, white shirts and red ties sat front row center, and a few sat in the pulpit.

Since it was the first Sunday, the Deacons donned their white gloves and served communion as the choir and congregation sang, "I know it was the blood."

When it was time for the invitation, the minister opened the doors of the church. The Deacons stood across the front of the sanctuary with their arms reaching out beseechingly. Church Mothers dressed in white stood. That was the time for those not saved to come forth. Anyone who wanted or needed a church home could come forth and be welcomed.

At one point, a member got up from his seat to go out; he raised his right hand and pointed his index finger heavenward as if to ask "May I be excused?" It was a sign of respect to the minister and the congregation and to God, I suppose. It brought back memories from the few times I had attended a country church during my childhood. It made me remember the fervent prayers of old black men who lived simple lives and appreciated life's basics. They often kneeled before a bench and said prayers of supplication, thanksgiving and praise in a rhythmic tone with a sincerity that made you believe they knew God. The singing of hymns, the call and response style of preaching, and the raised index finger all date back to slavery.

Uncle Frank continued, "Daddy's maternal grandfather was Indian. They called him "Troop." He didn't respect white folks and wouldn't work for them. He preferred to spend most of his time in the woods living off the land. If he went into a store to buy something and the clerk was slow in waiting on him, he would tell the clerk that he was walking out with the item. That got him some service."

Uncle Frank then turned his attention back to his mother. "Mother threatened to spank me once, and I said to her, 'I don't know why you want to whip me. I do everything you say.'"

You were just an obedient child I guess. Most of us were spanked at some time.

"Once Mother had to go downtown or somewhere, and she left me with a neighbor telling her, 'watch Frank for a little while for me.' The woman said all right, and she went back into her house and left me in the yard playing. When Mother came back, I was still in the yard playing. It didn't take much for me. I was a loner. I could play by myself for hours."

I guess obedience is the best course, but it's hard to stay out of trouble when you're little. Changing the subject, did Big Mama and Big Daddy go to school?

"Mother and Daddy didn't go far in school; however, they wanted their children educated. Daddy worked in the fields when they were in Arlington. Mother wasn't much of a field worker; she was an entertainer and would often be sent home from the field to keep from interfering with the others."

Big Mama was a character. She could make you laugh. When did you all leave Arlington and move into the city?

"I was about six months old; the other children were much older when Mother and Daddy knew they needed to get to the city. They came up with a plan. Daddy would pick cotton at night and hide it until the next morning when he would sell it. He saved up a few dollars; they packed a wagon with what they could carry and drove to Memphis. I don't know how Daddy got that wagon and those mules back to their owner."

You mean they didn't own the mules and wagon.

"No, no," Uncle Frank said as he fell back on the sofa laughing, "they belonged to that white man they worked for. He owned the land and everything on it."

"We rented a house on Vollentine before moving to Manassas Street. All of us children went to Manassas High School. One day I was coming home from school after football practice, I went into the house, had no books in my hands; Mother asked, 'where are your books?'"

"I left them at school." I said.

"Go get them." She said.

"I walked through the living room headed for the kitchen to get a drink of water. Daddy was sitting at the table reading the newspaper. He put down the paper and said, "Did you hear your mother?" "Yes Sir." "Daddy picked up the paper without saying another word. I had to get some water down at the filling station on my way back to get my books. Mother and Daddy supported one another when it came to disciplining. They weren't very strict except Daddy was only strict about time. If he said to be somewhere at a certain time, you had better be there."

"Mother told Clint and O.D. that she and Daddy would be gone from the house for a while, and she didn't know who was going to be in charge. Then she told them to go out in the yard and wrestle, and the one who wins will be in charge. They went out and started wrestling. O.D. was muscular and Clint was not. Clint was also smaller. O. D. picked up Clint, started twirling him around, and Clint yelled, 'Don't drop me.' Clint was older but O.D. was stronger. I was in the fourth grade then."

Uncle Frank gets more animated as the stories kept coming, "There was a time when Daddy went to Indianapolis, Indiana to work. I don't remember where Mother was, but we had to get our own dinner. O.D. had a rifle or a BB gun, and he was sitting on the porch when a chicken started across the yard. O.D. took his gun and shot that chicken. Clinton cooked it, and we had chicken for dinner."

I laugh and wonder whose chicken they ate, but Uncle Frank is on a roll. I let him continue.

"Before Thanksgiving one year when we lived on Ayers Street, either Clint or O.D. worked at a store and bought a live rooster. The rooster got in with the neighbor's chickens, and the neighbor kept it.

Clinton and O.D. had been watching the rooster all the time. The night before Thanksgiving, they went over to the neighbor's yard and got their rooster. We had rooster for Thanksgiving dinner that year."

I guess Daddy and Uncle O.D. were chicken thieves huh. I asked if they were ever without food.

"No, we never went without food. Mother was resourceful. We could take a quarter during the Depression and buy neck bones for a penny a pound. Five cents would get enough cornmeal to make a big pan of cornbread. We always had food to eat. Mother and Daddy saw to that."

When I asked about church, Uncle Frank reminded me that Big Mama had grown up in the church since her daddy William Harrison Hammond was a minister. Big Daddy also grew up in the church. He added, "Sister and I attended church all of our lives."

Did my daddy and the other brothers go?

"No. My brothers didn't go to church unless it was with some girl. Clinton never had much to do with the church."

I change the subject, and ask, why didn't the older brothers go to college?

"For economic reasons, there was no money."

I had been curious about what led my folks to seek higher education when they had no money. How did you, my daddy and Aunt Virginia afford to go to Lane?

"Scholarships, working, and helping each other."

I had always wondered who inspired them. I knew their parents knew nothing about college or fraternities and sororities. How did you all even know about college and fraternities?

"When I was at Manassas High School, one of my teachers, Mr. Tarpley, used to bring the Sphinx magazine to school and leave it on his desk, and I would read it. It inspired me to want to attend college, and of course, I would pledge Alpha Phi Alpha. When I was in high school, I was mentored by my teachers. Male teachers from Booker Washington and insurance men and others would come to Manassas through what we called Go to High School/Go to College

Campaign. Clinton and Sister had had similar experiences, and they were already at Lane; therefore, I had to go to college."

Uncle Frank earned his Bachelor of Science Degree from Lane College and his Master of Arts Degree from Memphis State University, now University of Memphis.

I always said that Uncle Frank enjoyed his retirement more than anyone I ever knew. He taught biology at Douglass High School for thirty-five years. I didn't realize what a distinguished career he had until I attended his funeral in 2008. There were many comments about the kind of teacher he was. He was a man of character. Former students, friends, fraternity brothers and neighbors all held him in high esteem. They praised him as an inspiring and dedicated educator. They lauded him for his fashion sense and style, and as a loyal friend and overall good person. His manner was kind, calm and cool. He was all of that and more.

I felt so proud to be related to such as man as I sat there listening with tears running down my checks. I couldn't stop the tears. I was apprehensive about my world void of my uncle. I had one elder of the Gray family remaining–Aunt Virginia.

I think I was close to Uncle Frank because he reminded so much of Daddy. When I was in summer school after Daddy died, and I was crying every day missing him, I saw Uncle Frank walking across campus to visit me. I thought it was Daddy. I ran to meet him with tears in my eyes. When I realized it wasn't Daddy, I hugged Uncle Frank harder trying to squeeze back my tears.

Once Uncle Frank retired from teaching, he didn't miss it. He did the job well while he was there, and he enjoyed about thirty years in retirement only working in his yard, his fraternity and St. John Baptist Church where he was a member for more than sixty-five years. Uncle Frank was able to play golf and fish for many years. He loved fishing. He came to Mobile with Charles in the late 1980s and they went deep-sea fishing with Joel.

I visited Uncle Frank several times when he was sick, but not bedridden. My last visit was two weeks before he died. By then he was lying peacefully with his eyes closed. I knew he was aware of the goings on around him. I stood at his bedside and spoke a few words letting him know I was there. I held his hand and caressed his face. I kissed his forehead knowing that it was the last time I would see him alive.

Aunt Virginia was there to check on him, perhaps to say goodbye. She was sitting in the living room when I arrived. When I came out of Uncle Frank's bedroom, I told her to go in and see her brother. I tried to assure her that he was okay. By that I meant that he was satisfied with his life and was ready to make his transition. He was at peace with the process.

She wouldn't go in to see him. She couldn't bear seeing her baby brother in that state. Aunt Virginia had always looked after him even when they were adults. Sometimes she would treat him as a child much to his chagrin. They had a good relationship all of their lives. She was not ready for him to leave. She knew she would be next. My aunt was afraid to face her own mortality.

Uncle Frank's first wife was Dorinda Collins, July 26, 1925-July16, 1978, his college sweetheart. They were married in August of 1949 and were together for twenty-eight years. Her friends, neighbors, church members, students and everyone knew her as the teacher, who loved to dress. She was fashionable. I thought she was so stylish and attractive until arthritis gnarled her fingers and hands and crippled her. The steroids she took made her face swell, and then none of those clothes, furs and jewelry mattered.

Aunt Dorinda attended Lane College on a scholarship. She was a soloist in the Glee Club, a majorette, and a member of Delta Sigma Theta Sorority, Inc. She received her Bachelor of Science degree from Lane College in 1947 and taught at Hyde Park and Cypress Middle School until arthritis forced her to retire in 1971. Aunt Dorinda loved teaching as much as she loved wearing beautiful clothes.

I enjoyed my relationship with Aunt Dorinda and loved visiting her beautiful home on Evergreen. They built their small, brick house in the early 1950s when housing was improving for black people. Subdivisions for the black middle class were coming up throughout the country. Owning a piece of the American Dream was becoming a reality for some black people.

Aunt Dorinda had a decorator named Poindexter who furnished her house with beautiful antiques, luxurious custom draperies, and a crystal chandelier. Sometimes he was there when I visited as a child. He was colorful and fun. They laughed and talked like girlfriends. Uncle Frank didn't seem to mind him being around.

When Anita and I were college sophomores, we were visiting Uncle Frank and Aunt Dorinda at the same time. We spent most of that time talking to Aunt Dorinda. Anita was curious about much in life and was anxious to learn. We could talk to Aunt Dorinda about anything. Without warning Anita said, "Aunt Dorinda, do you believe in sex before marriage?"

During her youth, women were admonished to be chaste before marriage. Her generation was trying to impose that same standard on our generation. Aunt Dorinda looked at Anita and replied, "You try on a pair of shoes before you buy them, don't you?"

Although she was in pain most of her later years, Aunt Dorinda was in good spirit whenever I saw her. She never appeared to be angry about her condition. I remember her beautiful smile and warm spirit and the way her eyes would light up when I walked into her room.

When I was a young child, I visited Aunt Dorinda and Uncle Frank with Mommy and Malcolm many times when we were in Memphis shopping or doing business. Both of them liked Mommy and were supportive of her even though she and Daddy were no longer together. They always seemed to be happy to see us. Aunt Dorinda was a generous person. She always had something enjoyable for us to eat.

There are no saints in my family, but Uncle Frank comes close. He took care of his sick wife during the last years of her life, and he took care of his mother. He didn't seem to come into life with any great agenda or any real beefs about life. He seemed to take it as it came and he made the best life that he could. He and Aunt Virginia were dedicated Christians all of their lives. Aunt Virginia sang and played the piano in her church when she was young. Uncle Frank was a deacon, and he sang in the choir.

On that last visit while Uncle Frank was still getting around and doing well, I sat in his living room admiring him and noticing how contented he was with his wife Carolyn. I felt that he was satisfied with the family and the life he had lived. I asked him about his talent and skill other than teaching.

Uncle Frank answered, "I don't have one. I don't know what it is."

Carolyn interrupted, "Frank sings, and I can sing too. We sing together at church. They call us Ashford and Simpson."

Oh, really, sing Uncle Frank. Both of you sing before the tape runs out. I pleaded, sing "Amazing Grace."

The tape ran out before they finished, but each time I listen to it, I feel pleased, happy and sad. I miss my uncle and all of the Grays each time I hear his voice.

I forgot to ask Uncle Frank or Aunt Virginia about their aunt Virginia. I don't know where to place another William Gray who was her father. He was married to Mary Ketchum. I remember Great Aunt Virginia and believed her to be Big Daddy's sister; however, I can't imagine that Wash would have had two sons named William. This Aunt Virginia also lived in Nashville and her niece, my Aunt Virginia was her heir. Aunt Virginia enjoyed a good relationship with her aunt until her death.

Virginia Ardis Gray Westbrook

January 30, 1916-April 2, 2011

I could write volumes on Virginia Gray Westbrook, the princess of the Gray family. She was born on stage with all of the people she met on her ninety-five year journey as her audience. She bounded into life with both feet hovering somewhere above the fray. If the harshness of life touched her, it was hard to tell. She aimed high and most of the time she hit her mark.

Being the only girl meant she got everything she needed and most of what she wanted. Her parents and her brothers catered to her. She was close to her parents and her brothers until the end of their lives. She was proud of her brothers, their professions, their families. Maybe she wasn't as proud of her favorite brother Clinton where his family life was concerned, but she was proud of him. She freely expressed her love for her family and spent many of her later years trying to pass on to her children, nieces, nephews, grandchildren, and great grandchildren the importance of family.

Aunt Virginia cherished her role as matriarch of the Gray family for many years. She would invite the family for Thanksgiving dinners and gather all of us in the family room to talk to us about family history and the importance of education and Christianity. Her desire was for us to start an education fund to help family members with education costs.

Besides the year I lived with Aunt Virginia, I have spent many days, weekends and holidays with her. She wanted Anita and me to grow up together like sisters since we were the same age and grade. We also were the only girl in our respective families. I also think Aunt Virginia wanted to make sure I grew up with some lady-like sophistication and grace. She was obsessed with making us "ladies," which meant being cultured and refined. She had felt that so much of that was missing from her upbringing, and she was determined that her daughter was going to be a lady. She hoped to help her niece also.

Of course times, "they were a-changing." We were not as concerned with all of that; however, Anita had to fall in line and submit, and so did I when I was around my aunt. Now, I appreciate the things she taught me; I am certainly grateful for the exposure to the arts that she gave me.

When I was a young married woman, I moved back to Nashville while the Westbrooks were still living there. Aunt Virginia took me to my first two touring Broadway shows—"Fiddler on the Roof" and "Hair." From that time forward, I was hooked on theater. I couldn't wait to go to New York and see a show live on Broadway. It was a few years before I did that, but each time I go is like the first time.

Aunt Virginia was an amazing friend. She kept her friendships from high school and college. When she was a young married woman beginning life in Nashville, she and a group of friends started a bridge club. They would take turns meeting in different homes to have their bridge parties. Those same friends met until their deaths. As one would die, another person would join. Aunt Virginia had lost much of her concentration during the last year or two of her life, yet she was still attending those gatherings.

Shortly before her ninety-fifth birthday, I went to Nashville to make plans to honor her. When I went to Harper's Restaurant to plan her celebration, Aunt Virginia, dressed in a white pantsuit with hair and makeup done, was sitting with her friends after their weekly bridge club meeting. By that time, the members were no longer hosting the parties in their homes. They would select a location and meet there. It wasn't really about bridge anymore; it was about enjoying some company.

We celebrated Aunt Virginia's ninety-fifth birthday on January 29, 2011 with lunch, a program highlighting her life, and sentiments from family and friends. We had a slide show presentation and music playing from the 1930s and 1940s.

I had to get her permission before planning the celebration. When I asked if we could do it, she said, "Yes, how much money do you need?"

I said, "Aunt Virginia, you are not paying for this. You have paid for enough."

She said, "All right then."

Aunt Virginia was always paying for everything. She was free with money and some took advantage of her generosity. Once she sent me a check for my birthday, and I sent it back. I did that because I didn't want her to treat me as though I needed money. I should have accepted it as the gift that it was; however, she had done enough for me when I was a child. Besides, when she gave money, she tried to control. I didn't want that. I was in my thirties at the time. I later accepted small gifts when she offered them. My gifts to her over the years were usually flowers. She loved receiving fresh cut arrangements for Christmas and Mothers' Day.

Many years ago, Aunt Virginia passed on to me an antique punch bowl and glasses and other crystal that my daddy had given her in the 1940s. She wanted me to have them while she was alive. When she died, she left some blue antique glasses for me that she had received from her aunt Virginia and one of the rings she wore every day. I will pass the ring to one of her granddaughters.

At Aunt Virginia's birthday celebration, I spoke about her teaching career. She started teaching in Shelby County right after graduation. She taught in Arlington, Tennessee. On her first day of teaching, she went to school dressed as though she were going to church, anxious to start her career. She wore a green tweed suit, stockings, and high heel shoes to the little dusty, country school. The principal let her know that she was overdressed and that she needed to wear something more appropriate for teaching young children. Aunt Virginia had wanted to look cute on her first day.

Aunt Virginia had some kind of fever that kept her from playing with her classmates when she was in first and second grades. She would go home at lunchtime and returned afterward. She missed associating with her classmates and was so happy to get over that fever.

My aunt was motivated to excel. Her parents encouraged her to achieve and to get involved with extracurricular activities. She was in drama club and performed in Christmas plays. She enjoyed participating in May Day activities. Aunt Virginia said, "All the schoolchildren dressed in white on May Day. We had sports competitions, food and fun. School, church and home were fun."

She continued, "My fifth grade teacher, Miss Anderson impressed upon me that I should go to college and major in English. I liked her and I listened to her. Since I was valedictorian of my graduating class, I received a scholarship to Lane College. The scholarship came from the National Youth Administration (NYA), a New Deal agency established by President Franklin D. Roosevelt." It operated from 1935-1943 as part of the Work Progress Administration (WPA).

The scholarship wasn't enough to cover all of her expenses. The family also helped

Aunt Virginia learned to play the piano when she was young. Pearlie Gassaway was her first piano teacher. Later, Dr. Gassaway became a professor at Tennessee State University.

Aunt Virginia kept up her piano playing skills. When she was ninety-four, she told me that playing the piano helped her keep her mental faculties. Playing the piano and playing bridge were what helped her stay alert and enjoying a good memory for so long.

My family and I went to Nashville to visit Aunt Virginia on the weekend of the flood in May 2010. I had taken food and we were spending the day with her. We didn't know they were expecting a flood; however, as we drove into Nashville, the deluge greeted us. Aunt Virginia was happy to see us as always. She was especially happy to see my grandson Kashiim who had just turned five and loved playing the piano in his own way. After lunch, Aunt Virginia sat at her piano in the family room and started playing and singing "Danny Boy." Kashiim got up on the bench beside her and played right along with her. She loved having her great grandchildren, my grandchildren and other little children around.

Aunt Virginia taught school for over thirty years beginning in Shelby County at Barrett's Chapel, then Brunswick Junior High, and Woodstock High School. She also taught at one Memphis city school. From there she and Uncle Fred moved to Nashville where she taught at Washington Junior High School.

During school desegregation, Aunt Virginia was the first black teacher selected for the English faculty at Apollo Middle School. She said, "They sent the best black teachers to the white schools and sent the worst white teachers to the black schools." She wasn't at all impressed with the intelligence of the white teachers. She didn't see in them the work ethic that was present in black teachers.

Apollo was an experimental school including team teaching and module scheduling, and individualized study in open-air classrooms. The students were "sort of select" the school was in Antioch "where the people were white, independent financially and motivated, also not many disciplinary problems. It was an ideal setup.

"White people got paid more than we did, and they got the best positions. They gave us sensitivity training during desegregation, but it was not effective. It wasn't done right. There was no input from the teachers."

About desegregation, Aunt Virginia said, "It didn't work because it wasn't done correctly. Whites were not ready. Black people were ready to do whatever was necessary, but whites weren't. They didn't have anything to gain."

Her last school was Overton High, located in the wealthy area where country music singers and other rich folks lived. She enjoyed working with the students at Overton as at each of the other schools. However, I got the feeling that she enjoyed the rich areas more. She had grown tired of buying lunches, shoes and school supplies her students needed when she was at Washington Junior High and the other segregated schools.

Aunt Virginia was not shy about bragging on herself. She often talked about how much her students liked her. She also would say that she liked them. She endeared herself to her students by finding some quality about each one of them that she liked and letting them know about it.

During her senior year at Lane College just before graduation, Aunt Virginia and some of her college friends chartered Beta Chi chapter of Alpha Kappa Alpha Sorority on campus. Alpha Kappa Alpha Sorority, Inc., was the first Greek-lettered sorority for black women. The sorority was founded on the Howard University campus January 15, 1908. It was incorporated January 29, 1913.

One of her high school teachers had talked to her about the sorority. Virginia always wanted to be the best. The AKAs had a high academic standard at that time, and they looked for the smartest and most moral girls. It was not about skin color as some have said; it was about morality and academics. Aunt Virginia loved the AKA sisterhood all of her adult life until she became an "Ivy Beyond the Wall."

As a young woman, my aunt was involved in many activities. She was a high school and college cheerleader. She played the piano at several churches, sang in the Lane College Glee Club, and in 1941 she had the honor of being the first Spirit of Memphis Cotton Makers Jubilee. Her picture hangs in the Pink Palace Museum in Memphis.

When I asked how she got such an honor, she told me, "Dr. Venson, who started the Cotton Makers Jubilee, was looking for a young girl with high moral standards." Ta Da! Look no further Dr. Venson, Virginia Gray is the one.

Aunt Virginia was always on stage. She thrived on attention and often stole the stage from others, even from her own daughter. I came, late in my life, to love and appreciate her for who she was. She was well intentioned in all that she did even in the things that brought pain and suffering to others.

Other than a case of Bell's palsy developed some time after she suffered a burn, Aunt Virginia had no illnesses and was on no medication. In the 1970s, a waiter at the Barn Dinner Theater in Nashville spilled hot coffee on her, which caused serious injury. In 2008, she was hospitalized while on her last visit to see her brother Frank. She was upset over his condition and paramedics carried her to the hospital for observation. They released her the following day.

Aunt Virginia was from a generation that tried to live up to a certain standard. It was as though that generation, born barely fifty years post slavery, had the burden of uplifting and redefining a people. Many of them believed in education as the way to improve. They were often concerned with appearances, what others thought and said about them. They wanted to have a good name and reputation, the community's respect. They wanted to be a "credit" to their race.

Aunt Virginia did not believe in being weak or flawed. That made her unsympathetic when she needed to be otherwise. She was always true to her beliefs. She was a good poster child for the generation dubbed "The Greatest."

In 1944, Aunt Virginia married Fred Emerson Westbrook, Sr. also from Shelby County. He was in the U.S. Army at the time of their marriage having enlisted after earning his Bachelor of Science

Degree from Tennessee A&I State University where he became a professor in 1956.

They met at a party where each had come with another person. When Uncle Fred saw Aunt Virginia, he said, "Aren't you the Miss Gray I met before?" From that moment, they spent the evening and the rest of their lives together. I was surprised to learn that Uncle Fred's ancestors were not slaves. The Westbrook family owned thousands of acres of land in Shelby County near Fullview Baptist Church.

I remember when Uncle Fred earned his PhD from Michigan State University. When Mommy told me that he was Dr. Fred Westbrook, I couldn't understand why he didn't have any patients.

Dr. Westbrook had a great career. He was head of the Department of Agronomy at Tennessee State from 1957-73. In 1973, he went to Washington, D. C. to work with the Department of Agriculture. President Jimmy Carter appointed him the task of organizing the USDA Extension Service. After retiring in 1989, he and Aunt Virginia returned to their home in Nashville.

Uncle Fred received many honors during his career. Perhaps Tennessee State University bestowed the greatest when they named a building in his honor. It was previously the Dairy Barn. They had renovated it in 1988. In 1992 the building was renamed the Agricultural Research and Extension Complex and housed research programs. They renamed it James E. Farrell--Fred E. Westbrook Agricultural Research and Extension Complex on May 4, 2000.

As a young person, I remember Uncle Fred as a calm, easy-going, unruffled sort of man. He was the typical professor of his day with the eyeglasses, pipe and serious, studious, professorial manner. In the evenings, he would be dressed in a smoking jacket in his den reading. He watched the news on television, but not much else. Seems he was always busy preparing for work, church, or his fraternity, Omega Psi Phi. He was always busy, yet available to his family.

Being an expert in plant science, Uncle Fred had the most beautiful yard in the neighborhood. He enjoyed working in his yard until the summer before he died. He made a koi pond in the back yard 1950s that still exists.

Uncle Fred and Aunt Virginia remained to some extent in the traditional male/female, husband/wife roles. Even though Aunt Virginia worked, she still took care of the household chores, shopping, cooking, and party planning. She planned activities for the children, corresponded with family through telephone calls and letter writing. My aunt loved to write letters. She and I often wrote to each other. Anita and Freddy helped with household chores, as did I when I lived there.

After the children were grown and gone, Uncle Fred and Aunt Virginia traveled to five of the seven continents. They enjoyed an Alaskan Cruise and a ride on the Orient Express, which ran from 1883 until 2009. Some of the places they visited were Osaka, Japan; China including communes and rice paddies; Australia; New Zealand; Acapulco; and eight islands in Hawaii. They met many interesting people from all over the world during their travels. They and their children traveled the United States extensively to sightsee, visit relatives and friends and to attend conferences. I certainly enjoyed my trip with the family to California, Utah, and Mexico in 1963.

Aunt Virginia and Uncle Fred appeared to have a wonderful and charmed life together for more than fifty years. However, like any marriage there were bumps in the road. Those that I know of will go unmentioned. The important thing for any marriage is that the partners love each other enough to work through any challenge they face, to smooth out any bumps in the road, or to find ways to maneuver around them together.

Aunt Virginia could be difficult for family to live with at times. She had issues with boundaries. It was not easy for her to see her children, nieces and nephews as adults. When Anita and I were in our mid-fifties, we tried to talk with her as adults, but she wasn't having any of it. In her eyes, we were still fifteen. It didn't matter that we had husbands, children and grandchildren and that we had spent years working to help others improve their lives. She had to be in charge always.

When Anita was sick, Aunt Virginia could not accept that reality. She would not hear us when we asked for some space for Anita. Anita needed some quiet time without interference from her mother. Our discussion and pleas fell on deaf ears. We didn't know how to reach her without her feeling either rejected or attacked.

Aunt Virginia had no patience for sickness. When it was time for her to make her transition, she fell to the floor while walking and talking to her granddaughter. I thought seeing her lifeless body would overcome me. I was sad that my last Gray elder was gone, but I knew she had grown tired and had made peace with life in the best way she could.

Death was not her friend. She was afraid. I spoke with Aunt Virginia shortly after Uncle Frank had passed. She was down in spirit thinking about her own mortality. I felt for her. Even though she had been a churchgoing Christian all of her life, she still had some apprehension about what was on the other side. I tried to allay her fears by speaking as if I knew for sure what was waiting for us when we transition. I just felt that transitioning would be okay, and that she would be ready when the time came.

I don't believe death caught my aunt off guard. She had been fading for a few months. Aunt Virginia had spent her last two months reading the article I wrote about her. I thought it was fitting for Black History Month. Rosetta Miller-Perry published it in her newspaper *The Tennessee Tribune*. She had written other articles on the Westbrook family throughout the years, and she was glad to publish my article.

Aunt Virginia read that article, my speech, and a letter I had written. She kept going over all the favors and things from her celebration. When I would call, she was going on and on about the pictures of her during her early years that were enlarged for her celebration. She couldn't stop expressing how she felt about the whole event and about everyone who helped and who attended. I surprised her by inviting two of her cousins, Melvin Shaw from Memphis and Freddie Irons Holeyfield from Omaha. She had not seen them in many years. Aunt Virginia had done so much for so many people during her lifetime; it was time for us to celebrate her. She had never felt honored and appreciated.

Her once sharp mind was quickly becoming dull. I could sense that she would not be around much longer. I was glad we had had the celebration and so was Freddy. He didn't want it at first, but he relented. That night as I was about to leave Nashville, Freddy walked over to my car, stuck his head in through the window and kissed me on the cheek. He said, "Thank you. Everything was nice. Mother loved it and so did I."

Over the years I had often thought of the time I lived in Nashville with the Westbrook family. I thought they lived a mostly ideal family life. They had more order than I was used to. Their roles were clearly defined, husband, wife, daughter and son. Things ran rather smoothly. There were little things I noticed that I didn't like, such as, Aunt Virginia "loving" and babying Freddy too much while being too hard on Anita. She tried to make Anita the perfect young lady, someone who would always make her proud. She didn't know how to praise Anita and encourage her. Her daughter had so much talent, grace, dignity and beauty. Aunt Virginia knew that, but she didn't let Anita know how she felt. Anita got great amounts of criticism. Aunt Virginia always said when she was berating or belittling us, especially Anita, "It is constructive criticism."

She wanted Anita to marry the right man, have the right house, social life and everything that would put her in the upper class, or would certainly keep her where they were. She wanted her daughter to have a good life, to have the best as she had tried to give her.

Sometimes when parents are ambitious, high achievers, social climbers and pretty spectacular in their own eyes, it is difficult for their offspring to please them. Parents don't want to accept their children's interests, ideas, dreams and paths in life. Children want to choose for themselves and fashion their own lifestyle.

There was so much good in my aunt. I believe she always acted from a place of goodness. Her motives were good, yet she didn't always express in the most beneficial way for the recipient.

After Daddy died and I had completed summer school, Aunt

Virginia invited me to go with then to the West Coast on vacation. Actually she said, "Barbara, we're coming to get you and take you with us this summer. You need to get away."

I didn't object. I packed my things and joined the Westbrooks on the longest and hottest trip of my life. We took Route 66 and were on our way. Their Oldsmobile wasn't air-conditioned and going across the Mohave desert was almost unbearable. Still, the trip was a wonderful experience for me.

Uncle Fred had his annual conference in Logan, Utah that summer. I think the participants were agronomy or agriculture professors. It seemed we were the only black people in Utah. It was a nice experience. The conference had prepared a reception for the attendees' children. Anita, Freddy and I went and mingled with the white kids. Some of the children were our age but most were younger. I wore a black sheath, the one I wore after my senior prom. I didn't get new clothes very often. Anita wore a black and white tiered dress with spaghetti straps purchased for the occasion. It was a nice evening.

In Logan, we received many stares while we shopped. I guess people hadn't seen the likes of us in their area before. They were nice enough. The highlight of our trip to Utah was seeing the Mormon Tabernacle Choir. Aunt Virginia insisted.

Los Angeles, Disneyland and Dodger Stadium were calling me. That was the fun part of the trip. Under a pavilion at Disneyland, a Bluegrass band was picking and playing some foot stomping music neither Anita nor I could resist. There were no young men for us to dance with. Freddy was no use. We were in college then and didn't want to dance with each other any longer. However, after listening to another number we got ourselves up and danced with each other. Both she and I had on our denim skirts and coordinating shirts with white socks and tennis shoes. We coordinated our clothing on each outing since our taste was similar.

I went to see the Dodgers play the St. Louis Cardinals with Uncle Fred, Freddy and some other men. That was not something Anita wanted to do. She stayed with the ladies and visited. In San Diego, we met our adopted cousin from Palestine and went to the Zoo.

Since Tijuana, Mexico was so close to San Diego we drove across the border and had some fun in a foreign country. It was my first trip out of the country. I had learned enough to know that the Mexican guys were flirting with us while we shopped. It was fun. We had our picture made with a donkey and cart. I wanted to get on the donkey but Anita beat me to it.

Aunt Virginia was a fun loving person. Sometimes all of us could have a good time together. It wasn't all criticizing. I knew then as I know now that my aunt was generous and that she enjoyed helping her people. She knew I was having a difficult time adjusting to life without Daddy and so was she. That trip helped me realize I had a life to live. I knew that I wanted to see more of this country and some of the world. I was forever grateful to Aunt Virginia for including me in their vacation plans that summer.

I felt about Aunt Virginia's driving skills the way I felt about Daddy's--both scared me since I was six. They tailgated. My scariest time in a car was the night Aunt Virginia picked us up from an event. Anita and I were not where she had told us to be when she came back for us. When we got to the car, she started yelling at us. Anita tried to explain, but Aunt Virginia wasn't having any of it. She kept looking back yelling while we sat mute. Since she was somewhat distracted, she drove across tracks in front of an oncoming train. Anita and I saw the train coming. She yelled, "Mother!" I screamed and we both fell to the floor. There were no seatbelts then and no railroad crossing gates. Aunt Virginia kept yelling saying she saw the train. She accused us of being dramatic.

I thought I would see my aunt one more time before she passed, perhaps in a hospital bed. That was not to be. She surprised us all and went suddenly, or so it seemed. I think she took her time transitioning. It was months in the making.

Her grandchildren asked me to write something for her funeral program. They knew our relationship and knew their grandmother would want it. Aunt Virginia and I had written many letters to one another over the years. I would write one more, my last.

Aunt Virginia,

Born a princess, you became Queen and Matriarch of our family. You expected the best from life, and life rewarded you greatly with love and prosperity in all things. You have inspired me in so many ways as you lived your life with grace and dignity and with a love for beauty. You made it your duty to uplift your family and others by encouraging them to value and pursue education, good family relationships, honest work, and moral and spiritual development. Aunt Virginia, I continue to celebrate you today and always. I love you, I appreciate you, and I thank God for you.

Niece,
Barbara Gray Armstrong

I AM MY BROTHERS' KEEPER

Am I my brother's keeper -- King James Version Bible, Genesis 4:9

Cain and his brother Abel presented an offering to God. Abel offered the first-born sheep of his flock, and Cain, being a farmer, offered grains and vegetables. Abel's offering was acceptable to God while Cain's was not. Cain became angry and confronted his brother Abel. They must have argued and Cain allowed his anger to overtake him; he killed his brother and hid his body.

God asked Cain, "Where is Abel thy brother?"

Cain replied, "I don't know. Am I my brother's keeper?"

From that sarcastic response Cain gave, it must have been some attitude, quality, characteristic, or spirit that caused his offering to be unacceptable to God. That old green-eyed monster jealousy had entered the world and set up residence in Cain's heart.

Sibling rivalry must have started at what some believe is the beginning of the human story. There was also the idea of selfishness as Cain was only concerned with his own life and not his brother's. Of course, Cain was lying to cover up his crime. However, he had no love for his younger brother.

I never experienced sibling rivalry, envy or jealousy. Perhaps it was because I had three brothers, and I felt no need to compete with them. Being the only girl in the family gave me many privileges.

Even my brothers made sacrifices for me. They often called me "the queen" since it appeared that I always got my way. I didn't. Yet, our parents treated me differently and seemed to show more concern for my welfare.

My relationship with each of my brothers was different due to their ages and personalities. The oldest, Clinton was born the year the Japanese attacked Pearl Harbor. I grew up calling him "Sonny." He was almost four years my senior and his role was that of big brother—protector, mentor—not an equal or a friend.

Sonny loved playing football and socializing with the girls. He was popular in school and enjoyed his status. He was never afraid of anyone or any work. As soon as he was old enough to work, Sonny looked for jobs. He wanted to have his own money. He wasn't studious as I recall, yet he did what he needed to do to graduate. Instead of going to college, Sonny enlisted in the Army. He was the ideal soldier because of his work ethic and sense of order and discipline.

When he was stationed in Germany, we wrote letters to one another. I still treasure the Polaroid camera he sent me. He also sent me mohair sweaters that were popular then. Sonny was always giving. He worked during summers while living with Mommy and helped with household expenses. I think he felt it was his responsibility to help Mommy.

Sonny served in Vietnam and earned the Bronze Star Medal for Valor. As the report goes, the Viet Cong opened fire on his Battalion, killed and wounded several soldiers. Sonny rescued a wounded soldier. The Citation stated, "Disregarding his own safety and without a moment's hesitation, Corporal Gray rushed into the killing zone to find the wounded man. Ignoring the heavy enemy fire falling around him, Corporeal Gray then carried the wounded man on his back to safety." The citation lauded my brother's personal bravery and devotion to duty.

The Army also awarded Sonny the Purple Heart. The Purple Heart is given to soldiers wounded in battle. His wound ended his second tour in Vietnam in 1968. Any thoughts Sonny had of becoming a career soldier ended. He suffered the wound as he was getting back into the helicopter to leave a war zone. The Army sent him to Walter Reed Hospital for extended treatment. Although his wound left him partially paralyzed and crippled, Sonny bought a motorcycle in D.C. and rode it to Nashville. I was in Mt. Pleasant, having moved from Charleston, awaiting the birth of my daughter Alysa. Sonny drove the motorcycle to Mt. Pleasant in the snow to see his niece when she was three days old.

That injury didn't prevent my brother from doing all kinds of farm work and hard labor. As the years passed, he had to slow down and leave the work to others. That war took a great toll on my brother as it did on so many more. Since Sonny had planned to be a career soldier, had it not been for the injury suffered in war, his life would have been so different. He was the macho, competitive type who always welcomed a challenge.

During a summer when we were in the country, we heard that if you kill a snake and hang it in a tree, the tail wouldn't die until after sundown. In addition, there would be a big storm as long as the snake hung in the tree.

Sonny was always daring as a youth. Snakes were not difficult to find in the country. Sometimes they would venture too close to the house for me. Sonny killed the snake and hung it on a limb. That afternoon a storm rose suddenly; I was so afraid I hid under the kitchen table. I begged, "Sonny, please go get that snake out of the tree." For all I knew, the storm could have been in the weather forecast. At that time, I thought the snake caused the storm. I never wanted him to do that again.

As I sat in the Kingdom Hall February 8, 2014, during Sonny's Memorial Service, listening to the minister speak about a person I did not recognize, I decided to remember my big brother as I had known him during the early years. I thought of how neat and clean Sonny used to be as a teen. He kept his room immaculate. Images of Sonny ironing his starched pants and shirts and shinning his shoes to perfection entered my mind. There he was waxing and polishing floors, fixing things, driving me to Memphis, hunting rabbits, squirrels and quail. I saw him riding the mule, plowing, planting, playing football, swimming, running, chasing girls, growing up fast, and leaving home for a military life that would redefine and reshape the brother of my youth.

The second born was Charles. He was somewhat sickly as a child, which must have taken a toll on his energy. He was studious, a bookworm who spent much of his time reading. Charles loved reading the World Book Encyclopedias Mommy had bought from a door-to-door salesman. Everybody thought he was smart. He liked school. I think Aunt Virginia tried to program him early in his life to become a doctor. He thought about it when he was young, but it must not have been a burning desire for him. I believe Aunt Virginia greatly wanted a doctor in the family and thought Charles might be the one.

Mommy told me Charles was trying to teach me to ride a tricycle when I was two, and I fell off. He tried to help me get up, but I said, "Leave me 'lone. I do it myself." My stubbornness made me independent early in life. I did ask him to teach me to tell time when he was eight.

Charles attended Austin Peay State College but dropped out to enlist in the Army. He didn't go to Vietnam. Instead, he was stationed in Germany. Charles wasn't a gung ho soldier. I think he was simply taking a break from college, and perhaps fulfilling his duty to his country in the process. After serving in the Army, Charles returned to school and earned his undergraduate degree in chemistry, and his graduate degree in economics from Memphis State University.

Charles was proud of his intelligence. I believe he always thought he was the smartest person in the room. I guess joining MENSA gave him bragging rights.

Malcolm, the youngest of the family and two years my junior, was more of a companion and playmate to me. He and I became friends when were children. We played well together and got into trouble together. Since I was older, I could boss him around and be in charge. I also felt maternal and protective towards him. Yet, we would sometimes engage in name-calling and even fights. It was always about something small and insignificant and our anger would end as quickly as it began.

Malcolm Thomas Gray was a lovable child, sweet and innocent, yet mischievous. People were drawn to him and not so much to me. I was distant, not at all trusting of people. His loving, trusting nature made him vulnerable to abuse by several people during his childhood and youth. I was not aware of the abuse until we became adults.

Malcolm was a fearless little boy who played rough and seemed to enjoy every minute of it. During the summer we spent with Daddy, I tried to keep him safe, but one day when he was running very fast on gravel he slipped, and as he stuck out his hands to break his fall, rocks lodged in both palms. I took care of his injuries, cleaning, putting on mercurochrome and bandages. I bathed and dressed him for a couple of days until the soreness eased.

Malcolm enjoyed playing at home and at school. His playing instead of doing his schoolwork caused him to spend two years in third grade. Mommy was his teacher. She was tough on him as she was on me. There was no nepotism from her.

Malcolm could play for hours under the hickory trees at our grandparents' house. He would be quite content with his little trucks, cars, soldiers, and improvised toys. Many times, we played together. I loved playing with my dolls, and sometimes Malcolm would join me. I don't remember if I ever joined him in playing in the dirt. Probably not.

One day we decided to put a doll dress on our puppy. We bathed him and dressed him in a pink dress. We then grabbed each front paw, and took the puppy for a walk. It didn't matter that the puppy was male; the dress looked cute on him. Good thing Mommy didn't see us.

Malcolm and I chased chickens and pigs and ran away stray cats. Don't know why we didn't like cats. Dogs were okay with the exception of Spikey. We roamed the fields, swung on vines, hid between rows of tall corn stalks, tried to find rabbits, and avoid snakes. We goofed off in Brother's field when we were supposed to be picking cotton.

Malcolm and I visited Aunt Pat and Uncle Alf often and tried to get Walter to play with us. He felt he was too old; he would say, "I'm not equal with you." Besides, he was always working. Walter was somewhat mysterious to us. We didn't know where he came from. Neither did we understand why he was different. We knew he wasn't Uncle Alf and Aunt Pat's child. Walter was our "Boo" before Harper Lee's "Boo Radley."

In 1963, I was at Lane College when Malcolm did as Daddy had done twenty-seven years prior. Malcolm got into trouble at Fayette County Training School, and the principal expelled him. Just like Daddy, he wanted to play football and finish high school. I think that was a way Malcolm could feel some closeness to the daddy he had never really known and would never know. He came to Jackson, rented a room, and attended Merry High School. Daddy had told Malcolm that he was going to live in Clarksville with him that year. Malcolm was so excited because he was living for the time when he could be with his daddy and play football. His dream ended with Daddy's death.

Daddy had written Mommy a letter in 1962 that stated, "I would like for you to let me have Malcolm." Mommy was going to let Malcolm go because she knew he needed to know his daddy. He needed male guidance. Brother and Papa were around, but Malcolm needed his own daddy. I know if life had given my brother that gift, then the course of his life would have been different. He suffered greatly for not being able to live with Daddy, for not knowing him. Malcolm was a baby when Mommy and Daddy separated; therefore, he only knew his daddy through short visits and one summer.

Like his big brothers, Malcolm enlisted in the Army when he was nineteen. He was stationed in Germany at first, then went off to Vietnam, the war of our generation. That war had a devastating and detrimental effect on him. He told me of many atrocities he witnessed and some in which he participated. He never learned to integrate those things into his life. He couldn't forgive himself. He tried religion as a means of escape, but it didn't work. In fact, it made matters worse. He became fanatical about his approach to religion.

Losing him was difficult for me. I used to feel that I should have known his pain and helped him in some way. I always tried to help my brothers when they were in need; however, I was not equipped to help Malcolm when he needed help most.

Malcolm was a writer and poet. He attended Lane College, but did not graduate. He wrote a book about the Viet Nam War in the early 1980s, and took the manuscript to Hollywood to shop around. A woman in show business took it under false pretenses. He never could connect with her after that. When the movie *Platoon* came out in 1986, Malcolm swore that it was his work, and he was adamant that the woman had stolen it.

Malcolm wrote hundreds of letters and commentary on scripture, mostly Bible prophecy. He also wrote poetry and published two poems in the 1970 Lane College yearbook, *The Lanite*.

DADDY'S GIRL

Clinton Claude Gray

May 17, 1913-April 9, 1963

Honor your father ... that your days may be long upon the land which the Lord your God is giving you.-- New King James Version Bible, Exodus 20:12

It happened on a Thursday. Physical education and humanities were the only classes I had that morning, so I spent the afternoon on the old clay court hitting tennis balls with a young man named Ron. Neither of us were players, nor was the court playable; nevertheless, it was fun just hitting the ball back and forth over the net without keeping score.

In the early evening, Betty and I were coming out of Cleaves Hall trying to get to Carol's Restaurant for barbecue sandwiches before dark. I saw Brother walking towards us. I turned to Betty and said, "That's my uncle. I wonder why he's here."

"Your mother wants you to come home," he said without a hello, as he approached.

"Why?" I asked, not wanting to know, but thinking how strange for Mommy to send for me when the weekend was a day away. Not wanting to hear any bad news, I asked no more questions.

"She just wants you to come home for a while, so get a few things together and come on. I'll be in the car."

Betty and I looked quizzically at one another, turned around slowly, went back inside, and started upstairs.

"I'll help you pack," she offered as she rushed up the stair ahead of me.

I stopped at the window in the stairwell, stared out onto the empty football field where Daddy used to practice and let my mind go to each brother in the Army. Then my mind settled on Daddy. "Oh Daddy," I whispered. I turned around and ran up to my room to pack. I refused to think anymore. I did not want to know anything before I got home.

I eased into the front seat of Brother's black and white Chevrolet and noticed Malcolm sitting quietly in the back. My baby brother was not quiet. He was always playing and joking, always happy to see me. He said, "Hi," and we rode in silence to a nearby service station.

Brother got out of the car. Malcolm started to cry.

I turned around and asked, "What's wrong?" I had to ask, but I didn't want him to tell me.

"Daddy's dead."

My mouth opened wide. I heard someone far away screaming. I realized it was I when no more sound came and my throat was dry. The pain of eternal loss was a chainsaw cutting through the middle of me as if I were a sapling. I was inconsolable. I screamed, hollered, cried and thrashed around on that seat until all of the shock and pain drained out of the hole that the chainsaw had made. I don't remember getting home, but there I was swiftly walking past Mommy who was frying some woman's hair. I did not speak. I headed for the seclusion of my room to bury my face in the pillow and sob.

I was Daddy's girl. I got many of my ideas about life from Daddy. He lived as if life should have more fun-filled and leisure times than times spent working and slaving. No, Daddy wasn't consumed with the mundane things of life like paying utility bills, a car note and such, which made life a little unpredictable and challenging for me at seven.

Daddy taught civics at Burt High School in Clarksville, Tennessee until he made his hasty departure from life in April of 1963. He never taught me, but from what I have heard from Charles, who was in his class in ninth grade, Daddy was especially tough, and he showed Charles no partiality. Charles had to dot every "i" and cross every "t" to get a good grade.

Clinton Claude Gray was also a tough and strict coach. Coaching was his passion. He, like any coach, wanted a winning team. He coached girls' basketball during the time girls played half court. Even though girls' basketball was quite different then, it was exciting and very popular. That was because of the skills of Wilma Rudolph and other girls. Daddy was a demanding coach, and the girls were fierce in competing against their opponents.

When I was ninth grade, Daddy told me to try out for the team. I didn't think about it for a long time. I thought it would allow me to have more time with Daddy if I were on the team. Of course, I would have to share him with the other girls, but that was okay.

I was there in shorts and sneakers on the designated day with all the other skinny-legged girls ready to show what I could do. I had fun playing basketball in gym class and participating in intramural games. I knew the basics. In fact, I already had a basketball injury that happened when I was jumping up to catch the ball, and it jammed my right index finger. It hurt beyond words, but I pulled it immediately hoping it would pop back into place. It didn't. I talked Daddy out of taking me to the doctor.

The tryouts were more grueling than I had imagined; however, it was Daddy yelling and hollering at us that I didn't like. What was motivational for the other girls was a big turnoff for me. My daddy was not supposed to yell at me. I couldn't take it, not even for the team. I quit before Coach Gray made his selections.

Daddy must have inaugurated the girls' Track Team shortly after noticing Wilma's speed on the basketball court. It must have been obvious to him that she needed a larger arena to demonstrate her speed and grace. Half of a basketball court could not do that. Even Daddy was shocked at her speed when she ran in her first track meet. Coach Temple of Tennessee State University, where they held the track meet, noticed her and wanted to work with her during the summer. I went along with Daddy one time when he drove Skeeter to Nashville to work with Coach Temple and his team the Tigerbelles.

I would like to think that I was the highlight of Daddy's life, but I do know that the highlight of his career was discovering, perhaps witnessing, and surely working with the talents of Wilma Rudolph.

As a seventh grader, Wilma had an older sister on the basketball team. She was ever-present running with the big girls. Daddy likened her peskiness to that of a mosquito and started calling her "Mosquito," which morphed into "Skeeter" and "Skeet." I always called her Skeeter.

Alex Haley wrote a story about Wilma entitled "The Queen Who Earned Her Crown" in 1969 for a ninth grade textbook, *Voices in Literature, Language and Composition 2*. In that story, he wrote, "she played with such fervor that during one game she collided with Coach-referee Clinton C. Gray. 'You're buzzing around like a "skeeter"' wherever I turn!'"

Skeeter treated me as she did her younger sister who was my classmate and friend. I looked up to her. I spent many nights at their home when Daddy was out of town.

When I jammed my finger and couldn't comb and style my hair, Skeeter met me at school before classes started and took care of it. Once I wore a cotton skirt to school in the wintertime, and Skeeter scolded me, "Barbara Jean, why are you wearing that skirt? It's too cold for that. Don't wear that skirt again until spring." I didn't.

Skeeter went on to have a successful career as a Tigerbell and as an Olympic track star. She won a bronze medal in the 1956 Olympics in Australia. In the summer of 1960, Wilma won three gold medals for the U. S. Olympic team in Rome, Italy. After winning three gold medals, Wilma came home to the cheers of her hometown. Businesses closed so both black and white citizens could celebrate her accomplishment.

Daddy had joined with others to plan the celebration. Mayor Bill Barksdale of Clarksville wrote a letter to Daddy dated October 10, 1960, thanking him for helping to make "Welcome Wilma Day" a success. The Mayor hailed it as "a milestone in the development of our community relations."

As Alex Haley and others wrote articles, books and movies on Wilma Rudolph's life and her outstanding achievements in track, Daddy's name appeared. He was her first coach. Aunt Virginia used to say, "My brother didn't get enough credit for Wilma's accomplishment. Without him, where would she be?"

In a letter from Sterling W. Fisher, Director of Public Relations at *Reader's Digest* magazine, he wrote to Daddy, "As Wilma Rudolph's first coach, you share the glory handed out by Alex Haley in his tribute to "The Girl Who Wouldn't Give Up" in the May Reader's Digest." He sent the letter to Daddy along with a copy of the magazine with compliments and good wishes.

Daddy got a congratulatory card from his mother and father after she had read an article in in a Nashville newspaper. Big Mama wrote a note in the card that read, "I am so very glad for you...I am sure you are proud of what you have done. Of all of my children, you are my greatest. I have been watching the Olympics in Rome. I have seen this girl run. She is great...I can say for true, you have done great."

Big Mama goes on to bless his family and ask about me. She closes by admonishing him, "Go to church, Church of God in Christ. You will be glad you did."

I don't know if Daddy went to any church in obedience to his mother's advice, but I do know that Big Mama saw to it that her son did go to church one more time before his body left this earth. On April 14, 1963, she had his funeral at Community Temple Church of God In Christ where she attended. The burial was in Oak Spring Cemetery, Arlington, Tennessee near the church his grandfather Pastor Hammond founded.

April 9, 1963 was Daddy's last day on earth. Wilma has just gotten into town. She usually went by the school to see Coach before she went home, but that day she was tired and went home to rest. When she heard of her coach's death, Wilma said, "He was just like a father, and I'll never forget what he did for me." She went on to say that, "Coach Gray was proud of her Olympic achievement, but he would have been prouder when she graduated from college. (*Clarksville Leaf Chronicle*, April, 1963)

Coach Whitney of Burt High said, "He was not a soft-spoken man, but he got results from his youngsters. He demanded loyalty to team members and to the principles of winning and making good grades." (*Clarksville Leaf Chronicle* April, 1963)

Daddy had many winning teams. He was president of the Region II Athletic Association and on the Board of Control of the Tennessee High School Athletic Association.

Daddy smoked Pall Mall cigarettes and drank bourbon whiskey. He sometimes came home late at night, fell asleep, and snored loudly enough to wake the dead. I know because sometimes I slept in Daddy's bed. I liked sleeping with Daddy because it made me feel safe. I didn't know then that some father's abused their daughters, and I am thankful that Daddy was sane, if not always sober.

I think whisky made Daddy sleep very deeply. It was dangerous and sometimes very scary. On more than one occasion, Daddy fell asleep while smoking a cigarette. This could have turned out deadly if I hadn't been sleeping in his bed. I felt the smoldering mattress and woke Daddy on two occasions. Another time Daddy burned his fingers when he went to sleep holding a cigarette. I learned much later that Daddy was diabetic, which could have accounted for his coma-like sleep and slow healing fingers. Diabetes was probably responsible for Daddy's death. It may have been a diabetic coma, which caused him to lose control of the wheel, and run off the road. There were no adverse driving conditions such as weather, road, or traffic. Daddy was on his way to the doctor in Kentucky just past the Tennessee line, and for some reason he turned off the main highway near Fort Campbell onto a country road where he lost control and ran into a small embankment.

One summer Mommy needed some "me time" so she packed Malcolm and me off to Clarksville. Sonny and Charles lived with Daddy from elementary through their high school graduations. All of us spent summers and holidays in Somerville with Mommy, Mama, Papa, Brother, and Aunt Penny, and later their sons two sons joined the household. Summer in the city with Daddy was fun and completely different from the country. I enjoyed having girls to play with. I was ten and Malcolm was eight. Daddy worked at a country club, and I looked after Malcolm. Sonny and Charles were responsible for both of us. However, Sonny, who was a very industrious teen, often worked.

I was motherly and responsible, so I had charge of a neighbor's children sometimes. I knew how to bathe, dress, and keep little ones safe. The children ranged in age from three to seven. I was trusted to take the children for walks and even to the movies.

It was that summer of 1955, when I learned an important lesson about money. My motto was, "Have money, will spend." My favorite morning greeting was, "Daddy can I have dime before you go to work?" He was going to the Clarksville Country Club where he worked as a cook during the summer. Daddy was employing the skills he used as a Pullman Porter in earlier times. The hickory smoked chicken breast, Daddy sometimes brought home, would entice and gratify my senses completely.

Daddy lectured me about my spending habits, as if he had a right. One morning, he said, "I'll give you a dime, but you can't spend it." I looked at him cross-eyed. He continued, "If you still have it when I get home this evening, I'll give you a dollar." My eyes relaxed, the corners of my mouth crept up. I gladly took the challenge thinking of all I could buy with a dollar. A dollar went far in those days, eighteen cents for a loaf of bread, three cents to mail a letter. Gas was twenty-three cents a gallon. I could buy a Baby Ruth candy bar, Lay's potato chips, and my favorite Nehi orange soda pop, and still have change. *Okay*, I thought, *I can do this*. I should have known that I could only wait as long as it took Daddy to get to work. Besides, I reasoned, what was the good of having the dime if I couldn't spend it right away?

I took the dime and put it away for safekeeping. I really did want to show Daddy I could stay away from the corner store for one day. Since I could spend the dime plus the dollar the next day, I thought I could meet the challenge, but my will crumbled at the thought of salty potato chips and a sweet candy bar. I failed. There I was about to disappoint Daddy after I had already let myself down. What was a girl to do? I did the only thing I could think of: I borrowed a dime from Charles who was not a big spender, and I lied to Daddy. I was not proud of myself, but I was a dollar richer even if I did become so by crook. I think Daddy knew I had cheated. He couldn't hold onto money for any length of time either. In money matters during my early years, I was truly my daddy's daughter.

Daddy didn't claim any piety, which meant he didn't seem like a hypocrite to me. He came from a family who was mostly religious, having a maternal grandfather who was a minister. I remember going to church with Daddy only one time for a regular Sunday service and twice to funerals. Daddy believed in love, yet he had no formal religious practice. He didn't push me away from hell or towards heaven. I was comfortable spending Sundays playing, watching television, and lying around reading as I did on any other day.

When I first went to live with Daddy he had a housekeeper who was a little muddle brained; she didn't last long. I don't know if it was that Daddy couldn't pay, or she couldn't find her way back to our house. A woman two houses down combed my hair before school each morning. I was friends with her daughter Hattie. Her son's funeral was the first of a young child that I ever attended. I didn't want to go, but Daddy insisted I go and pay my respects. He took me, against my will, to the casket to view the body. The boy was nine and suffered from rheumatic fever. I saw great care his mother had given him, but that disease was a killer of children. I heard his mother crying so many times when I visited my best friend. I could hear her loud cries even when I was in my house. I was so sad for her.

The thing about living with Daddy was that I had to learn self-sufficiency early in life. I learned to take care of my personal needs, and even learned how to do housework earlier than most other children. I could stay home alone without being scared. I loved experimenting in the kitchen when everyone was out. Cooking generally meant opening a can of beans or corn and heating it, or making cheese toast under the broiler, but when no one was home, I would try to make a cake. I knew nothing about a recipe. I would put in the ingredients I saw Mommy and Mama use when they baked. Of course, nothing was edible, and cooking without supervision was a dangerous thing for me to do then. People used to say, "God takes care of fools and babies." Mommy used to tell me how much she and Mama prayed for us.

C. C. Gray, as some called him and as he often used for his signature wasn't the most conscientious person when it came to taking care of his bills. Sometimes he either forgot to pay or he ran out of money before he could pay the water or the electricity bill, and we would have to go without one or the other for a couple of days. That became difficult to deal with, as I grew older. It was embarrassing to have to borrow water from a neighbor.

Daddy was overprotective. He worried that I would get involved and become pregnant at an early age. That was almost the worst thing that could happen to a young girl in those days. Unlike today, it brought shame on the girl and on her family. It meant early marriage in some cases. For some it meant dropping out of school and friends shunning her. I had no thoughts of having a baby before I was married, and I hated those talks; however, they were prevalent throughout my school days. Even teachers and others would admonish students about the pitfall of teen pregnancy and venereal diseases. The village was at work then.

There was the pretense of morality at that time. Some thought girls should be virgins until marriage. It was okay for boys to have sex before marriage. I always wondered with whom the boys were to have sex. Daddy wanted to make sure it was not with me. There were two categories of girls—good and bad. Most boys wanted a "bad" girl at some point during their youth, but they often wanted a "good" girl to marry. Therefore, I suppose any girl could be in the good category if she was discreet and did not get pregnant. "Kissing and telling" was not necessarily the order of the day. No girl sported a firm round belly as though it were a badge of honor. Ministers put some out of their churches; others had difficulty within their own families. It was as though the generations before had not had sex before marriage and brought "illegitimate" children into the family. Legitimacy was only for those children born in the confines of marriage. I didn't want to bring shame on Daddy by becoming a pregnant teen. Moreover, I did not want to become pregnant.

Daddy loved sports and not only coached girl's track and basketball, but was also an assistant football coach. Before we had a television, on some Sundays we would visit one of Daddy's friends and watch the Green Bay Packers, Cleveland Browns, the New York Giants and others with an eye out for the few black players like Lenny Moore, Dick "Night Train" Lane, or Joe Perry, San Francisco 49ers fullback and the first African American MVP. I didn't like football. I didn't understand the roughness of the game. I just liked hanging out with Daddy.

Daddy had been a star football player at Manassas High School in Memphis before they expelled him for his disobedience. According to Uncle Frank, Daddy was suspended and had to sit out a game. The team was losing and Daddy was anxious to get in the game. The coach said no. Daddy was going to put the uniform on and go in against the coach's will. Uncle Frank said, "Mr. Cotton told Clinton not to touch that suit." Uncle Frank fell back on the sofa laughing as he remembered the story, "Clinton touched it anyway. He just had to touch it. Mr. Cotton must have taken Clinton's hand off of it because Clinton hit Mr. Cotton, and for that, he was expelled from Manassas High School."

Daddy was determined to graduate; he had to come up with a plan. He had messed around long enough. Seems Daddy was so interested in sports during eighth grade that his class had moved on without him. He said to Aunt Virginia, who was a year younger, "Sister, you may have caught me, but you won't pass me."

Sadly, Daddy had to leave his family, friends and schoolmates in Memphis. He took off walking the forty plus miles to Jackson to attend Merry High School. Many young people left home and made it on their own in the 1930s. There were people who would rent rooms to them and many black people, during that time, were willing to share food and resources. Daddy knew the Ford family and stayed with them for a time and with whomever else he could. In spite of having to work to provide for himself, Daddy was able to play football there and do well enough academically to graduate.

When he was in college, the house he lived in burned and destroyed his Merry High diploma. When Daddy went back to Memphis for a visit, he went to Manassas High and apologized to Mr. Cotton for his past behavior. That impressed the principal enough that he awarded Daddy a replacement diploma from Manassas.

Daddy went from Merry High up Lane Avenue to attend College. He played football and lettered in the sport. I have several newspaper clippings that mention Daddy's exploits on the football field. Daddy wore number 25, weighed 150 pounds and was fast on his feet. When the Lane College Dragons crushed Fisk 33-6, the newspaper reported, "Gray, acclaimed Lane's most accurate passer, completed several long passes to Sims."

Daddy pledged Alpha Phi Alpha Fraternity, but he didn't have much free time to participate in extracurricular activities. He was an English major with reading and writing to keep him busy. Aunt Virginia finished Manassas and followed her big brother to Lane College. Resources were limited and Daddy helped her financially. Daddy should have finished Lane in 1937, but he dropped out to work fulltime so he could help his sister her last year. She was a more serious and motivated student than her brother. It was a good arrangement because after Aunt Virginia graduated and started her first teaching job, she helped her brother. Daddy received his Bachelor of Arts Degree the year Hattie McDaniel won the Academy Award for Best Supporting Actress. She played Mammy in *Gone with the Wind*.

Not finding a teaching position immediately after graduation, Daddy joined the ranks of the proud black men who were Pullman Porters. The Pullman Company was one of the biggest employers of black men. It made it possible for many of them to move their families into the middle class. In 1867, industrialist George Pullman designed a sleeper car so passengers would be comfortable and rested on long cross-country trips. He hired black men as servants. They greeted passengers, cooked and served food, shined shoes, cleaned, and did whatever chores passengers requested. While they got no respect on the job, they were highly regarded in their communities. They were well-dressed men who traveled, had good communication skills, and were often college educated, as was Daddy. The porters also assisted many black people from the South who were heading North, East and West between 1910 and 1969 during the Great Migration. They also helped to distribute the *Pittsburgh Courier* and the *Chicago Defender* throughout the country. Under A. Phillip Randolph's leadership, the porters made up the first black labor union, Brotherhood of Sleeping Car Porters. The union helped to improve working conditions and salaries. It took more than twelve years of negotiating to bring about that change.

Daddy liked to read and to write, therefore, I can just imagine him reading while on break when one of the white passengers takes notice and asks, as the Senator asks Pullman Porter Dixon in *From "Superman" to Man* by J. A. Rogers, "Reading the Bible George?" White passengers didn't bother learning their porter's names; they simply referred to each of them as "George."

It was difficult for some white people to think of black people reading. Moreover, if black people did read, what could it possibly be except the Bible? Those passengers did not know that some of those porters and perhaps some of the few Pullman maids were formally educated and others self-educated and well read.

Of course, Daddy could have been sitting there writing poetry and dreaming of the job and the life he really wanted. He must have become a porter in 1939 or 1940. I don't know how many years he spent on that job and whether the entrepreneurial spirit was beckoning him or if his boss suggested he might be more suitable elsewhere. I don't see him doing that work for many years in view of this poem he wrote in the 1930s or early 40s.

Some One

Someone has got to wield the pick,
Use the ax and run the train.
Someone has got to mine the coal,
Build the roads and plant the grain.
Someone has got to do hard work—
This world can't get along without it,
But I'm darned sure it won't be me,
For I had rather write about it.

Daddy grew up under the loving care of a father who did not want his children to do hard labor. He wanted them educated, and he took the steps necessary to make that possible. I don't remember Daddy fixing anything—not a faucet drip, or a toilet, or his car. I never saw him with a wrench, screwdriver or any kind of tool in his hands. No, Daddy wasn't a man who fixed material things. He wanted a different life.

Sometime after his Pullman Porter days, Daddy, along with a partner, bought a dry cleaner, which was located close to where we lived in Memphis. A dispute arose between Daddy and his partner that must have ended his entrepreneurial quest. I think his partner was Mommy's Uncle Caleb and the fight was about money. Uncle Caleb shot Daddy with a shotgun. Good thing Daddy turned in time for the buckshot to spray his arm and elbow. Otherwise, it may have been a fatal shot. When I was a young girl, I would sit on Daddy's lap sometimes and feel the buckshot in his arm.

Both his work as a porter and running the dry cleaners took place between 1939 and 1949. In 1949, Daddy started teaching and coaching football at Fayette County Training School in Somerville. I met one of his former students some years ago who related to me just how strict and exacting "Mr. Gray" was as he taught her English.

Daddy only taught one year at the Training School. He and the county agent got into a physical fight. Seems the county agent was a favored son of the establishment. After it was over, Daddy rushed to the Board of Education to resign. Word of his actions must have preceded him. When the superintendent came out to fire him, Daddy said, "You can't fire me. I quit."

Daddy was a dreamer. He didn't know you had to plan and work a dream. When I was born, he wanted me to go to Spelman College. Even if he had known how to plan and save money, there would not have been enough on his meager salary to provide such an education. He settled on Lane instead and took me there against my will. I don't hold it against him. In fact, I'm glad he did. If Lane College was good enough for Daddy and Mommy; Uncles Frank and William; Aunts Dorinda, Virginia, Penny; and Cousins Ernestine, Maureen and Melvin, it was good enough for me.

The last time I saw Daddy alive was when he came through Jackson to pick me up so we could go to Big Daddy's funeral. Daddy had been drinking whisky. I could smell it. He was upset that his dad had died; he needed a drink to steady his nerves. He was sad because of where his dad had died. Big Daddy died in Western State Hospital for the mentally ill. It was painful for Daddy to have his father there. It was painful for me. Big Daddy was there because Big Mama had become afraid of him. I think he was starting to have Alzheimer's or dementia. They didn't know what to do other that put him in a mental institution. Aunt Virginia said Big Daddy had had a brain aneurism when she was a teen, and the doctors didn't expect him to live; therefore, it could have come from that.

I don't know why Daddy had been drinking before or during the trip. He was able to drive. I wasn't afraid. I was with Daddy; therefore, what could go wrong? Everything.

As we were passing through Bolivar where the police were notorious for stopping drivers, an officer got behind us with lights flashing. Daddy pulled to the side of the road. The officer was the typical white supremacist *du jour*. He came over to the driver's side. Daddy rolled down the window. Whisky aroma and fumes must have rushed from the car's interior and headed straight for the officer's brain via his nostrils. He ordered Daddy out of the car. "Git out there and walk that white line boy." Daddy tried to comply.

"I oughtta take you to jail. I ought to arrest you for drinking and driving. Anybody this gal can stay with? Git outta the car gal."

There is no way I can accurately describe the fear, shame, and disgust that came over me as the officer walked towards me, sizing me up, evaluating my worth to see if he should buy off the slave block or the block? I didn't move. I didn't breathe.

Daddy looked on helplessly. I felt sorrier for him than I did for myself. I was his little girl. He wanted to protect me. What could he do? He was a helpless black man, on the side of the road in the dark, in the 1963 American South with a power-hungry racist police officer out for sport.

After the officer pierced my trembling flesh with his stare, he spun around, regrouped, and ordered Daddy to, "Git back in the car."

"Gal, can you drive?"

"Yes sir."

"How old are you?'

"Eighteen."

"Do you have a driver's license?"

"No sir."

"Drive. Go."

I drove to Somerville in silence. Daddy sat in the passenger seat perhaps contemplating the weight of the evening. The residual alcohol made him drift off to sleep. The event settled in a deep crevasse. Nothing needed saying.

After Big Daddy's funeral, Daddy drove me back to Jackson without the whisky. He walked me to my dorm, gave me a few dollars and said, "Spend your money wisely."

"Okay, Daddy."

He hugged and kissed me and said, "Daddy loves you Baby."

A couple of weeks later Daddy sent me a message by a fellow student who had attended a conference and met him there. The next mention of Daddy was on the day he died. The *Clarksville*

Leaf Chronicle reported that he was DOA when brought to the U.S. Army Hospital at Fort Campbell at 12:20 p.m. He was forty-nine.

Mommy pulled up to the gates seeking permission to identify the man she must have loved during a time. Soldiers, standing perfectly with guns on their sides seemed to share my pain. The coroner walked over to the huge file cabinet, reached down and pulled out a drawer. Mommy and I approached cautiously as if we would wake a sleeping baby. I looked at Daddy, so peaceful, calm and ordinary, with a small cut on his forehead.

Mommy answered the coroner's questions while I stood blinking away pain, swallowing screams, wondering how I would move to the next step.

We stayed in Clarksville for the memorial service held at Burt High School. When I saw what had been my daddy, I wanted to scream, "Who is this stranger in Daddy's casket?"

Since I had seen Daddy before the undertaker went to work, I was shocked to see that swollen, distorted face. Daddy looked like someone I did not know. If he had resembled his living self, I probably would have defiled the sanctity of the occasion by trying to pull him out of that box.

I sat with Mommy and my brothers--dazed. Times with Daddy tiptoed through my mind in a melancholy procession. A boat ride on the Cumberland, when I was a reluctant passenger: A picnic in the park: Daddy letting me sit on his lap and pound his chest when I had a toothache: A trip to the dentist when I refused to get in the chair, and Daddy wouldn't force me: An outing to get milkshakes: Daddy trying to get me to taste shrimp: Daddy trying to get me to eat chicken livers, telling me they would make me pretty: Christmas shopping with Daddy to buy a scarab bracelet for Mommy: Daddy telling me not to drink coffee because it would make me black: Me making watered down coffee for Daddy and him drinking it, telling me how good it was: Making fried pies with juicy canned peaches and Daddy eating them: Trips between Clarksville, Nashville, Somerville and Memphis: Daddy frying fish, making French fries and coleslaw: Daddy cooking greens with cornbread dumplings, and making vegetable soup with a beef bone he got from the butcher: Daddy grocery shopping, house cleaning, doing laundry: Daddy wanting more for me than he could give: Daddy teaching me that I had value: Hellos: Goodbyes: Hugs: Kisses: Missing Daddy: Missing Daddy: Missing Daddy.

FROM SLAVES TO LANDOWNERS

Thomas "Tom" Jefferson 1847-1921
Ann Jefferson, 1843 or September
1851-May 11, 1940

Remember the days of old; consider the generations long past. Ask your father and he will tell you, your elders, and they will explain to you. -- Deuteronomy 32:7

Papa's father Thomas "Tom" Jefferson, born October 1847, came from the plantation in Virginia previously owned by Thomas Jefferson, the third U.S. President. A man named Thomas Jones Cocke acquired Tom and Caty, who must have been Tom's mother and brought them to Tennessee. Cocke became a landowner and planter in Fayette County.

Tom and Caty had the name Jefferson when they came to Tennessee; however, their new owner must have changed it to Cocke. My grandfather, Will Jefferson said Cocke was their family name at one time. His father, Tom, did not like the name, and changed back to Jefferson.

Tom Jefferson and Caty are listed by name in Fayette County Will Book A, 1836-1854 when Thomas Jones Cocke willed Tom and Caty to his daughter, Amy Elizabeth Cocke. She married Dr. Josiah Higgason, and they lived in Somerville. Higgason became a prominent name in Somerville. The Higgason house called, "Frogmore," circa 1830, still stands on South Main Street today inhabited by Higgason descendants.

Tom Jefferson married Ann Macon June 6, 1873. The 1900 Census lists Ann as born September 1851. The Tennessee Deaths and Burial Index, 1874-1955 shows her birthdate around 1843. My great-grandfather Tom and great-grandmother Ann had five children—Lizzie, Mary F, Mary Bell, Will (Willie) who was my grandfather Papa and Alfred. Uncle Alf was named after Ann's father Alfred Macon. I only knew Papa and Uncle Alf since the others died young. Lizzie was married to Allen Watkins. They had no children. She died at 44 years of age. Great Grandma Ann had a sister, Hattie, who, according to the same Census, also lived in the household.

When Mommy wrote about her grandfather Tom and grandmother Ann some years ago, she thought Tom and Ann had come to Tennessee from Virginia as a married couple after 1865. She did not know that Tom was brought to Tennessee as a young slave boy.

Tom and Ann made a good life for themselves and their children. They farmed the land with their children, and Ann did some day work to help make ends meet. She worked in the Charlie Dickerson home. Mommy said, "Grandma Ann was a hard working woman and a good cook." Tom was a farmer. They saved money to buy their land.

Tom Jefferson was literate and was a capable businessman. His skills skipped Papa and Uncle Alf, and passed down to Tom's namesake and grandson Thomas.

Tom and Ann looked quite different from each other. Tom appeared to be of mixed race and Ann was more African. Tom died January 20, 1921 at the age of seventy-six satisfied after realizing his dream of becoming a landowner. Ann died May 11, 1940 and buried May 13. Ann was between ninety-seven and ninety-nine according to the Census reports. Both Tom and Ann are buried in the Somerville Cemetery where the Higgasons are also buried.

Tom wanted to be buried in the white cemetery. As he put it, "The colored cemetery is not kept up."

When people died during those years, they would often have a hasty burial after laying the body out on the cooling board for a while before they prepared it for burial. They didn't always embalm. Moreover, it was necessary to wait a little while before burial to ensure the person was actually dead and not in a coma.

In 2002, I was at Mommy's house when I notice great-grandfather Tom's portrait and thought it should hang in the elementary school named for him. It bears his name because he once owned the land where the school sits on Highway 59 about three miles from Somerville. Tom supported education and saw a need to foster education for his people.

Tom donated the first plot of land for the building of the school; he later sold additional land to the county for expansion. Many years later, the school became Jefferson Consolidated School. As one and two room schools in the surrounding area closed, some students rode the bus to Jefferson. When I was young, Jefferson was a three-room school.

The original name of the school was Hard Side. The first teacher was Tom's daughter-in-law, my grandmother, Ethel B. Howell Jefferson. They also used the school as a church on Sundays. They named it Hard Side Primitive Baptist Church.

I contacted then school superintendent Myles Wilson and told him my idea of donating Tom's portrait to Jefferson School. He and the principal Dr. Chandler planned a program on November 13, 2002 where I spoke to the Jefferson Elementary School students about my great-grandfather and presented his portrait to hang in the hallway.

Tom was highly regarded and well respected in the community by black and white people. Tom didn't live to see his three grandchildren; Thelma, Ophelia, and Thomas; however, Ann spent many years with them.

Will J. Jefferson, October 10, 1875-November 15, 1972
Ethel Bell Howell Jefferson, November
5, 1891-March 7, 1958

I didn't cry when Mama died. My best friend in the entire world, yet I did not cry. I was thirteen. The summer of 1957 was strange and empty for me. I knew something was wrong. The grownups were whispering; I was wondering. One day, I asked Mommy, "What's wrong with Mama?"

"She's sick."

That was no answer. I could see that. "But what's wrong with her?"

"She has a tumor growing inside her stomach. It's cancer."

I didn't know what cancer was, but I knew it was terrible and that there was no hope for Mama. That was the first and last time I heard the word cancer uttered that summer. It seemed that if you said it aloud, it would grow faster.

When Mama got sick, the whole family was sad and scared. We washed Mama's dishes separately from ours for fear we might get cancer. The atmosphere in the house changed as the summer wore on; things got quieter and scarier, and Mama got thinner and weaker. Summer moved at a slow, creepy pace after we got the news, and then Sonny, Charles, and I went back to Clarksville with Daddy to start another school year. Mama passed away the following spring.

The undertaker brought Mama's body out of her room into the central hall, which contained a dresser with a mirror. Someone, perhaps the woman who took care of Mama during the day while Mommy and Aunt Penny were at work, covered the mirror with a quilt before they brought her body past it and out of the front door feet first in obedience to a superstition about the spirit of the dead seeing its reflection in the mirror. I guess they thought the spirit hung around waiting for humans to do their thing.

I was closest to my maternal grandparents Ethel Bell Howell Jefferson and William "Willie" or "Will" Jefferson who I lived with starting at age three or four when Mommy and Daddy decided they could no longer share the same abode. Mommy and other folks often told me that I looked like Mama and that I had many of her ways. As it happened, they were not the ways Mommy admired.

Mama was serious and stern. She liked to keep a neat home. She was not happy when others didn't respect that. Mama preferred a "proper" lifestyle complete with manners, decorum, respect, and civility. She was born near the back edge of the Victorian era hanging on the precipice of the Modern era. In the 1940s and 1950s when I was a child, good manners and respect were still present.

Relationships were more formal during my childhood than they are today. Papa always referred to Mama as "Miss Ethel" even in their everyday interactions. Not one time did I hear Papa say, "Ethel." I didn't hear any terms of endearment either. I don't know if Mama required that Papa used "Miss" or if he was just carrying over the manners from their courtship days.

Mama didn't have a college degree; however, she taught school when her children were young. A college degree wasn't required for teaching during that time. In another life, Mama would have gone to college and become a professional. Mama was smart and she loved to read.

When I was nine or ten years of age, Mama took a correspondence course in nursing from the University of Chicago. At the end of the course, she went to Chicago by train and spent three weeks training onsite. We were so happy and proud when Mama became a Licensed Practical Nurse. She took care of patients in their homes before her diagnosis with cancer.

The following summer was so different with Mama gone. I had an odd feeling being in her house. I didn't like to pass by Mama's room even when the door was closed. I knew Mama would never hurt me if she did appear as a ghost. Folks always said a ghost wouldn't hurt you. It would just make you hurt yourself running away. Death was scary to me then; therefore, I didn't want to see any image of Mama since I knew she was gone forever. I had seen two dead people, a nine-year-old boy and Mama's brother Herbert. I went to Uncle Herbert's funeral with Mama when I was a little girl, and for days afterwards, I was afraid to go into a dark room alone. It took a long time to get his image out of my head.

That summer, reality set in. My best friend was gone when I needed her most. My fun summers in the country were over. Being in the country had been full of activities, cousins visiting, too much work peeling, shucking, shelling, and canning one fruit or vegetable after another, but it had been fun. I went to movies, baked cookies and muffins, read comic books and romance magazines, and dreamed of being in the city with friends. Yet, I liked the freedom of being in the country. When I became an adult, I wrote poetry to capture memories of being at my grandparents' home.

Summertime down South

> Sitting on the front porch
> Swinging – breeze cools sweaty body
> Sweet ice tea with lemon and
> Spice trickles down my throat to quench thirst
> Smells of pig pens and cow manure
> Sometimes, but mostly
> Sweet honeysuckle blossoms
> Sweet jasmine
> Sweat of men working in the fields coming late for
> Supper of fried pork, biscuits and
> Sweet potatoes
> Summertime down South

Papa was a dashing fellow in his youth with a head full of easy to comb hair and brown skin darkened by years spent in the cotton and cornfields. Old age and arthritis made Papa short in statue. Painful arthritis caused him to take short steps and walk slowly. Papa was handsome in old age when he dressed in his suit and tie ready for Sunday school. Old women were interested in him after Mama passed, but Papa didn't bother with them.

I don't know how Mama and Papa met, but I would like to think that they met at church. However, since Mama wasn't much of a churchgoer, at least not when I knew her, I guess that didn't happen. Mama had four brothers, and one of them could have known Papa and believed him to be a decent man of some means who would be a good mate for their only sister. I do know that Papa drove his horse and buggy the seven miles from the Jefferson farm to the Howell farm on Sundays to court Mama. Even though Papa was a handsome man, I don't see that as a reason Mama would have been attracted to him. I don't think it was a love match for Mama. Nevertheless, they produced three children—Thelma Queen Odessa Jefferson, August 28, 1914: Ophelia Alberta Jefferson, November 22, 1921; and Thomas Albert "Brother" Jefferson, December 18, 1926.

Papa seemed happy with what he and Mama had together, but Mama wanted more materially and perhaps in other ways. I don't think she was happy from the beginning. During their time, there was so much work to do, such as taking care of the children, parents, house, land and livestock. There was plowing, planting, harvesting, slaughtering livestock and chickens, preserving meats, and canning fruits and vegetables. They washed clothes on a washboard in a tin tub and hung them on the clothesline to dry. Living on a farm was hard, backbreaking work, and there was so little time for leisure. There was little time or energy for developing relationships.

Mama and Papa got along well. They shared the same bed until Mama became ill, then Papa slept on the horsehair, stuffed divan in their bedroom. I seldom went into their room. No one went in there much. The door stayed closed, and the room stayed neat. They had a carved wood double bed with a dresser and chest of drawers to match. Mama had starched white scarves on the dresser and chest of drawers. My grandmother wasn't a frou-frou, crocheted-doilies type. Her style was more streamline moving toward modern except for the beautiful organ. I loved hearing her play it. It was an ornate oak Victorian organ from the 1920s. She also had an oak Singer sewing machine that required pedaling to make it work. Mama let me sew doll clothes on it. Mommy saved one of Mama's 1920s occasional tables for me.

I enjoyed going into Mama's room for our little talks on occasion.

Her room was much nicer than the one Mommy, Malcolm and I shared.

Papa ran the farm until his son came of age and took over. In the early years, Papa helped some, and in the later years, Papa seemed content sitting on the front porch nodding off throughout the day. Sometimes he would make a bucket of slop and walk down to the hog pen, and feed the hogs. Slop was a concoction of table scraps and dishwater. Papa went to bed early in the evening and got up at 4:00 a.m. Life for Papa was slow and easy, or so it seemed to me.

On Saturday nights, Mama would heat water in the teakettle and pots on her wood burning stove and fill the tin tub for Papa to bathe in preparation for Sunday school and the rest of the week. Papa would use a shaving brush to apply soap to his face and an old fashion razor to cut his beard. He rinsed the utensils in a wash pan of hot water. He often cut his face while shaving. Papa wore long johns, long-sleeved, cotton work shirts and overalls during the week. He smelled of newly plowed earth, corn piled high in the crib, and cotton fields.

Outside the family, Papa's greatest achievement was serving as Sunday school superintendent at Mt. Zion Baptist Church for thirty years. My grandfather was always at Sunday school; however, he didn't stay for church services. Aunt Thelma said, "Papa didn't go to church because he didn't want to sit in there with a bunch of hypocrites. Papa was critical of ministers. He used to say, '"There are plenty of devils in church.'"

Papa didn't drive after the horse and buggy was passé, therefore, Brother would drive him to Mt. Zion, pick him up at the prescribed time, and take him home where, after dinner, he spent the day, sitting on the porch when the weather was good. The church gave Papa a plaque to commemorate his thirty years of service.

On a recent trip to Somerville, I stopped by the old Mt. Zion Baptist Church, and for the first time noticed the small rectangle of concrete that interrupted the brick front. I decided to stop and read it. It had been there since the year I was born. It read, "Mt. Zion

Baptist Church, renovated October 22, 1944." It listed the minister and deacons. Papa's name was there as "W. Jefferson."

Papa didn't smoke or drink alcohol except homemade wine at Christmas. Mama dipped snuff, a tobacco powder held in the bottom lip. Saliva would mix with the powder and the dipper would spit it in a container or on the ground. I remember one time when Malcolm and I got Mama's tin of snuff and tried to dip. It was strong and tasted awful. We spit it out and ran to the well house for water to rinse our mouths.

Mama was very clean with her unclean habit, but it must have contributed to her illness. It must have caused her stomach cancer. Mama was a sickly person when her children were young. Aunt Thelma had to help raise Brother. She told me that Mama had given birth to two children, Jerry and Leah, who died in infancy. Those deaths must also have taken a toll on her health.

Malcolm and I were often in Mama and Papa's care. We didn't give them much trouble, but sometimes Mama would get after us for some infraction like the time we were trying to make oatmeal muffins while she was in the garden. When we heard her coming to the door, Malcolm grabbed the bowl, and we went running through the dining room trying to hide it before she came in. In our scurry, the etched glass in the china cabinet door was broken. Mama fussed at us for the longest time. That was her way of disciplining us. Both of us hated it. We would make faces behind Mama's back after she had finished and walked away. Our nickname for her was "Fuss Fuss" when she fussed at us. I don't remember Mama ever spanking me.

Mama raised chickens, and sometimes we would help her gather the eggs. Other times we would run the chickens and try to get them to fly over the fence. If Mama heard chickens clucking and looked out the window and saw feathers flying, she would rush out fussing, "You hard-headed children leave those chickens alone. Haven't I told you chickens don't fly? Leave those chickens alone, or you're going to get a whipping."

Actually, chickens could become airborne for a few seconds, but they didn't fly like birds. Besides, Mama would clip their wings to prevent them from flying over the fence and out of the chicken yard. We knew not to bother the setting hens or they would tear into us with a fury. The setting hens were the breeders. They sat on their eggs to keep them warm so they would hatch baby chicks. We weren't too keen on messing with roosters either. Sometimes they would turn and run after us. When it was time for a special dinner with chicken as the entree, Mama would pick an old hen that had stopped laying eggs, put her in a small coop or pen and clean her out for the kill. The cleaning out process involved only a special kind of chicken feed, not the stuff a chicken would eat as she forged on the ground. Since we didn't bond with our food, we had no problem eating the chickens.

I enjoyed the times I spent in the kitchen with Mama as she cooked. When she made biscuits or teacakes, she would let me cut them out and arrange them on the baking pan. We would talk about everything while we worked. I could complain about Mommy or my brothers, and Mama would listen. I liked watching Mama and Mommy cook. They cooked from the heart and soul, not needing to measure, just adding what they needed at the right time. That was how I learned to cook.

Mama was a dignified woman who had a strong sense of price. When I was ten, Mama and I were in the garden on the side of the house one day when we heard a car horn. Mama said, "I wonder who that is." We didn't get many visitors during the week; therefore, she wasn't expecting anyone. I followed Mama to the front yard, and there was the Watkins man, a door-to-door salesman who worked rural areas selling spices and flavorings and such. I was happy to see him.

The Watkins man walked towards us all jolly and smiling as he offered a friendly, "Good day auntie."

Mama was not smiling, jolly or friendly. She stopped in her tracks, placed her hands on her hips and cut him off before he could utter another word. "I am not your mother's sister. I am Mrs. Jefferson."

White people didn't use titles when addressing black people. They just came into your yard uninvited and spoke to you however, they saw fit. They acted as if they were entitled to whatever it was they wanted.

Many white people referred to older black women as "auntie" and older black men as "uncle." They may have considered it an upgrade from "boy" and "girl" and a sign of respect. They called younger men "boy" and younger women "girl." Some white people used a first name if they knew it, but hardly any used titles such as Mr., Miss, and Mrs. when dealing with black people. During the early part of the twentieth century, some black parents named their children titles such as Lady, Princess, Missy, Queen, Lieutenant, Duke, King, Chancellor, and such. Historically, black people have found creative ways to get over on white people.

I remember Mama as a woman of pride and dignity. She stood straight and tall to me as a child, and she was what people referred to as stout. Many black women were stout, not fat, a little thick. Mama was particular about her appearance. She dressed neatly in a housedress and wore an apron every day when she was not working in the garden. When Mama worked in the garden, she put on one of Papa's long-sleeved shirts over her housedress and cotton stockings. She wore a wide straw hat to keep the sun off her face.

Another thing I enjoyed doing with Mama was listening to the radio. We would listen to *Queen for a Day*. The show featured four women with compelling stories. The audience selected the Queen after they heard each story. The Queen would get her crown and robe and a bouquet of roses before taking her seat on the throne. She would then receive several wonderful gifts such as household appliances.

My favorite show was *People are Funny* with Art Linkletter. He believed that ordinary people were funny; he would have scenarios to demonstrate that. There were also prizes given. Although we could not see the people, listening to them was very entertaining. After all, we were not used to television then. We didn't have television while Mama was living.

I see Mama as I see myself, a displaced soul, born at the wrong time and place. Mama made do in the country, but she was more suited for the city where she could have exposure to a cultured lifestyle. She liked beautiful things, and desired a nicer and bigger house. While Papa's life seemed simple and uncomplicated, Mama's was just the opposite. Her morality was wedged between the prim and proper ways of the Victorian era and the free spirited age of Jazz, Prohibition, and the Speakeasy. Mama was young and vibrant when she and Papa married on May 5, 1913. She must have desired a taste of that life. Given a choice between being a Gibson Girl or a Flapper, I think Mama would have been a Flapper. She read about the Harlem Renaissance and all those wonderful jazz artists and black writers such as Claude McKay, Arna Bontemps, Langston Hughes, W.E.B. Dubois and Zora Neal Hurston. Mama knew there was a life more interesting and satisfying than hers, and I believe she longed for it during a time.

To me, Mama was a fine wine served in paper cups to people who preferred beer. When I think of Mama, I think of her gingerbread with the thin, sweet sauce poured over it. I think of the zinnias, petunias and the cannas she grew. I think of elegance, sophistication, and lavender.

Mama's family migrated from Charlotte and Goldsboro, North Carolina to Tennessee and bought a large farm on the west side of Somerville. The Howell family was four brothers: Herbert, Jerry, Caleb and Leo and, one sister, Ethel. Their parents were Eliza and Albert Howell.

I visited Mommy's favorite first cousin Earnestine in 2003. She told me a few things about the Howell family. "Grandma Eliza was a schoolteacher, and I became a school teacher because of her."

Earnestine Howell McFerren taught home economics for many years at Fayette County Training School before moving to Memphis where she finished her career. Earnestine was among the first group of teachers to integrate Shelby County Schools. She taught at White Haven High School. Earnestine received her masters at the University of Mississippi, Oxford campus in 1970.

"Grandma Eliza also inspired her own daughter, my Aunt Ethel, who in turn inspired her daughter, your mother Ophelia, to teach.

Another thing I will always remember about Grandma Eliza is she told us girls never to smoke. Grandma Eliza lived with us when I was young, but she would go and spend weeks at a time with Aunt Ethel. She died while living with Aunt Ethel."

Earnestine continued, "I don't remember much about Grandpa Albert because he died when I was young. He was cutting down a tree the tree fell on him and killed him. Albert was half Native American Indian. Both Grandma Eliza and Grandpa Albert are buried in Warren Cemetery."

Earnestine was the oldest of seven girls and seven boys born to Jerry Howell and Bessie Neal Howell. Her siblings were James, Lettie Bea, May Liza, Jessie Lee, Rafael, Harold, Caleb, John, Lafayette, Rosebud, and twins Geraldine and Jerlene, and Joyce. Some of them and their descendants still live on the family property in Fayette County.

Another of Mama's brothers was Herbert who also had a large family. With his wife Mary Bell, he had Virginia, Herbert Jr., Clara Bell, Mildred and Joyce. With his wife Eldora, he had Bobby and Sherman.

Caleb had a daughter named Canary; Leo fathered LaNell and Marie. Ethel gave birth to Thelma, Ophelia and Thomas.

I think Papa found God's Kingdom right here on earth. He seemed satisfied. He didn't go anywhere after his Sunday school years ended. He just read his Bible, talked to family or whoever came by, ate what Aunt Penney prepared or what Mommy sometimes sent. I don't remember Papa going to town for anything other than church. His world was small. I think Papa only wanted to be around family, the workers on the farm, and a few relatives and neighbors who came to visit. Papa was born only ten years after slavery. That history must have been with him in a poignant way. I believe he didn't want interactions with white people. I believe he resented that his mother worked for white people, and that's why he was determined that his daughters wouldn't work for them. In his later years, Papa sat on the sofa in the small den and watched television. He remained alert until his passing with prostate cancer in 1972.

A few years ago when I was visiting Aunt Thelma, I said to her, "Papa was sort of quiet wasn't he? He didn't bother anybody."

"No," Aunt Thelma said, "Papa wouldn't bother a soul, but he would shoot you."

"What!"

"Yeah, if someone came around up to no good, Papa would get his shotgun. They had to move on, or he would have shot them. He didn't stand for foolishness. I saw him get his shotgun a couple of times. Thank God he never shot nobody."

Papa was a man of few words, but when he spoke, we listened. Sometimes he would get after Malcolm for some mischief. I can still hear Papa, "Mike, catleggit! Boy, stop digging in the yard." That was harsh language for Papa. He didn't curse, other than say "catshit" when he was angry. He didn't smoke, chew, dip, or drink. Papa liked fried slab-bacon and Mama's biscuits with home-churned butter and the sorghum molasses he made.

In the fall of the year, after the sugarcane was gathered from the field, Papa would cook it in a large flat pan made for the process. I remember the sweet substance we poured over biscuits, cornbread and hotcakes. Mama used it to make molasses cake and gingerbread.

Papa used to pour his heavily sugared coffee into a saucer and blow on it to cool it before sipping. Papa loved anything sweet. When he got a taste for sweets and there was nothing around, I would see Papa take a spoon to the sugar canister. When he got indigestion, Papa would put baking soda in a glass of water, let it fizz and drink it. He didn't suffer from diabetes or high blood pressure or anything other than arthritis until he was in his nineties.

Mama, Mommy, and Aunt Penny grew greens, cabbage, okra, bell pepper, corn, potatoes, tomatoes, peas, string beans, onions, beets, squash, garlic, and perhaps a few other foods. Papa and Brother killed hogs when the weather turned cold. Other men would join in and help. Hog killing time was a big deal. They would separate the intended victim from its peers and fatten it for weeks before the slaughter. On that fateful day, the men would take the hog out of his private little pen, cut his throat and hang him up by his hind legs.

They would scald the hog and scrape its hide off before splitting open its belly. Then they would remove the innards. It wasn't a pretty sight.

Papa cured hams and shoulders with salt and hung them in the smokehouse. Mommy made the best sausage with sage and other herbs and spices and it hung it in the smokehouse to cure. We ate some of the meat fresh such as pork chops, pork loin and chitterlings. Mommy spent what seemed hours outside cleaning and washing chitlins--the intestines, which were unappetizing to me. In later years, they preserved much of the meat in the deep freezer.

Rabbit, squirrel, and sometimes possum were hunted and eaten. I was a fussy eater and was not fond of meat especially the wild game.

Papa had two mules, Roadie and John. Papa used them for plowing before Brother modernized the farm. My cousins, brothers, and I used to ride gentle and slow john. Roadie was not slow or gentle, but Sonny was bold enough to ride her.

Papa died in 1972 when I was one of Jehovah's Witnesses; therefore, I didn't go to his funeral. I had bought into the idea of keeping separate from the world and "false" religion. The Witnesses taught that all religions but theirs were false. Since I didn't see Papa lying lifeless in a coffin, I remember him with his arms folded across his chest sitting on the front porch or on the sofa in the den. I often expected to see him sitting there when I went back for visits after 1972.

Papa and his brother Alfred inherited the land from their father, Tom. Papa proved to be a good steward of the land, while tobacco-spitting, whiskey-drinking, woman-chasing Uncle Alf was less so. In his youth, Uncle Alf was arrested several times for drinking and fighting. Papa would mortgage the farm to get him out of jail. When the crops came in, Papa would pay of the mortgage; however, since Uncle Alf was a repeat offender, the process would take place often. When it happened just before the crash in 1929, the banks failed, and Papa lost all the money he had. He still had to pay off the loan. He lost about 200 acres of Jefferson land during that time.

Uncle Alf was born about 1882. He married Patty Mason who was born about 1892. They had children who died in infancy; however, they took in a boy who was eleven years of age in the 1920 census report. The census listed Walter as adopted. I don't think he was adopted since he never had the Jefferson name. His last name was Perkins. The Census also says that Walter could read and write. He may have gone to school and learned to read when Mama was teaching.

I remember Walter as a houseboy, a servant, not a son. I don't know where Walter was from, but he must have been injured as a young child or born with a birth defect as he walked a little bent over and with a limp as though one leg was shorter than the other. He didn't seem bothered, and it didn't prevent him from doing his work. Malcolm and I would sometimes try to get Walter to play with us. He didn't have time for childhood foolishness, but he was always nice to us.

According to the 1940 Census, Uncle Alf lived in a rented house on Jefferson land; therefore, Papa owned all of the land then. He must have owned it all since the loss. . Walter took care of household chores and the yard. He was always working. Their house and yard were always immaculate. In later years as Aunt Pat began to lose her eyesight, Walter helped her with the cooking.

Uncle Alf's house had bigger rooms than Papa's. It had a central hall, and to the right as you walked in was his and Aunt Pat's bedroom. Walter's room was behind theirs, and across the hall from their room was a guest room. The guest room had a large dark walnut bed with a tall headboard and a shorter footboard. On it were beautiful colored quilts and pillows in lace-trimmed pillowcases. There were crocheted doilies on the dresser and a porcelain washbasin on the washstand. Lace curtains and rollup shades adorned each window.

There was a closed-in back porch where the wringer style washing machine sat. The most intriguing and scary part of the house was the upstairs. Malcolm and I would sit on the bottom step and dare one another to go up the stairs any further. We would go only so far slowly taking one-step at a time. I never knew what was up there. We liked thinking it was haunted. Later, I learned it was only an empty attic.

Uncle Alf was too old to farm when I was a child, and I'm not sure he ever did much. He owned two horses, which he probably used in his "catting around" days. He probable hitched them to a buggy or wagon. On the other hand, perhaps he just alternated riding each horse when he wanted to venture out. The horses graced the pasture close to the house with their beauty. Malcolm and I were concerned about Uncle Alf selling them to a soap factory because they had gotten old. We had heard they made soap out of horses.

Uncle Alf must have had diabetes. I remember his leg developing gangrene and Aunt Pat taking care of it, trying to keep it clean with peroxide and covering it with gauze. He was a bit cantankerous. He must have forgotten about the earlier days and how his youthful lifestyle, especially the whiskey drinking, might have led to such an end. Aunt Pat and Walter took good care of him until he passed away.

Though Aunt Pat was blind, she liked to come to Mommy's house for visits some Sundays. One Sunday after her visit, I had to walk her back home. It was late evening, not quite dark, and we were walking on the side of the road even though there was very little traffic on that road since they had built the new Highway 59. Along came a car filled with white boys, and although I guided Aunt Pat to the shoulder, the driver forced us into the ditch. I was too busy reacting to become frightened. After they drove away, I became angry and scared for what could have happened. When I got back to the house and told Malcolm, he grabbed the shotgun and headed for the door. I stopped him and told him that they had already driven off.

Sometimes Walter would visit Mama and Papa on Sundays. When Mommy built her house, he would walk down to visit some Sundays, especially if Mommy had made ice cream. After Uncle Alf passed away and Aunt Pat went to live with relatives in Memphis, Brother took care of Walter and provided a place for him to live. He lived there for many years, then one day Walter went for a walk in the woods and never came back. George Burns found Walter's body. George, his father, and his brother Joe had come to work for Brother in 1956. Joe moved to Detroit after high school. Mr. Burns and George remained there until their deaths.

While Papa's life seemed so simple and uncomplicated I often wondered what he was living and reliving inside his head during all those years of seeming solitude. Papa just sat and watched life unfold around him. He appeared to be okay with Brother running the farm and taking care of all the business.

Perhaps Papa was having some regret or feeling some sadness for losing so much of his father's land. Papa knew the pride his father Tom had in land ownership. He knew the esteem Tom had in the community. Papa had spoken of incidents about his father, such as this one, "Two white men were talking and one man said, 'I think Tom Jefferson owes me a $100.00.' The other man said, 'You must be mistaken, Tom doesn't owe you any money. If he did, he would pay it.'"

Tom's reputation was sterling, and I am sure Papa wanted to keep his that way. He wanted to leave a good legacy for his children and grandchildren.

Maybe Papa regretted helping his brother Alf when he got himself into trouble. Maybe he wished he had let him stay in jail and finish out his sentence the first time. I will never know that for sure, but I believe Papa had held on to his pain over losing the land. I think he didn't trust white people after the banks failed, and he still had to pay off his loan or lose the rest of his land. I believe Papa felt like he had disappointed his father and tarnished his legacy.

Papa lived out his days in the ranch style house with Brother, Aunt Penny, and their sons. Papa didn't complain. He kept up his spirit and his faith in God.

The Jefferson family was small compared to the Howell family. Aunt Thelma was six years older than Ophelia, who was six years older than Brother. They were not close enough in age to be friends as they were growing up; however, they did develop their relationships as young adults. In Brother's later years, he grew closer to Thelma. I think it was because she didn't judge him in his philandering like Mommy did.

Brother was a handsome dark skinned man. He smelled of Lifebuoy soap and Old Spice. He would walk out of his room dressed in the most perfectly starched, creased and pressed pants imaginable. My uncle was sharp. I loved getting a whiff of him as he dashed out of the door many evenings to go where a married man was not supposed to go. Mama and Mommy took note of his actions early on; they were not happy with him. I don't know if Papa ever said anything to Brother about his philandering, but I imagine Papa may have cited a couple of scriptures pertaining to the matter. On the other hand, perhaps it was an acceptable practice for men. Neither Mama nor Papa wanted to interfere with their grown children's lives even if the children did live in their home.

Mommy had no problem chastising her baby brother, "You know you shouldn't be going out and leaving your wife the way you do."

Mommy had little talks with Aunt Penny who she seemed most disappointed with in that situation. I remember her saying, "Penny, don't allow Brother to treat you that way. You need to stop him right now, or it will get worse." Mommy gave Aunt Penny a good picture of the situation, naming the girl involved, when it started and everything.

Aunt Penny did not look delicate. She was tall and big-boned, but she was a nice size. She took pride in her appearance, and people considered her pretty with her light tan skin and straight hair. Aunt Penny had come to Somerville in 1944 from Lexington, Tennessee to serve as Home Demonstration Agent. She worked with homemakers in Fayette County before she became a schoolteacher. Her beauty had captured Brother, and he married her after a short courtship. She was a "good wife," an asset to him.

When I was little, I didn't like something about her. In fact, neither my brothers nor I called her Aunt Penny. We called her by her maiden name, Miss Henry. I only called her Aunt Penny after I became an adult. I think what I didn't like about her was her cowardice. Neither did Malcolm. We used to mock her when she would cry while Brother was verbally assaulting her. We wanted her to stand up for herself and talk back to him.

Mommy pleaded with her to speak up to him. Penny wouldn't. She was like Spikey, the little black and white dog that took up residence at our house and Mommy claimed as hers. Spikey was always cowering when we called him or simply looked at him. He would come haltingly with his tail tucked between his legs. Neither Malcolm nor I could stand that. One day we put Spikey in a Croker sack or burlap bag, and carried him what seemed like miles away from the house. We set him free telling him, "Go away Spikey and don't ever come back." When we returned home, to our dismay, Spikey was there to greet us with his head bowed and his tail tucked between his legs.

The summer Mommy was in St Louis, I fell going up the steps to the back porch and hurt my shin. It hurt badly, was swelling, and I started crying. Aunt Penny came to my rescue. She checked my injury, and then told me to wash my face and ride to town with her. I guess she figured a little distracting was in order. A ride and a sweet treat would do it for me every time. She enjoyed having children around.

Aunt Penny was so different from Mommy. Her family, the Henrys, was unlike the Jefferson family. They were a lot more interesting and fun to be around. Mommy used to refer to them as hillbillies. I never felt that she did that in a demeaning way. She saw them as a clan all living under the same roof, sharing and united in a way that the Jefferson family was not. The Henrys lived on their own land and farmed.

As a young child, I loved going to the Henrys for weekend visits. Aunt Penny would sometimes take Malcolm and me before the boys were born. I looked forward to those times because there would be a house full of children to play with and many good sweets to eat. We had the run of the place. Children and noise did not bother the Henrys. The men hung around outside telling stories and spitting tobacco juice; the women spent their time in the kitchen cooking all sorts of dishes and enjoying one another's company. Mrs. Henry made delicious cakes using her five fingers as the mixer. They sent us to the root cellar for onions, squash, and other vegetables they stored there. We played wildly and freely all Saturday and Sunday until it was time to go home.

I remember attending a Homecoming at their church one Sunday.

People who had moved away would come back to their home church, to visit with family, friends, and neighbors. There would be food in abundance. Women would bring pots of peas, beans, and greens. Some would have potatoes, okra, tomatoes, corn, and every other vegetable that grew in a garden. There would be ham and fried chicken, homemade breads, cakes and pies. It was a fun time for children and adults.

Mommy thought Aunt Penny went home too often, allowing Brother too much freedom. I noticed that Brother didn't wait for the weekend to go out; he often went out during the week.

There were those times that the Henrys came to visit. As they were driving up to the house, Mommy would whisper, "Here come the 'Squatleys.'" I think she referenced the word "motley" in view of the Henry's mixed coloring of black, white, and perhaps Native American. She then threw in the hillbilly people portrayed in the *Li'l Abner* comic strip. Mommy enjoyed reading that comic, and she was very creative with names. She may have been a little jealous of Aunt Penny's relationships with her relatives.

However, Mommy and Aunt Penny got along well. Mommy was with her on the night she passed away February 12, 1991. She had one sister and two brothers. Aunt Penny was respected in the community as a hard worker and a person who was always willing to help. She adored her sons and grandson.

When I was young and thought of home, I would think of the Jefferson house and land. Even after Mommy built her house, I still thought that way. Mommy's new house didn't feel like home. Everything was new. It had no soul, no history. I longed for the weatherworn frame house with its porch swing, the house of my early childhood. I started living there when I was three or four after Mommy and Daddy separated. I have vague memories of our house in Memphis, but my fondest memories were made at Mama and Papa's house.

My grandparents' house was home to me until Brother tore it down and built a brick ranch home for his family. He changed the landscape, and I had difficulty recognizing it as the place I once loved, the place filled with memories of childhood innocence.

As a child, I thought the house was large. It was only after I was a young adult and saw a picture that I realized how small the house was for the number of people who lived there. I stared at the picture at first wondering whose house it was. It looked shabby, in need of paint. I never thought of my grandparents as being poor. Food was plentiful and Papa dressed nice on Sundays. Why did they live in that shabby looking house? Then I remembered that most of the houses in Fayette County were far more distressed, especially houses on white peoples' land inhabited by black sharecroppers and tenant farmers. Sharecropping was that unfair practice that kept black people poor and dependent on white people for a living.

Mommy was one of the first in Fayette County to build a nice, brick home. In the 1950s, black people learned they could get FHA loans from the government to build homes. Housing in the area started to improve in the 1960s. Brother was on the forefront of the building boom. He became a contractor along with being a commercial farmer. He built many houses in the community. He built a small subdivision on Jefferson property we referred to as "the other place." Brother used to keep cows on that land when I was a child. It's located on Jefferson Drive off Armory Road. Brother also built the New Mt. Zion Baptist Church. He was busy in the 1950s-70s with building and farming.

Papa didn't want any of his children to work for white people. His reason for not wanting his daughters to work in white folks' homes was as he said all those years ago, "There is too much miscegenation." Brother never wanted to work for anyone. The only time he did such was in Uncle Sam's Army. He came back from Korea and took a course in agriculture before he began farming. Many in the community depended on Brother for employment. There was much planting and harvesting of crops such as soybeans, corn, purple hull and Crowder peas, and cotton. There was cotton to chop in the summer and to pick in the fall. Sonny and Charles chopped cotton for Brother; however, they were in Clarksville when it came time to pick the cotton. Brother paid $3.00 per day for chopping cotton when white farmers were only paying $2.50.

Malcolm and I picked cotton in Brother's fields. We were not serious cotton pickers, and no one but Brother would have hired us. We used to go to the field to socialize with the other children who were serious workers. They often worked to help their families. Brother indulged us. Some children our ages could pick more than one hundred pounds of cotton per day. We fell far short. Our favorite time was lunchtime when we could dine on liver cheese or bologna with crackers, a Hostess cupcake or Twinkie, and a Nehi soda pop. Brother or one of the workers would take our lunch orders, go into town to Taylor's store, and buy the food.

I liked it when Brother made trips to Memphis for business; he would always bringing us snacks such as roasted peanuts from the Planters store on South Main or Krispy Kreme donuts.

One summer when all of us children were in Somerville, we had a big scare, or I should say, Mama had a scare. In the country, when the mail carrier had a package too big for the mailbox or a telegram to deliver, he would blow the horn and someone would go out to the road and get it. That was the summer Brother was in Korea. I think it was 1952.

We were playing in the front yard when we heard the mailman blow the horn, Mama came out of the house ringing her hands in her apron and tearing up. Mommy took off for the road. We stood in silence waiting. At first I didn't know why Mama was reacting as she was; however, I soon learned that she was in constant fear of getting a telegram from the Army saying that her son had been injured or killed. Mama was crazy about her son. He had come close to death once before when he was four years of age and had an appendicitis attack. The doctor was able to save him through that, but Mama lived in fear that something would take him away. Mama was afraid that Brother had been killed.

Mommy came down the driveway with a box almost too big for her to carry. She announced, "It's from Clinton. I wonder what he has sent the children. I hope it's clothes." I got excited. We tore into the box, pulled out the big ball and other toys and played the rest of the day. Mommy took a deep breath and expelled the air forcefully. She fussed about Daddy sending toys instead of clothes or money. Mama wiped her eyes, thanked God, spun around and went back into the house. My brothers and I had a good time playing with the toys that our daddy had sent.

Brother lived until 1983 when his womanizing ways caught up with him. He died at a woman's house under suspicious means. When Mommy called me she said, "Brother got himself killed." Of course, I reacted as I always did when hearing such news about those close to me, I screamed and cried. Later, I thought about how Mommy had phrased the news. I understood her pain and her anger at him for living that lifestyle. Her baby brother was gone and all for some senseless reason. It didn't make sense to her. She blamed him just as some people blame a girl when she gets pregnant before marriage. They say, "She got herself pregnant" as if she did it all by herself. Sure, Brother did share some responsibility, but he did not kill himself. There was never any real investigation. It was a small southern town, and all involved were assumed black.

His life was relatively short, but he did many good things along the way. He was quick to help others. My uncle's only fault, that I could see, was that, like many people, he was not monogamous. He was like many other men of his time and perhaps all times. He loved his wife and his sons and wanted to stay with them, yet he wanted to enjoy the company of several other women.

Aunt Thelma was a fun loving woman who was accepting of all. She lived in town with her husband, William Henry "Jack" Anderson and their three children Jean, Jack, and Dorothy. Aunt Thelma and Jean, who was married and had two sons, decided to move to Memphis when I was about thirteen. Aunt Thelma wanted to get away from her husband because she had gotten tired of his tom catting ways. Uncle William was a schoolteacher. I remember him being a nice, gentle man who had patience with children. When I was nine, he let me steer the car on a country road; I thought I was driving.

Aunt Thelma and Uncle William had married young during a

time when that was what a girl did to get away from home. When she was a teen, she wanted to have male company, but Papa wouldn't allow it. She threatened to run away. Instead, she met William, fell in love, and married on May 27, 1934. Aunt Thelma didn't like life on the farm.

As the oldest child, she had to do most of the housework, laundry, and cooking. She also was responsible for taking care of Brother when Mama was not feeling well. Mama often told Aunt Thelma to comb her sister's hair. Mommy had long, thick hair she did not want to comb. That was a time when children did what their parents told them without questioning or talking back. Aunt Thelma did as she was told, but she resented it all the while.

Aunt Thelma worked for a restaurant when she lived in Somerville and for a hotel after she moved to Memphis. She spent her later years helping with grandchildren and great grandchildren and enjoying her life.

After Mommy has passed away, I was visiting Aunt Thelma when she was still up and getting around well. We talked about many things. I took that time to ask her a few questions about her life. I asked her why she never married again after Uncle William died. He lost his life in a car wreck a few years after they separated.

Aunt Thelma said, "I didn't want anyone over my children."

"You could have married after they were grown."

"I didn't need a man after my children were grown. But, I had my chances."

"I know how much you like to drink beer; did you ever smoke?"

"I tried, but I didn't like it. I just liked my beer when I could drink it. I can't drink it now."

"Are you okay with that?"

"I guess I had enough."

I knew Aunt Thelma enjoyed getting dressed up, putting on her stockings and high heel shoes, and going to the corner club to drink beer and listen to music on the jukebox. She was very sociable and always had male friends. Aunt Thelma and Jean lived close to one another; they seemed more like sisters than mother and daughter.

They socialized together and so did Jack. They were a close family. After Dorothy had her children, she moved to Fayette County to raise them; however, she would go to Memphis to see her family often.

I asked my aunt about Dr. C S. Powell (January 26, 1881- July 10, 1932), a black doctor who came to Somerville in the early 1920s. He had an office on the square and each day he used to take his "morning constitution," as he called it. What he meant was his early morning walk around the square before he opened his office. Either this practice or simply his presence incensed the white people in town. Dr. Powell was the grandson of a white master and a slave woman. Aunt Thelma said he was a good doctor. He treated her when she had typhoid fever. I think he must have been the doctor who treated Brother when he almost died of appendicitis at age four. I was curious about Dr. Powell. He might have had another connection to me. I always visit his vault when I go to Mr. Zion Cemetery.

Aunt Thelma was a person who was at peace with life. She had not been ambitious. She took life as it came to her. I wonder if she had any unfulfilled dreams. She said, "I have had a good life.'

When she died November 4, 2008 at the age of ninety-four, she left two daughters, Jean and Dorothy, ten grandchildren, twenty great grandchildren, and six great-great grandchildren. I visited Aunt Thelma at Dorothy's house a few weeks before she died. She was not talking much then. I just stood over her bed wistful about a life and time and the people I had known. I knew the passing of the last Jefferson elder was nearing.

Aunt Thelma's greatest pain was losing her son Jack in 1995. Jack was the middle child, the only son, and a jewel in his mother's eyes. He was named after his father. We called him "Junior" when we were children. After he grew up, he wanted us to call him Jack like his father. After his divorce, Jack and Aunt Thelma shared a house together.

Jack was one the most diligent workers I have ever known. He worked for the Memphis sanitation department for over twenty years. He was conscientious about getting to work on time, doing the job well, and never missing a day until near the end of his life when cancer overpowered him. What made Jack's life so remarkable to me was that he drank beer every day after work and on weekends, yet he took care of his responsibilities. He left this world debt-free and with all his business in order.

When Jack was young, he often worked for Brother on the farm. Brother trusted him to drive his John Deere tractor, a task not given to just anyone. Jack must have been fourteen when he started driving the tractor. He developed his work habits and a sense of accountability early. It must have been premature marriage and early fatherhood that drove him into a different reality and caused him to rely heavily on alcohol. I never thought Jack was living his dream, but he must have made peace with the life he had. He lived it well.

The Jefferson family was small since Papa was the only child of Tom and Ann Jefferson to have children. Extended family I remember were Papa's cousin Edmonia who lived in town with her son and his large family. The older children worked in Brother's fields chopping and picking cotton, and Malcolm and I used to play with them.

Then, there was Lucy and Arthur Williams who lived down the road from Papa. I think Lucy was Papa's cousin. We used to call her "Cuttin" Lucy. She was a character, not like Mama or Aunt Pat, and she was in love with her husband Arthur. When he died, I could hear her crying and calling his name for days. She always spoke of him fondly.

I knew these people in my own way. I spent much time with them and saw many of them for years after I moved away and went back for visits. They were the family I was closest to and whose passing I mourned. These people in one way or another helped to shape me- -people who were products of slavery, Jim Crow, Fayette County and Somerville in West Tennessee. These are the people on whose shoulders I stand. Mama and Papa lived in Fayette County all of their lives, and so did brother. It was Aunt Thelma and Mommy who wanted to get away from those small town attitudes and move to the city.

All of the Jefferson elders have now passed into the realm of the ancestors. Mama and Papa, Brother and Aunt Penny, Aunt Thelma and her son Jack are buried in the Mt.

Somerville is the most memorable place I have lived. It is the first place I knew as a young child. When we moved to Fayette County, I was a toddler. As a young child age nine to twelve, I could walk around town by myself without being afraid. I could do grocery shopping for Mommy, go to the post office or the courthouse doing errands.

When I was a little older I loved shopping at Two Sisters, a store that sold fabric, notions, accessories, socks, even dolls at Christmas. I saw twin dolls there when I was nine, and begged Mommy for them. They were a boy and a girl. I was so happy when Mommy surprised me that Christmas with the twins. I named them Merelyn and Jerelyn. Another Christmas, Mommy bought a black doll for me from Two Sisters. Black dolls were rare in the 1950s, especially in small towns. When I saw her, I had to have her. I believe the Sisters brought her in just for me.

I was ten when I had bought ribbon and socks at Two Sisters to wear Easter Sunday. I didn't discover that the package was missing until that morning. Mommy had me call the Sisters at their home and ask if I had left my package at the store. The sister who answered the phone told me to come to their house and get my package. Mommy drove me to their house on South Main Street. It was a white antebellum house, circa 1830. The original owner named it "Frogmore." I walked right up the tall steps to the large front door and knocked.

That was one of the good things about a small town even then. Of course, not all white people were mean spirited and hateful towards black people.

Somerville was a courthouse in the center of town with stores on each side. The courthouse faced Highway 64, which we took when we traveled to Memphis. We lived in Fayette County two miles north of Somerville. Around the Square was Farmer's Hardware, which still operates today. Two Sisters was a few doors down. My favorite store was Cooksey's, which came to town when I was about twelve. There were offices, and Rexall Drugs, Powers Jewelry Store, Shinault's Grocery Store. We would buy groceries at Shinault's or Taylor's grocery located just off the Square.

The 250-seat Fair Theater was built in 1935 on Market Street. They now use it for a number of community events such as plays, puppet shows, graduations, religious services and movies.

Somerville was a neat little town built around the courthouse square like many other towns in the South. Its appearance, however, contradicted its character. People who embraced the customs of the segregated South ran it. Black people didn't have the rights and privileges that white people enjoyed.

One night Mommy and I were driving back home after a day of shopping and visiting in Memphis when we noticed a group of people gathered near the corner of Market Street and South Main in front of Farmers' Hardware. There was music playing. It was a festive event. Mommy was curious and wanted to see what was going on. I wanted to go home. She parked the truck; we got out and walked towards the crowd. A booming voice came towards us, "Y'all go on home, girl. You don't belong here. This ain't for you."

A number of black people lived in town in an area called Winfrey Bottom on the north end of town. Some also lived on the south end; however, most black people lived in the county on their own farms or on rented land. Many were sharecroppers.

It was the custom for black residents to go into town on Saturdays unless they had business to take care of during the week. Young black people had an interesting ritual "Uptown Saturday Night." It was a rite of passage. On Saturdays, the adults would dress up and go to town to do their shopping during the day. Teens would come to town on Saturday evenings and walk the streets around the square. There would be a procession of young people, couples, and groups. Some would be looking for someone they knew or someone they were supposed to meet. They would be talking, laughing, flirting and enjoying themselves. It was a time and place for socializing. There was no other place for young people to meet one another outside of school, church, or perhaps the cotton fields. Merchants kept stores open until ten on Saturday night whereas they closed at six throughout the week. Some parents would park their cars near Taylor's Grocery Store on the edge of town and wait for their daughters.

Jack, Sonny, and Charles were regulars who joined the ranks of eligible young men on the prowl for girls. Jack and Sonny were very popular and had no problems attracting girls and women. I was too young to participate; however, Malcolm and I could go to a movie on Saturday night. We had to leave town immediately after the movie was over, walk to Aunt Thelma's house nearby, and wait for Mommy.

Fayette County gained some notoriety during the Civil Rights Era when black residents attempted to register to vote. Although the Fifteenth Amendment to the Constitution gave Americans of African descent the right to vote in 1870, the reality was that black people were prohibited from voting in many states until the Voting Rights Act of 1965. It was difficult even then. Officials used many tactics to prevent black people from voting such as having to pay a poll tax, literacy tests, intimidation, threats, and violence prior to 1965. Later, they made it inconvenient for black people by having voter registration only one day a week in some places, fewer than that in others.

When President Lyndon Johnson was trying to get the Voting Rights Act passed, he made a speech March 15, 1965 before the joint session of Congress and urged expediency on their part in passing voter legislation. The President started his speech by saying, "I speak for the dignity of man and the destiny of Democracy." Johnson had paid attention to the Selma March and what happened to the marchers. He knew what was being done throughout the South to keep black Americans from voting was wrong. He knew all the tricks local officials were pulling on black people such as telling them they have to recite the Constitution before they could register. They would ask such questions as "how many bubbles are in a bar of soap" and "how many jellybeans are in a jar?" There was much chicanery going on in southern cities and towns to keep black people out of the American political process.

President Johnson said, "There is no moral issue. It is wrong, deadly wrong to deny any of your fellow Americans the right to vote in this country. There is no issue of states' rights or national rights. There is only the struggle for human rights." The President called for protection of voting rights in federal elections and protection for every American in every election. "We have already waited 100 years and more. Time for waiting is gone."

President Johnson spoke of the outraged conscious of a nation and the harsh judgment of history on our acts. He said, "Even if we pass the bill the battle will not be over. What happened in Selma is part of a larger movement that reaches into every state of America. It is the effort of Negroes to secure for themselves the full blessings of American life. Their cause must be our cause too because it's not just Negroes, but really, it's all of us who must overcome the crippling legacy of bigotry and injustice. And we shall overcome."

During the winter of 1959, many black sharecroppers and tenant farmers were evicted for registering to vote. White farmers had waited until after their crops were harvested before they evicted the farmers. With nowhere to go, Shepherd Towles allowed what became known as Tent City to be erected on his land. Many families lived there for two years and more. Gertrude Beasley set up a second Tent City on her property.

Living in those tents was challenging, especially in the winter when it was cold and wet; however, some of the residents said the tents were warmer than the houses they had to leave.

Living conditions for black people in Fayette County were substandard, almost primitive. Not all white farmers evicted their black workers even though the White Citizens Council tried to put pressure on them to do so. Some white people even donated to the cause. One Somerville merchant donated tents; however, he did so anonymously. Those were fearful and violent times for black people in Fayette County and other areas. It was time for change, and there were enough courageous and determined people to move forward in the struggle no matter the obstacles or the consequences.

Frederick Douglass said, "Power concedes nothing without a demand. It never did and it never will." He also said, "If there is no struggle, there is no progress." The black people of Fayette County knew they were in a struggle to gain the power of the vote, and they were committed for the long haul.

The architects of the Fayette County struggle were John Meferren and Harpman Jameson. John's wife Viola and many others joined immediately to fight for voting rights. Their fight grew out of a desire to serve on the jury when they noticed that an all-white jury had convicted a black man for killing a white man. Due to circumstances, the black man could not have been guilty of the crime brought against him; nevertheless, they sentenced him to twenty years in prison. Jurors were chosen from the list of registered voters.

Somerville was and still is a bewildering place to me. It must have an energy passed down from its founders and old-guard residents which has caused it to stagnate. There has been little growth and few improvements since I was a child. In recent years, there has been a General Dollar Store, a Family Dollar Store, and Fred's Discount Store. For a short time, there was a scaled down copy of Wal-Mart. It had an awkward name. When I saw the name Pamida, I knew it wouldn't last. There was a Hardee's fast food restaurant for a short time. Only the Scenic Drive-In restaurant has lasted for over twenty years. In the last year so a McDonald's restaurant has come to town.

The city of Oakland is ten miles west of Somerville. When I was a child, it was hardly there. Now it has experienced much growth and development and is thriving. I think because many people from Memphis are now moving to surrounding areas and causing growth. Perhaps the same will eventually happen in Somerville.

During the years my mother was sick, I spent much time in Fayette County; therefore, I had the opportunity to experience Somerville in a different way than I did as a child. Since I took care of all of my mother's business, I got to know the banker, pharmacist, and store clerks. One Sunday when the drugstore was closed, I realized that I had forgotten to refill a prescription. I had no other choice but to call the pharmacist and ask if he would fill it. I didn't want to impose on a Sunday, but what could I do. He had known my mother from many years of her patronizing his store. I found his number in the phone book and called his home. I was so grateful that he immediately went to the drugstore and filled the prescription.

Somerville is still a lazy, sleeping town tied to the past. Since people from Memphis are looking for quieter places to live and raise families, some have begun to move to the area. Perhaps others will follow.

DEAR MOMMY

Ophelia Alberta Jefferson Gray

November 22, 1921-December 16, 2001

Honor your ... mother: that your days may be long upon the land which the Lord your God is giving you.—New King James Version Bible, Exodus 20:12

Ophelia Alberta Jefferson Gray was my mother. I always thought God had sent me to the wrong woman. Once I asked Mommy, "Did you adopt me?"

She said, "Yes."

Mommy liked to joke; I didn't. I was a much too serious child.

She later added, "If I had adopted you, I would have sent you back long ago."

Once I said to my mother, "I hate you!" She knew I was angry. After a few moments, I let it go and all would be okay.

When I was a little girl under the age of twelve, I thought Mommy was so beautiful. That is, when she dressed up, had her hair curled, and put on lipstick. She did not wear much makeup. Mommy wore the worst clothes she could find when she worked in the garden. I didn't like that look.

I was always glad when Mommy came to visit us in Clarksville. She would bring Malcolm, and all of us would be together for a weekend or a holiday just like a picture-perfect family. Mommy would cook wonderful meals, and life would be ideal for a while. She and Daddy would get along well as far as I could tell.

I was so sad when it came time for her to leave. That's why Mommy kidnapped me one weekend. It was not that I wanted to leave Daddy; it was simply because I missed Mommy. I would miss Daddy when I lived with Mommy. I think Daddy liked having Mommy come for visits. I don't remember them arguing when I was a little child. I never got a true sense from either of them as to why they could not live together, not even for the sake of the children. I have my own ideas. Mommy did tell me several times that she and Daddy would have fared better if his mother and sister had not interfered. Mostly, they were cordial when all of us were together. I always had the feeling that Daddy wanted Mommy to stay. I never thought their breakup had anything to do with me, or my brothers. My parents never badmouthed each other to me. I appreciated that fact more and more as I grew older. I preferred separation to chaos and disharmony.

Mommy believed in working hard and saving money. She managed well on the salary she made as a teacher, but that was hardly enough for her to get ahead. She wanted to have her own land, build a house, and have animals and a garden. Mommy was in her thirties and still living in her parents' home with two of her children and all four of them during some holidays and summers.

Mommy struggled. I later came to believe that she enjoyed the struggle and defined herself through it. She did manage to save and buy a few acres of land down the road from her parents' property. In 1958 with the help of the Federal Housing Administration (FHA), a master carpenter named Tommy DeShields, and Sonny, Mommy was able to build her three-bedroom, brick ranch house on five acres where she had plenty of room for a garden and chickens. She even planted a small orchard with apples, pears, peaches. There were nut trees, grapevines, muscadine, persimmons and more to come over time. The house was to cost $8,000 according to the plan; however, Mommy added some upgrades, which brought it to about $10,000.

Ophelia had big dreams for the place she called Hillcrest Acres. When I moved to Somerville temporarily to care for Mommy after her stroke in 1996, I was cleaning out her closet when I came across a box of stationary with Hillcrest Acres on the letterhead. Sadness overtook me as I ran my fingers across the embossed heading and felt her unrealized dream forever gone. Mommy had planned to grow organic vegetables, fruits and nuts and sell them to supplement her retirement income.

Over the years, Mommy had done much gardening and sold or given away vegetables to neighbors, relatives and friends; however, it was small-scale compared to what she dreamed of doing. Mommy loved working in the dirt. Gardening was her thing.

It was not my thing. I had no desire to get dirty and sweaty. I did not appreciate her efforts to get me involved. Mommy knew I didn't enjoy working outside, and so, most of my work entailed cleaning the house, doing laundry, and cooking. She insisted on all of her children working. Sonny was the only one of us children who liked working in the dirt and taking care of farm animals.

I came to appreciate gardening many years later after my children had grown up enough to learn that our food did not originate in the grocery store. I planted tomatoes, green beans, and squash so they could observe the growing process. I always planted blooming flowers outside and green plants inside. I inherited the Jefferson green thumb.

Having a mother and two brothers who were not concerned about tidiness affected me greatly. I wanted them to clean up after themselves. Mommy was not a housekeeper; she made no pretense at such, yet a couple of times a year she would do a thorough cleaning. She did not relish working inside at all. An unmade bed, scattered clothes and shoes, and dirty dishes were the order of her life. She also read many books, magazines, and newspapers and left hem scattered about; mail, often unopened, added to the clutter. Mommy was unorganized when it came to the house in spite of having a mother who was extremely neat and particular about her environment. I got tired of cleaning up after my mother and brothers. I decided when

I had my own home I would always keep things neat, and teach my children to do likewise.

I don't know at what age I started finding it difficult to handle clutter, but during my teen years when I lived in Memphis, Clarksville, and Nashville, I would come home for visits and dread opening the door to my mother's house. I knew I would find a mess, and immediately become a different person than I had been all week. My personality would actually change. I would become sullen, withdrawn, mean-spirited, and hateful. That was mostly how Mommy saw me. I fussed a lot about how she kept the house. The condition of the house meant nothing to Mommy and everything to me. We were so at odds in most ways.

There were good times. There were times when all of us children were together with Mommy. Holidays were times when Mommy baked for days making the best coconut cake with pineapple filling between two white layers. It was my favorite. She also made a yellow cake with caramel icing. Mommy made everything from scratch. I used to help peel and grate the coconut, sift the flour and cleanup, but she did most of the work herself. Mommy put so much love into her cooking. We always had good home-cooked meals at Mommy's house. During the summer, there were fresh greens, cabbage, string beans, peas, squash, okra, tomatoes, beets, radishes, onions, and more.

Mommy was the absolute best ice cream maker in the whole world. Bluebell homemade vanilla is the only brand that comes close. She made lemon, black walnut, strawberry, peach, and just plain vanilla. I could taste her love in each spoonful. We would have ice cream on Sundays. Mommy cooked the custard, a mixture of milk, eggs, sugar and flavoring, in a double boiler careful to stir continuously until it thickened. After it cooled, my brothers and I would take turns freezing it. The process involved a wooden bucket maybe two feet tall, a metal can with a dasher inside it to hold the custard. The dash rotated as you turned the handle. Mommy would pack ice and rock salt around the metal can. She would insulate the ice by packing crumpled newspaper on top. Malcolm and I would start the freezing process since it didn't require much strength. As the custard started to freeze, turning the handle became more difficult. Mommy would add whatever fruit she was using and a can of chilled, whipped Carnation milk. Charles and Sonny would take over, and in a short time we would have delicious ice cream.

Mommy loved fishing. There were ponds nearby where we could catch brim that Mommy would fry until they were crisp and they would eat the fish and the bones. I did not like fish or fishing. I was afraid of the earthworms we used for bait. One day Mommy, Malcolm, and I went fishing; I almost fell into the pond trying to get away from a little fish that was dangling on Mommy's pole.

Mommy didn't spend time teaching me how to cook, but she would allow me to go into the kitchen, find a recipe and make something—cupcakes, cookies, or a cake. I loved baking.

I got in trouble the Sunday Mommy let me bake my first cake.. The cake was good; however, what I remember most about that Sunday was that something happened and Mommy was trying to teach me a lesson. After she made her statement, my response was, "I don't care."

Mommy said, "Don't say that again. You need to care." For some reason I repeated it. Mommy gave me one of those memorable whippings. The pain of the whipping has long vanished. What I remember is the occasion whenever I say, "I don't care," especially if it's something about which I should care.

I remember every whipping I got from Mommy. Perhaps not, but I do remember the ones I got during my school years. I got one for something I did not do. That one really hurt, not the pain of the switch, but being whipped for something I did not do. Aunt Penny had put a saucer of sardines on the kitchen table. She went out of the room to get something. Curious about the taste with that awful smell assaulting my nose, I stuck the tip of my finger in the broth and tasted it. Malcolm picked up several of the smelly little fish and ate them. Fearing what was about to go down, we fled from the room. Both of us got in trouble, but I got the whipping. Malcolm admitted eating the sardines while I kept denying that I had eaten any.

Whatever anger or ill feelings I had towards Mommy always

dissipated in a short time. That ability to let unpleasant feelings and situations go serves me well as I move through life. Many people today would call what I experienced child abuse. As I look back, I don't label it that way. It was a method of disciplining in some families during that time.

Mommy gave me my last whipping when I was twelve. It was punishment for my last fight with Malcolm. He and I loved one another and were good friends. We did not argue and bicker like many siblings, but we did have an occasional fight, nothing to hurt either of us, just the passing of a few licks. Mommy whipped both of us. By then I thought I was much too old for such discipline.

I always thought Mommy was easier on Malcolm than she was on me. I was two years older; therefore, I was the one who should have known better how to stay out of trouble. Malcolm was the mischievous sort. If there were trouble around, he would find it. Usually, he was creating it. Sometimes I would have a small role in it, but I would pay the bigger price. We had lots of freedom to be kids, to explore, and to experiment.

I deplored going places with Mommy. My mother took an incredibly long time getting ready. I would be ready and waiting in short time, then I would sit, pout, wait and wait. After what seemed an eternity, I would knock on the bedroom door and whine, "Mommy, hurry up and get dressed so we can go." I wanted to go and come back quickly.

Once the meeting, church, visit, or shopping was over, Mommy would stay and talk to everyone she knew while I would stand around sulking and waiting. She didn't mind keeping me waiting. After all, I was a child with nowhere to go and nothing to do. When she visited one of her cousins or a good friend, she would stay into the night. If there were children to play with I would be okay; otherwise I would be bored and would pester Mommy about leaving.

Just like Missy, I wasn't a sweet child. Mommy let me know that on more than one occasion. She didn't like my personality, attitude, or disposition most of the time. She often accused me of being mean and fussy just like my grandmother. She would tell me that I looked, sounded, and acted like my grandmother Ethel. I took that as a compliment since I was fond of Mama and she was fond of me. We understood one another.

I wasn't a disobedient child, but sometimes I got in trouble. For example, the time one of Mommy's friends was visiting. They were walking to the hog pen to look at the baby pigs. I ran along in front of them and climbed the fence where the mama sow, her piglets, and some other pigs were.

"Get down from there girl. Get down before you fall."

I could see the piglets through the wire, but for some reason I wanted to climb that fence that Sunday evening. Before Mommy could say another word, I fell over the fence, face first into the mud hole where pigs cooled off in the summertime. Pigs were squealing and the mama sow was running towards me as I tried to get up. I was screaming as loud as the pigs were squealing and the hogs were grunting. Mommy reached over the fence and pulled me out before the sow could vent her wrath on me.

After Mommy pulled me out of the pen, she and her friend burst out laughing while I screamed through the foul smelling mud that covered me. I must have looked a dreadful sight. After the laughter, Mommy realized the mess she had to clean up, then nothing was funny anymore.

"Look at yourself. You are so hardheaded. It serves you right. I told you to get down from that fence."

Mommy had to clean up another mess when I dropped a kitten into the toilet. I was four. It really was nasty, but Mommy was an animal lover and was always rescuing. Like the time she put stitches in a pig's belly after another pig or a dog attacked it. She was not afraid of anything. She once told me that she picked up a toad frog and ran Daddy with it just for fun. Daddy wasn't a country boy.

I noticed how Mommy handled herself when we went into the marketplace dominated by white people. She didn't allow herself to be treated disrespectfully. On a trip to Rexall Drug Store, the sales clerk said to Mommy, "What do you want, girl?" Mommy, in her early thirties by then, pointed in my direction and replied,

"She's a girl. I'm a woman." That was one reason we did most of our shopping in Memphis. The attitudes among white sales clerks were a little different at stores such as Goldsmith's where we shopped for clothing, and linens and towels during the White Sale after Christmas each year; Lowenstein's department store, and Lady Oris where we bought hosiery. Mommy wanted me to be able to make my way in this world. She wanted me to live without the struggles she had had.

When I was nine years of age, Mommy would send me to the school superintendent's office to pick up her paycheck because she didn't want to endure the humiliation of receiving it from the superintendent. I had been with her and I understood; therefore, I didn't want her to suffer humiliation.

I would walk right past the "white only" and "colored only" drinking fountains and go into that huge courthouse. One day I just had to taste the white water to see if it was different from the colored. Then I would climb the wide staircase to the superintendent's office and say, "I came to pick up my mother's check." The Ichabod Crane looking superintendent would scowl at me across his enormous desk and say, "Who is your mother, little girl?"

"Mrs. Ophelia Gray." I used her first name to distinguish from the other Mrs. Gray.

He grinned at my innocence and perhaps at Mommy's shrewdness. "Mrs." was not a title he would have used for a black teacher. He would look through the stack of checks not yet picked up, find Mommy's, and pitch it across the desk. I would take it from his desk and say, "Thank you."

Years later when I started working, I never liked anyone handing me a paycheck. I felt there was something demeaning about it. I welcomed direct deposit where my employer could send my paycheck to the bank.

I used to play Mommy's records from the 1930s and 40s. That was the best music. I would put the 78 rpm hard vinyl discs on the record player, get a belt and attach it to the doorknob, and dance to "Chattanooga Choo Choo," "Boogie Woogie Bugle Boy," by the Andrews Sisters. "Don't Sit Under the Apple Tree" and "Don't Get

Around Anymore" by the Ink Spots were two of my favorites. I played all that were not broken. There was Frank Sinatra, Glen Miller, Billie Holiday, Duke Ellington, and many others. I actually don't know if those records were remnants of Mommy's youth or Brother's.

Mommy would sometimes sing "My Buddy" and "Trees," a poem by Joyce Kilmer. She had a pleasant voice and could carry a tune. Mommy told me that when she was young she loved dancing. Her favorite dance was Balling the Jack. She also liked the Jitterbug and the Swing. It was hard for me to imagine my mother being young and dancing. Her high school boyfriend was Dave Hamilton. I have a picture of Mommy and a pilot, taken beside an airplane. I think that was when her love for flying began.

Mommy graduated from Fayette County Training School April 28, 1938. On May 14, she got a card from Tennessee State University saying a catalog was on the way. That tells me her first choice was not Lane College. I think she wanted to go to TSU because Dave must have gone there. He later became a professor at TSU. He used to bring his family to visit us during summer vacations. They remained friends throughout their lives.

During her teen years, Mommy's favorite songs were "What Will I Tell My Heart" and "Stardust." Her job interests were sewing, beauty culture, office work and waitressing. Ultimately, she wanted to be a stage and radio star or a pilot.

In her youth, Mommy also dreamed of going to Hollywood and becoming a movie star. California beckoned her presence more than any other place in the world. It was magical. She was as beautiful as Dorothy Dandridge, so why not go to Hollywood and try out for a movie. Mommy had held on to that dream for so long time that in 1970 after all of her children were adults she decided to trade Fayette County for Los Angeles. That was a gutsy move. She took her retirement money out of the system, packed clothes and a few personal items into her 1969 Ford, and took off driving across country with Charles' help. She had a cousin she could stay with until she found a job and a place to live. She and Charles made the trip in two days. Mommy lived to regret that quick trip. Being in the car without stopping for any length of time was what triggered the problems she later experienced with her back and legs.

While in Los Angeles, Mommy, like so many others with stars in their eyes, did try to audition. It was to no avail. She found a teaching job at a private school, and sometimes she would work with a friend who was a caterer. Once they worked a party at Aaron Spelling's home. Spelling produced *Dynasty, Charlie's Angels, The Love Boat, Beverly Hills 90210,* and many other television shows.

Mommy decided to move back home in 1987. Hollywood had lost its luster. Home was calling. She had allowed Sonny and his family to occupy her home in her absence, but it was time for them to move into their own home. She knew she could get back into the school system and live out her days in Fayette County.

Mommy traveled to Europe. She loved traveling. Being a teacher and librarian who read about faraway places inspired her to want to see some of them. She visited several European countries including Germany, Greece, and France. Mommy loved learning about different places, people, and trying new foods.

I was shocked and displeased when Mommy got married to Mr. Scott. I thought my mother would never marry again; however, she only promised not to marry while her children were minors. She did not want a man in the same house with her daughter. So there she was out on the West Coast and free as a bird. Why not marry. She had known Mr. Scott and his wife when they were at Lane College. Mr. Scott was a widower with a son and four daughters. I lived in Charleston and never met them. I met him when I went home for a visit after Mommy returned from California.

I wish I had been kinder to Mr. Scott. However, I resented his presence in my mother's home. Besides, I was angry that his daughters, who lived there for a short time, had destroyed my dolls, the souvenirs I brought from California and Mexico, and other mementos from my youth. Even though I had been married for several years by then, I didn't think my mother needed a husband. I was a selfish, immature child. I hated when a man would show interest in Mommy when I was a little girl. I still didn't understand why she married after all those years.

When I was a young adult, I learned that Mommy had questions about her parentage. She wasn't sure if Papa was her father. As a young child, she heard rumors that Dr. Powell was her father. She and his two sons Joel and Lowell grew up together as good friends and playmates. People said they looked like they were related. Mommy asked her mother if the rumor was true, but she never got an answer to that question. When my grandmother was near death, Mommy rushed in from work and begged her for the last time, "Mama, please tell me who my father is." Mommy lived eighty years without knowing. It ate away at her like cancer.

I believe Will Jefferson, Papa, was my mother's birth father. I think people looked at color and assumed that since Mommy, Joel and Lowell were the same color they must be siblings. No one considered Mommy got her coloring from her grandfather Tom Jefferson. In fact, I think she looked like him. I just wish she had known the truth, whatever it was.

Joel and Lowell moved to California as young adults, but they would often come to Somerville to visit Mommy over the years. The three of them had a good relationship and often joked about being siblings. They remained good friends until life made it impossible.

My mother had a great reverence for the land. She believed in owning land and keeping it in the family. I didn't realize how much the land meant to my mother until she became ill. She must have thought about how so much of her grandfather's land had been lost and how hard Papa had tried to save it. She suffered greatly when losing the Jefferson land became a possibility, and had a stroke after it became a reality. Mommy tried in every way she could to keep the land in the family; however, the debt was too great for her pocketbook. I believe the loss of the Jefferson land was what put Mommy over the edge. I promised her that I would do all I could to keep her land in the family. She wanted to leave her house to me to make sure I always had a place to live. I suggested she leave it to her first grandson, Michael, who had lived there most of his life and had done so much for her. I know she had a will, but I have not been able to find it.

Mommy had inherited sixteen acres from Papa that she was able to save. However, it is owned jointly with someone we don't know. Some shyster came in under the pretense of helping her save the Jefferson property and took advantage of the situation. We won a judgment against him, but he never paid. Mommy had also bought ten acres across the road from her house. She used to raise sweet potatoes and peas on it. She sold three acres to individuals who wanted to build homes.

It has been only recently that I have come to appreciate my mother's life of hard work and sacrifice. One day I was sitting at my dining room table with my grandson Benjamin sharing some entries from my mother's diary. As I read one, then two entries, I broke into tears of sadness and regret. I felt like the ungrateful child I had been so long ago. I felt as though I had loved Daddy and battled with Mommy. For a moment, I did not like myself. Though I had the diary since 2001, I read it as I recorded it here. My notes are in parenthesis. These are a few entries from Mommy's life during the summer of 1945.

Thursday, May 10, 1945, Dear Diary, Today I earned 50 cents for hair work. I also bought my baby (Barbara) a carriage that is costing $39.50. Clint would have a fit if he knew it.

Friday, May 11, Dear Diary, I missed school. I didn't have anyone to stay with Barbara. I did ironing and had a visitor. I also earned $1.00 for some work I did for Caleb.

Saturday, May 12: Dear Diary, Today I earned 75 cents. I also washed. Maurine came by. Clinton stayed out 'til 2:00 a.m.

Sunday, May 13, Dear Diary, Today is Mother's Day but I didn't get anything. Of course I never do. Clinton left for work and I went to church, carried Bob and Charles.

Wednesday, May 16, Dear Diary, Today Clinton's brother came to see me. I like him very much. He is very nice and friendly, not a bit like Clinton. His name is Herbert Gray.

Thursday, May 17, Dear Diary, Today I earned 55 cents. I fixed some lovely curls. I also called Herbert. It was his last day in town. I hated he had to leave so soon. Today is Clint's birthday.

Friday, May 18, Dear Diary, I earned $1.50. It was much needed...I got a letter from Clinton. (Daddy must have been on the train working as a Pullman porter.)

Saturday May 19, Dear Diary, today I got Barbara's carriage out of lay-a-way. It is very nice.

Sunday, May 20, Dear Diary, I had planned to take Charles and Bob out for a stroll, but my folks came for me to go to the country.

Monday, May 21, Dear Diary, I went fishing today, but didn't catch any fish. I also helped my mother work in the garden and I cooked dinner.

Tuesday, May 22, Dear Diary, I went fishing again and I caught three fish fair in size but I enjoyed myself very much.

Wednesday, May 23, Dear Diary, I pressed Mrs. Batts' hair and helped pick and can 14 pints of English peas. I also went to town.

Thursday, May 24, Dear Diary, I helped Mama do a big washing, helped cook and gave her a shampoo. I'll complete the job tomorrow.

Friday, May 25, I went up town to Thelma's, and completed my job, fixed Jean's hair and saw Mable Chatman's baby (Macy).

Saturday, May 26, Dear Diary, I had quite a lot of work to do, but I found time to go to Brown's Beauty Shop to work. Had one customer, made 50 cents.

Sunday, May 27, Dear Diary, I wore my first pair of slacks. I worked quite a bit and tried to learn to ride a bike. I also drove Mama's car a short distance. I hope I can learn to ride the bike.

Monday, May 28, Dear Diary, Today I tried to ride the bike again. I haven't learned yet, but I will. I also worked quite a bit.

Thursday, May 31, Dear Diary, Today I helped Mama wash and set out sweet potato plants. It was quite a job. Tomorrow, I go to Memphis.

Friday, June 1, Dear Diary, I caught the 5:15 a.m. train and went to Memphis to get rings for Mom's car. I went to see Mrs. Gray (Big Mama), went up town and bought some things for the kids.

Saturday, June 2, Dear Diary, I went to the shop around noon today. I made $1.95. I also ran into Miss Sally McFerren, an old friend and schoolmate of mine.

Monday, June 4, Dear Diary, Today we started chopping cotton, the first I've chopped in several years. But, I'm back in the swing of it again.

Tuesday, June 5, Dear Diary, I'm still chopping cotton. It isn't so bad. I went down to Aunt Pat's house, carried Barbara Jean.

Wednesday, June 6, Dear Diary, I'm still chopping cotton. Clinton came out her to see us. He is here for a few days. We have not fussed (argued) any yet.

Thursday, June 7, Dear Diary, We are still working in cotton. Clinton helped all day. I wish he could be here to help tomorrow.

Friday, June 8, Dear Diary, Clinton left on the early morning train. It also rained this morning, but we went to the field after it stopped.

Saturday, June 9, Dear Diary, I had to do quite a bit of work before I went to the beauty shop. I made $1.50. I'm on 50-50 basis.

Sunday, June 10, Dear Diary, Today I made a cake and ice cream. They were   good. I also went to visit my sister (Thelma) and cousin in town. We had a nice time.

Monday, June 11, Today, I cooked dinner, helped kraut cabbage and set out tomato plants. I am packing my things. I leave for home tomorrow.

Tuesday, June 12, Dear Diary, I left Somerville at 7:20 a.m. Am back at home in Memphis, brought all my kids. We are glad to be home after helping Papa chop cotton. (This entry leads me to believe that Sonny had been staying in the country with Mama and Papa for a while.)

Wednesday, June 13, Dear Diary, I carried the kids to the clinic for their second whooping cough shots. Barb doesn't feel so well after hers. I'm resting up after working in the country.

Thursday, June 14, Dear Diary, I had planned to go to school tonight, but I didn't have anyone to stay with my kids. Clinton left at 2:00 p.m. and hasn't returned at 12:20 a.m. (I am thinking that Daddy was not working on the train.)

Friday June 15, Dear Diary, I went up town today to have my glasses rechecked. I couldn't find a Father's Day gift, or we were too poor to buy one.

Saturday, June 16, Dear Diary, Clinton left this evening for work. I hope he can stay out a while. Thelma left tonight after several days here with me.

Sunday, June 17, Dear Diary, I had a good dinner today. Had planned to go to church but I didn't have the energy.

Monday, June 18, Dear Diary, I went back to school tonight for the first time in several weeks. I had to take my kids with me. Bonita kept them for me. It was quite a help.

Tuesday, June 19, Dear Diary, I went to the Ration Board today. Mary kept Bob for me. I took all of them to school with me. Bonita kept them for me.

The United States was at war--World War II. Rationing of goods such as can goods, gas, clothing, shoes, coffee, sugar, milk, cheese, butter, and many other items was taking place. Each person including babies had their own rationing coupon book. Rationing was the way the government controlled supplies during wartime. A person couldn't buy certain items unless they had their coupon for that item.

Wednesday, June 20, Dear Diary, Today I had two visitors, Mrs. V. Westbrook and her daughter (Aunt Virginia and my first cousin, Anita who was four months old) and Mrs. M. Porter. We had some good watermelon. They helped me clean up. I went to Mrs. Jefferson for class in anatomy.

Thursday, June 21, Dear Diary, I got up very early this morning about 4:45. I felt somewhat let down (depressed) all day. Didn't even go to school. Sonny doesn't feel well.

Friday, June 20, Dear Diary, tonight I had Barb's picture made at Mrs. Mary H. Porter's house. I also started a Victory Garden. I hope it does well.

Saturday, June 23, Dear Diary, I went to Sears and got Barb a playpen. She gets so dirty when she crawls on the floor. Mary kept her for me to go.

Sunday, June 24, Dear Diary, The proofs for Barb's pictures came. They are very good. I worked all day getting ready to go out home in the country tomorrow.

Monday, June 25, Dear Diary, Today, I had a very insulting time at the Greyhound Bus Station. I missed my train. Had to wait four hours. I finally made it with the kids, so I'm here and am I tired.

Tuesday, June 26, Dear Diary, Well I went back on the job of chopping cotton. I also earned 75 cents. I dressed Mrs. Chatman's hair. I enjoyed doing that very much.

Wednesday, June 27, Dear Diary, We finished chopping cotton the first time today at 12:30. Sure did chop hard but I rested most of the evening.

Thursday, June 28, Dear Diary, Jean took sick today. I helped Mama wash, also cooked and went after (to get) Thelma. I guess I'll be up most of the night. (My first cousin Jean was a teen then and she kept us while Mommy was working in the field.)

Friday, June 29, Dear Diary, Today was just another day. I didn't work so hard. I fertilized the watermelons and helped plow them. I'm really farming. Also, saw my cows. They are lovely.

Saturday, June 30, Dear Diary, I worked very hard today at home, then I went to Brown's Beauty Shop to work. I made $1.75 on 50-50 basis. My curls weren't so good.

Sunday, July 1, Dear Diary, Today Clinton came out to help us for a day or two.

Monday, July 2, Dear Diary, Clinton is helping us hoe cotton today. We are going back for the second time. We killed two snakes in the field.

Tuesday, July 3, Diary Diary, Clinton left this morning with Thelma. He gave me $20.00 and I had to pay Mom $15.00. I'll be glad when I get my debts paid. I chopped cotton today.

Wednesday, July 4, Dear Diary, I celebrated Charles' birthday. I cooked a good dinner, made ice cream and cake. We had a fine time. I didn't go to the field today. Clint came back.

Thursday, July 5, Diary My Dear, I went back to the field today. And did I hate to go back after such a fine time at home, eating the good food and enjoying the things Clint brought me.

Friday, July 6, Dear Diary, I washed today and had four heads to do. I made $3.26 from 5:30 p.m. to 9:30, all mine. I worked at home. I really do enjoy the work.

Saturday, July 7, Dear Diary, I baked Aunt Pat a good cake today and went to Brown's Beauty Shop to work. I made $2.75, 50-50. I don't like those terms but it's the best I can do.

Sunday, July 8, Dear Diary, Today I cooked dinner, dressed the kids, and Mom and I went over to Mrs. Hayes' for luncheon. We had a fine time. Also went to Mrs. C. Watkins.

Monday, July 9, Dear Diary, I went to town, came home and went to the field.

Tuesday, July 10, Dear Diary, LaNelle (first cousin from Ohio) came out for a few days visit, her first since 1940. How she has changed. It's for the better though.

Wednesday, July 11, Dear Diary, I really did chop some grassy cotton today. I'm about to get tired of the field. Tomorrow will be my last day to hoe cotton.

Thursday, July 12, Dear Diary, I finished hoeing cotton today at noon and helped Mama can fruit. I also attended a nice dinner in my honor down at Aunt Pat's house. It was given by Henry and Martha.

Friday, July 13, Dear Diary, Nelle left today. I went to town and bought some things for Sunday dinner. Also pressed Mama's hair. I really didn't feel like doing very much.

Saturday, July 14, Dear diary, I had to do a big washing. Cooked rolls and fish for dinner. Went to Brown's Beauty Shop and made 45 cents. I had some of the shortest hair I've ever had to fix—what a job.

Sunday, July 15, Dear Diary, I fixed dinner for the preacher and he didn't come. Well, we enjoyed it very much. I was busy all day but after I dressed the kids, we walked down to Aunt Pat's house.

Monday, July 16, Dear Diary, Today, I peeled and canned 18 quarts and 1 pint of peaches, which was a big job. I stayed up all night getting ready to take the kids back to Memphis.

Tuesday, July 17, Dear Diary, I left home at 5:15 a.m. on the train, arrived home about 7:00. Went to get my husband's check. Oh! Boy, am I sleepy and tired.

It was extremely difficult for me to record these entries. I felt so much sorrow. I understood much more about my mother. I understood why she loved the land and wasn't afraid of hard, dirty work. I learned why she was so insistent that we work the land. She wanted us to love it and the work it the way she did. She seemed to accept it as her duty to help her parents. I also understood why she preferred outdoors. I thought she was lazy about housework; however, now I believe she did so much fieldwork during her youth that she never got the chance to appreciate her house in the way of making a home for her husband and children. I understood her love for food and cooking.

I cried for that young "single" mother with the baby girl and toddler boy getting on the train early in the mornings. I felt her pain and humiliation at the Greyhound Bus Station. I was there with her during that four-hour wait after she had missed the train. She had to find a snack for Charles, and find a discreet way to breastfeed me. Mommy breastfed me until the day I embarrassed her on the streetcar by saying aloud, "I want *tittie* Mommy."

It couldn't have been easy getting her children dressed and fed to catch an early morning train. Yet, how many times did she do that? How many times did she go to the field and work hard and sweat like a mule? How many times did she go work in the beauty shop for so little money? How many trips did she make to the clinic without help from her husband? How many classes did she miss because she had no sitter even when her husband was in town? Where was he?

I felt her love as she worked for pennies to buy her baby girl a carriage and a playpen. I saw her love for Charles as she planned and made his birthday celebration. I saw her concern for all of us in the way she made sure we were taken care of when she worked in the field or the beauty shop, or when she attended classes. Mommy was only twenty-four years of age in 1945.

After I finished recording the entries from Mommy's diary, I understood her independent spirit, her fierceness in making her own way in life. Somehow, I understood how and why she worked so hard all of her life. I understood her never-ending debt and desire for money. I understood why she used to say, "I need to go to the hospital for a rest." She did not know of any spas for black people then. She couldn't have afforded one anyway.

I am no longer at odds with my mother. I am no longer judging the mother I knew. I did not know her. Neither did I understand what she truly wanted for me. Now I know that she wanted me to have my own and never to be dependent on a man for anything. My daddy had presented an example of a husband that was not acceptable to her. She did not want me to have such a hard and difficult life as she had experienced. Although Mommy did not want me to marry so young, she came to appreciate my husband and was glad I had married him. She was extremely upset with me when we separated. I always thought Mommy was a bit envious of my life. Now I understand.

I did not know any of those things I learned about my parents in Mommy's diary. How could I? I was a baby then and a toddler when they separated. Mommy knew I was crazy about Daddy. I believe she never wanted to speak ill of him and disillusion me because she hoped or perhaps knew that one day I would learn the truth about both of them, who they were before I came to be.

Why do children often idolize their fathers and demonize their mothers? Well, that may be overstating it a bit; however, children often adore even absentee fathers who do little or nothing for them financially or in any other way. Yet, they have little regard for the mother who is taking care of them physically, financially, and emotionally while she is often working outside the home to provide the necessities. The mother is often taken for granted as though she is doing what is expected of her. What is expected of the father?

Mommy was friendly to all; however, she had one close friend over the years. She was close with many of her first cousins, the Howells; however, Irene Riley was her best friend until she died. Mommy was also her hairdresser and colleague. Mrs. Riley died shortly after she retired from teaching. On the night she passed, she called Mommy and asked her to come to her house. Mommy went; however, she was slow in getting there and her friend passed before she arrived.

I don't know if Mommy delayed on purpose or if she was her usual slow self. I think she knew her friend was dying. I believe Mommy feared seeing her during her transitioning process.

My mother was afraid of death. She didn't want to be around it. She didn't attend funerals unless was a family member or someone very close to her. She told me about one of her college friends who passed away when they were young. Mommy did not attend her funeral. She couldn't bring herself to go. She said, "I was lying on my bed that day, and I felt someone touch my leg. I felt she did it. It nearly scared me to death." Perhaps the friend was letting Mommy know that it was okay that she didn't come to her funeral.

My mother didn't want to attend her own funeral. She told me many times that she wanted her body cremated. She did not want a funeral. I didn't plan a funeral for her, but I did have a small memorial service at the funeral home. I had to do something; however, I don't like funerals either. Like weddings, I think they are a lot of fluff and stuff for the onlookers. Both can be beautiful but financially wasteful. Funerals may bring comfort and closure to survivors, and they are opportune times to see family members and friends. I like a speedy service without sad songs and sad words. I choose cremation for myself.

In January 1996, Charles called to tell me Mommy had suffered a stroke and was in the hospital. I was already anxious about a graduate English class I had just enrolled in at the University of South Alabama. However, Joel drove me to Memphis through ice and snow to Methodist Central. I spent three nights with Mom in the hospital. Though her stroke was in January, I didn't write in my journal until March 24, 1996 after I had stayed in Somerville again for an extended period. My journal became my place of refuge, my best friend, my place to vent.

Dear Journal, I hated to leave, but I had to go back and continue my class. I'm glad that's over now and I got an "A." It wasn't easy, too much to read, especially with my state of mind—worrying about

Mom's mental and physical condition. I went through many changes, exploring feelings and remembering the past. It was sheer agony but I got through those periods, as Charles would call with encouraging news of Mom's condition. I almost gave up on school several times, but I decided to stay. Guilt was not a constant companion, though there were occasional pangs of it.

I found myself at one point taking two English classes, having to read fourteen books, write two short stories and critique about nine others while I was taking care of my four-year-old grandson Benjamin, and going to see Mom periodically. It was too much. I dropped one of the classes. Mom had many ups and down after two more strokes. I spent much time on the road between Mobile and Memphis and Somerville.

March 22, 1997, Dear Journal, It's rough. Watching my mom suffer is not easy. I don't even know if she is suffering. I just know that I am. She seems to rest well, doesn't complain, and speaks occasionally. She often makes a coherent statement unsolicited, which makes her seem okay...Mom doesn't respond well to me yet. Maybe it's my haircut, or maybe she didn't expect me to take care of her in her time of need. She always thought I didn't love her and she joked about me putting her in a nursing home. I didn't want that, and I thought it would never happen. I wanted her in her own home that she had worked and paid for.

March 28, 1997, Dear Journal, I keep trying to figure things out. I never was good at figuring, and I am having a hard time now. I left the hospital Wednesday night feeling very sad because I thought Mom looked so sad and pitiful. I had the feeling early Wednesday morning that she did not want them to put her in that ambulance. She did not want to go back to Methodist Central again. She looked frightened like a child not knowing what to expect. I had the feeling that she thought this might be her last trip. I didn't want to see her go alone, but I was too tired to follow. I said, "I will be there later this morning. I love you Mom and I want you to be well."

Mom was in and out of the hospital so often; I was making many trips trying to make sure she got the care she needed. There were many people in and out of the house taking care of her. Things came up missing. I knew I needed to be there, yet I had a husband and home to take care of. I had young adult children and a grandson who needed me. I had mixed feelings. My life consisted of caring for others mostly and neglecting myself.

I watched my mother as she lost so much. I was scared and helpless when my mother suffered her first seizure. I could not dial 911. Ebony, my nine-year-old great niece, had to do it.

June 20, 1997, Dear Journal, It has been a rough day...I told Mom we may have to put her in a nursing home because I couldn't do certain things anymore. I felt very bad afterwards and cried much of the afternoon. It is so difficult, tortuous for me to see my once "Rock of Gibraltar" mom in such a helpless and humbling state. I feel I'm the one being punish for something I didn't do. Why Lord? Why? I want Mom to have good care around the clock, but how can I continue to stay here?

August 3, 1997, Dear Journal, I had a flash back today. As I was caring for Mom, I had a flashback to when I was ten. I thought about Mom in her condition. Yet, I could not stand losing her. I said that if she died I would want her body to stay in the house, embalmed of course, because I couldn't stand the thought of her body being put into the ground. It was as if just having her body present, even though she had no life in her would make things okay for me. Well, when I looked at her sitting in the recliner today, I felt that I was living my childhood dream. It is as though she is dead, yet she is ever-present. I hate her condition, yet I want to keep her longer. Sometimes I wonder why she won't leave and give us release from the duty that we feel is ours. Charles wants her to keep living. I suppose in hopes that she will improve. I see little hope for improvement and sometimes I feel she is holding on selfishly without regard for our lives. It is as though she is punishing us for not paying enough attention sooner. We were busy living our lives with a measure of happiness and success she had never known.

Mom had lost so much. Her legs didn't work shortly after the first stroke. Actually, she had started to lose mobility before the stroke. Mom was not one to take medication. She should have been taking blood pressure medication regularly for years.

Mom wanted to get healthy the natural way; however, she lacked discipline. Her speech became less and less frequent. Near the end of 1997, it ceased altogether.

In January 1998, the paramedics came to the house again because Mom had had another seizure. They asked me if my mother had a Living Will. I had had that conversation with them before. I said, "If she didn't sign one when she could, then I won't. I'll talk it over with my brother."

I knew his answer. We wanted to keep our mother alive as long as possible. It was difficult, a lot of work, trying and stressful, but we loved her enough to do all we could do to help her.

January 12, 1998, Dear Journal, I deplore what this illness has done to my mother. Sometimes I am sure God is punishing her and me – me for not making a better relationship with her while she was up and going. How I wanted to so many times but we seemed too different and frankly, Mom seemed immature – an immaturity born out of her own unmet childhood needs. We are all fucked up. I'll do what I can to help my mom. The past doesn't matter to me. She is my mother. That's all.

February 20, 1998, Dear Journal, Well, my mom is in the nursing home, and I feel relieved. It is too much for Michael and that woman we hired must have been incompetent. ...I hate that my mother is in the nursing home. She always said she didn't want to end up there. I think. I have mourned the loss of my mother for over two years now. I think I'm ready to quit.

When I saw Mom in the nursing home for the first time, I wanted to bring her home. I wanted so much to bring her home to the brick ranch house she had worked so hard for so many years ago. I wanted her to spend her last days in her own house. Her care had become so complicated by then that it was impossible. I could not stay in her room for long because I was fighting back tears. I couldn't stand it. My tears flowed as a river after I got into my car.

February 27, 1998, Dear Journal, Mom was sleeping soundly, peacefully with oxygen flowing into her lungs. I was thinking that she could just sleep away. Mom was not one to welcome death. She seemed to fear it. I don't imagine she will face it head on.... I have to accept that I have wasted so much precious time that I will never see again. My mom seems to be leaving without getting to know me. I'm not sure I know her either. I only knew the things about her that I didn't like. I do appreciate her strength and her hard work to some extent. I love her as my mom.

September 9, 1998, Dear Journal, My mom is sick, very sick. I'm so afraid that she will not pull through this time. She has fought back so many times since January 1996. She is a strong and determined woman, but no one can cheat death forever. God, you have been good to her in letting her stay her for so long. We were not ready for her to go. Now we may be getting used to the idea that she will not be with us for much longer. The reason I'm crying is that I feel in my heart that my mother has not come to terms with her life. I think she believes that life has treated her unfairly. She looks outward rather than inward. She remains steadfast in her stubbornness while on her sick bed. I wanted so much for her to accept her condition and live out her life differently. It hurts my heart to see he go through so much humiliation, degradation and shame. It hurts that my mother has to suffer.

January 13, 2000, Dear Journal, Mom was asleep when I arrived at the nursing home. Aunt Virginia had wanted me to spend the night at her house, but I decided that she would not make that decision for me. Besides, I wanted to see Mom. I didn't know if she was glad to see me. I cannot read her too well sometimes. She did look sad one time. I thought she was going to cry. Her eyes filled and her face contorted, but nothing would come. I wonder if she can cry now. She has fought it back for so long. I keep going through the same torment wishing, hoping, and praying that Mom could, would talk. I feel so sad sometimes, most times for her. Moreover,

I feel sad for myself and wish that I had been a better daughter. If I had just had a better relationship with her and had known she was in such bad shape. I should have done more than simply tell her to go to the doctor. I should have come up to Tennessee and taken her to the doctor. Will I ever be able to forgive myself?

October 1, 2000, Dear Journal, I feel good about my decision to bring Mom to Georgia. ...I am worried about her care. It makes me so sad to think of her that I often push her out of my mind. She gave me life. What am I giving her? I was upstairs thinking about Mom and feeling conflicted and confused. I was caring for Benjamin in the mornings and afternoons wondering about my health (since being diagnosed with low white blood cell count), wanting to get on with some writing and other activities. I prayed aloud for God to tell me what to do about Mom and that nursing home situation. I said, "God, tell me what to do and I will do it." I then went back downstairs and told Joel of my conflict, my guilt, my desire to do more in the way of personally taking care of Mom. He said, "Bring her here to a nursing home." I accepted that as my answer and immediately felt relieved.

I became involved with my own health for a time and could not bring Mom to Georgia. I underwent many blood tests and bone marrow biopsies to learn what was going on inside my own body. It was a trying and difficult time. Not knowing is often as scary as knowing.

August 25, 2001, Dear Journal, Mom will be her in Georgia Tuesday. I am asking God to deliver her safely and let her be stable when she arrives. I know she will miss Michael, but I pray I can make life good for her. I pray it is a good thing, the right thing to do. I have to believe she will get better care here. I will see to it.

Mom seemed to be at peace when she came here. I went to spend time with her daily. I would comb her hair, cut her nails, clean her mouth and talk to her about whatever I was doing in my life. Charles, Virginia, Michael and Ebony came to celebrate Mom's eightieth birthday November 22, 2001.

Mom passed away December 16, 2001 less than a month after her birthday. On the Saturday night before she passed, I was visiting her. I noticed she seemed to want to say something to me. I kept asking what it was that she wanted to say. Of course, she could not speak then. She had a hard time trying to keep her head up. It was slumped. I adjusted her pillow and told her that I would get a neck pillow for her. I stayed a little while longer then told her that I would see her tomorrow.

Joel and I went to several stores looking for a neck pillow that night. We couldn't find one. After Mom passed, I saw neck pillows everywhere.

It happened that Sunday. We were having the Christmas program at church, which went a little long. Then after church, Alysa, Benjamin and I stopped by an art gallery for a little while. Afterwards, I decided to take a different route to the nursing home. I was turned around as I drove through town. We finally got to the nursing home. When we walked in, Mom's roommate was coming towards us in a wheelchair. She asked, "Is your mama going to be alright?" Alysa took off running to her room. Benjamin and I followed. The paramedics were working on Mom. I went to her bed and called her, "Mom, Mom." I touched her body. I could feel no life. All that week Mom wanted to say something to me. On either Monday or Tuesday, she had made some sound in her throat as I was talking to her about bringing her to my house. What did she want to say? I can only imagine. I think she wanted to say that 'it was okay."

As I stood over her bed and covered her body I said, "It's okay. It's okay." The paramedics took her to the hospital as though she were alive. I followed knowing that Mom was gone. I spent some time alone with her, making final my long goodbye.

Even though Mom had that big tube down her throat, she looked peaceful. Her body was still warm, and her skin was soft, very nice. I had sat at Mom's bedside many days caressing her soft skin for comfort. She still felt warm and comforting. I shed some tears because she was my mother, and she did the best she could. I was her daughter, and I did the best I could.

December 20, 2001, Dear Journal, The time is drawing nigh and I haven't written what I want to say. I want to be prepared with a script in a way, and I want to shoot from the hip in another way. I need to remember from longer than six years ago. And I want/ need the memories to be significant and/or pleasant. Mom had an interesting life. She was an adventurer or sorts. She took some chances and for that, I am pleased to be her daughter.

I made plans for Mom's body to travel to Tennessee for Charles and Michael and perhaps Aunt Thelma to view. Aunt Thelma declined. Charles and Michael had concerns about cremation; however, after they viewed her body, they knew she was no longer there. They were still not in favor of cremation even though it was what Mom wanted. I continued with the arrangements.

December 23, 2001, Dear Journal, We are leaving Somerville. Today is clear, beautiful blue sky and sunshine. It does lift my spirit. Yesterday started beautiful and clear, but before the service started, the sky began to "spit" and when we were on the way back to Mom's house, the sky opened, and the angels shed the tears we didn't shed at the service. I had been crying over Mom's condition for six years. I did not want to cry that day. That was a day to give her what she wanted. I think we succeeded. People said it was nice. I felt good about it yesterday and I feel good about it today.... I like the way I arranged Mom's pictures, the candle and rose on the altar with the Ashanti cloth I brought back from Africa. Last night I dreamed I had moved Mom home, but it did not seem like her house or mine. Yet, Michael and I were taking care of her. We were waiting for her to get a bed at the nursing home. I didn't want to move her there. I was thinking she would pass on before I moved her.

I sobbed many days after Mom passed. I questioned the care she received. I questioned whether I should have tried to find a naturopathic doctor and wondered if she could survive without the medicines she had been on for those six years. I had so many questions and no answers. I was sad and lonely. I no longer knew what to do with my time. I wanted to talk to Charles so I could feel close to Mom. I worried about Michael.

Christmas Eve 2001, Dear Journal, I have sobbed many times today. Why? Many reasons….I miss her. Yes, I got tired of making trips to the nursing home but I loved having my mama close. I thought it was what she wanted. I knew she wanted me to take care of her. I believe Mom had gotten tired of her condition. I felt she became frightened after losing the use of her hand. If I could erase what Mom went through these past six years, I would. I did not want her to reach that state. I said to Benjamin about three weeks ago, "I'm tired of taking care of old people and babies." Immediately after I said it, I realized what it meant and I took it back. I guess it didn't come back. I miss you Mom, and I wanted to take care of you.

MY JOURNEY HOME

Ghana, West Africa

A people without the knowledge of their past history, origin and culture is like a tree without roots--Marcus Garvey

This is only a glimpse into my African experience. I cannot put into words the deepest feelings about my journey, for it took place not just in my physical being but also in my soul where the English language has no expression. There was so much that I encountered—people, places, smells, sights, feelings, and sounds. I cannot express how being in Africa stretched my mind into the possibilities of "what ifs." I do not know how I could feel so perfect in such an imperfect land—a place in need of so much materially. Yet Africa's greatest need is the knowledge that would create a different mindset. I came away feeling responsible for the predicament of my brothers and sisters on the African continent and throughout the Diaspora.

Captor and captive must have shared a symbiotic relationship, a shared responsibility for the institution of slavery although I do not like to think that my African ancestors became complicit with the slavers. According to the Bible, God gave humankind dominion over every living thing except other humans. What made the Europeans decide otherwise? What made the African captors so willing to sell their brothers and sisters to the Europeans? What had happened to them as a people that they were not grounded in their own identity as Africans with pride in their soil and in their own way of being in the world? What made them so spiritually bereft that they needed to put a white face on God? Why did the white captor so easily sway their minds when he dared to set foot on the sands of Africa? Perhaps we will never know. These are just questions I raise. On a spiritual level, there had to be cooperation between the captor and the captured. Had African people turned away from their true nature?

Slavery and Beyond (1991)

A people torn away
Sold, bought, tricked
Stolen from mothers crying
From fathers trying
Not to remember their deeds
Wicked design for a new world
Foreign and far away
White devils came
For sovereignty to reign
Forever
Power hungry, greedy
Rapist, murderers, thieves
Owe the Motherland a debt
Not to be paid
For souls desolate
Souls growing more desolate
With generations coming and going
Going, going
Gone
Not yet
But coming to birth
Like fine wine
Becoming strong, smooth, refined

Finding their way back from the abyss
Missing some beats
But beating strong
Long
Longtime returning home for salvation
Birth of a new Nation

I think Africa needs to look within its own history, culture, religion, and self to find the answers to the questions that would propel them into a more developed and certain future. I do not have the answers to black people's plight in America and throughout the world. I just know that the fall from the top of the pyramids to the bottom of the political and economic heap has been long and hard. Getting up has been difficult and is still an ongoing process. However, black people are getting-up, but are bruised and blistered, tattered and torn -- and the hospital is not treating them just yet. They do not own the hospital.

The problem, though not completely owned by Africans and African Americans, is ours to solve. We cannot expect the one who captured and enslaved us to turn around and make us whole. After all, he let us go unwillingly. With the departure of the captured Africans, the continent became poor and ever more vulnerable to foreign invaders. The African continent has suffered greatly through European colonization. Europeans took much of the continents wealth in the form of precious gems, minerals and oil, along with its people. The African captors have greater responsibility for their part because they turned against their own flesh and blood, thus against themselves. That was probably the greatest occurrence of self-hatred since humankind's appearance on Earth.

These are some thoughts I explore as I try to understand my place in the United States and in the world. I believe everyone and everything has a purpose. Are we as African descendants in America fulfilling our purpose? Each group has a land base, a country they call home. African Americans are the only people who refuse to recognize a connection to land. Why?

For many years, I wanted to journey to the land of my people, my beginning -- Africa. I have the desire to cross the Atlantic to the African continent—to Ghana, West Africa on the Atlantic Coast. I visited the capitol city Accra, the Ashanti region Kumasi, and Cape Coast.

The entire time I spent in Africa was like a dream. Each morning as I awoke, I reminded myself I was there, and then I would see the streets were crowded with black people and my soul would become satisfied. I felt safe and secure everywhere I went. I was at home with people I did not know because of our long separation; however, we always knew each other through blood, history, spirit, and struggle. We were one.

Each day I breathed Africa and a peace of mind I had never known. I experienced what my ancestors were denied when they were captured. The country was so wide open. The air was so clean, unpolluted by capitalism. The land flourished with banana and plantain trees, yams, maize, and groundnuts. The beautiful waters of the Atlantic gave up many different fishes, crabs, and prawns.

The journey took about ten hours from Baltimore. I had an experience on the plane that I won't soon forget. First, I must say how thrilling it was to see Ghana Airways— African pilots and flight attendants. I was tempted to ask what Muhammad Ali asked when he flew to Ghana almost forty years ago, "What y'all did (sic) with the real pilots?"

Anyway, that night I had a difficult time falling asleep. The seats were too close. I must have dozed a little though because in the early morning hours, I felt I was suffocating, and I began to panic. I felt claustrophobic sitting between Joel and a woman who never got up the entire ten hours. I felt as if I was in an overcrowded elevator headed to the top of the Empire State Building at a very slow pace. My heart began to palpitate, my pulse was racing, and I had difficulty breathing. Then visions of slave ships passed before me with Africans packed spoon fashion in the decks just as in the pictures I had seen many times.

I woke and quickly got up from my sea. I stood in a roomy area behind a row of seats, affirmed divine order, and prayed for peace in my soul. After I realized I was dreaming, I almost lost control just remembering that I was somewhere above that huge body of water so many miles from land. I suppose I would have been one of those Africans who did not make the journey. For an infinitesimal amount of time, I understood how it must have been for my ancestors. I felt proud that my beginnings were rooted in such strength and determination to survive.

I was relieved when we landed, deplaned, and got on the trolley that took us about one hundred yards to baggage claim. We walked through a corridor with large murals depicting African life and a sign that read "Akwaaba—Welcome to Ghana, Gateway to Africa."

I was traveling with a tour group of seventy-eight. Since we were going to the land of our ancestors, our beginning, the name of our tour was "Roots." In 1977, Alex Haley wrote a book entitled *Roots: The Saga of an American Family*. That book and the television mini-series that followed inspired many African Americans to learn about their ancestry. The book is the story of Haley's family in Africa and America.

Trying to locate our baggage on the over-packed carousel was chaotic. It kept spilling and getting jammed. The airport was not like any that I had seen. Africa was not like anywhere I had been. Amazingly, we got our luggage and our guides loaded it onto two buses and a van that would transport us throughout the tour. While we were waiting for our buses, people selling various items approached us, as did those seeking donations for various causes.

The ride to the resort took us through the square and on a quick tour past the police barracks, municipal buildings, military hospital, war monuments, and homes. The roads were paved but dusty from the red dirt that prevails in Accra. The buildings looked rundown. There were few trees and almost no landscaping. I saw where the "lower class," according to our guide, lived. It was squalid like the townships in South Africa—shanties with dirt yards. There was a man showering outside in a partly enclosed concrete structure. I also saw men and women relieving themselves on the grounds near the streets and markets. It was a bit more discreet than it sounds. There were no public toilets as we were accustomed to in America. In one area there were many people, including teens and young children, on the streets selling gum, candy, pies, toiletries, and all sorts of items. What I was seeing of Ghana was not beautiful, but it was oh so fascinating, interesting, and so alive.

The LA Palm Royal Beach Hotel lived up to its four-star rating as it graced the bluff overlooking the Atlantic. How incongruous though, such a beautiful place set in the midst of a largely undeveloped country.

The first night, they welcomed us to Ghana with a reception complete with African drummers, dancers and the most delicious appetizers and fresh juice drinks of pineapple, citrus, papaya, and mango. Dinner was wonderful—fish, lamb stew, fresh vegetables, fresh fruits, plantains, salads and desserts--everything prepared to perfection. They set up a marketplace especially for us where we shopped for gorgeous clothing and crafts. Shopping soon became a sport for some and an art form for others on the tour.

On Wednesday, we visited Kwame Nkrumah University of Science and Technology, established in 1952. Kwame Nkrumah became Ghana's first president. In 1957, the country formerly known as the Gold Coast of Africa gained independence under Nkrumah's leadership. Ghana was the first sub-Saharan African colony to gain independence.

We also visited the Kente Weaving Village, Ahwiaa Wood Carver's Village, and Ntonso home of Adinkra cloth. In the authentic hand-woven Adinkra and Kente cloths, wood carved masks, Ashanti stools and other artifacts, I saw the true beauty of the African spirit.

Kente is an Asante (Ashanti) ceremonial hand-woven cloth of various colors sewn together in strips and used for important social and religious occasions. The different patterns represent the history, religion, ethics, moral values, social codes, and such of the Akan people. At one time only royalty wore some patterns of the cloth, but today anyone can wear the cloth.

In the afternoon after our tour, we traveled about 150 miles to the southern part of Ghana, the Asante (Ashanti) Region, home of the Ashanti people. The British colonial administrators used Ashanti to describe the Kingdom of Asante. The Ashanti resisted British colonializing until around 1900. After a series of wars, the British overcame them; therefore, English is the official language. Many villagers do not speak English. They speak different dialects of the Akan, Kwa, and Twi languages.

We spent one night in the capitol city Kumasi at Hotel Georgia. It had a two star rating. It was old, had not been updated, but it was clean and sufficed for one night. Accra was flat land; Kumasi was somewhat hilly. So many people were buying and selling. There were many furniture makers along the streets. They had bedroom and living room furniture that sat low to the ground. The buildings were taller than those in Accra.

The street vendors who had been following us throughout our tour stood outside the hotel calling for us until management ran them away. They were persistent in getting us to buy. It was a little disconcerting at times being surrounded by so many vendors thrusting merchandise in your face and imploring you to buy. Sometimes the vendors got into struggles among themselves. It was nothing major, as they all knew each other. The police used belts as a parent would to discipline a child, to run vendors away from our buses when we were visiting the Textile Market in Accra.

As I traveled throughout each region of Ghana, I noticed that the day begins around six in the morning for many of them. I would see women sweeping their dirt yards. I had not seen such since I was a child. Some women in the country would do the same thing. It seems that grass was a luxury back then and some people had yards of clay dirt.

Ghanaians do most of their living outside—bathing, laundry and cooking. It seemed that everyone goes to market daily to buy, sell, or trade. Their mud huts were too small and not equipped for refrigerators, cupboards and the like, so each day was market day. Women walked to market carrying eggs, peanuts, yams, and other goods in baskets on their heads. One morning I saw a young mother and a cute little toddler going to market with baskets on their heads.

Ghana is not all primitive. There are subdivisions in Accra with homes suitable for those who are earning decent wages. There are those who drive Mercedes and other fine automobiles. There are nice restaurants and even a mall. However, none of that is on the level of what we have in America. Some of our vendors wore Nikes, Adidas, FUBU, and such labels. They had little contact with the western world via television, books, and magazines. There was not much television to watch. I watched CNN and some Ghanaian programming when we had a few moments in the room. There was not so much leisure there, yet the Ghanaian people seem to live at a leisurely pace.

Many churches dotted the landscape along the route we traveled. They appeared to be only a mile or two apart. Each village had a small one-room church. I wondered what they were teaching.

The countryside was beautiful. There were no McDonald's restaurants or service stations where we could use clean restrooms and wash our hands. The one restroom stop we made was located at a couple's house. They had a little store out front where we bought soft drinks and snacks and used the one "public restroom" that was far from adequate. I was thankful for the hand sanitizers our travel agents advised us to bring. Still, there were few complaints.

Upon leaving Kumasi, we traveled to Cape Coast, the highlight of our tour. Fishing villages were nestled among the palm trees that lined the beach. It was quite magnificent. It made me dream of a simpler lifestyle. One morning as we were on the bus traveling up the coast, I saw five men with a huge fishing net they had cast out into the sea probably the day before. They were pulling the net ashore. Sly said that before that day ended many more men from the village would join them. It was an awesome sight, which reminded me of how it must have been when Jesus was selecting his disciples and saw Peter and James fishing.

When we got to Cape Coast, it was nighttime. We could see many fires along the banks of the water, and we could smell fish

cooking. We arrived at Coconut Grove Beach Resort in the evening. The staff greeted us with fresh coconut water served in the shell. After a delicious feast at the thatched restaurant located on the Gulf of Guinea, I went for a solitary walk along the beach. I contemplated life before the Middle Passage as I listened to drummers who were further down the beach. I sat in the sands of Africa and blessed my ancestors who crossed the Atlantic centuries ago. I closed my eyes and let the tableau of frightened Africans pass in solemn procession on their way to a land that would produce me. When I opened my eyes, I found the entire area shrouded in darkness. The resort had lost power, and all the lights were off. With moonlight above me, unafraid, I rose and walked to the water's edge and stood, half expecting the drowned Africans who chose death over enslavement to rise from the sea and greet me. The ocean roared quietly, its foamy waves lapped the shore and tickled my ankles. I could imagine young girls crying over futures they would never know. I could imagine fathers and young warriors without weapons to defend their lifestyle searching the crevices of their minds wondering what was happening. I saw villages torn apart by those in search of the "noble savage" looking for people they deemed not quite human, but who were trainable nevertheless. Those who would build their cities, raise their crops, clean their homes, nurse their babies, and provide them with entertainment and enjoyment.
Colonialism (1991)

I am Back

Let Victoria cleanse my wicked designs
I want what is yours
Lush green valleys
Concealing wealth untold
You may have my treasure
Give me yours
We are one
I am your child

Your wayward child
Returned
To your warm, black bosom
Voluptuous hips that carried humanity
Your shoulders strong held civilization
I will show you a new way
Your crown does not fit
Your scepter is not sharp
His Majesty is hungry
For lush greens
Buried treasure
And thrones
Your child demands his inheritance
Motherland!

After a few minutes, the lights came back on and knocked me from my reverie. I went back to my room and turned on the radio hoping to find a talk show. I did. The host and guests were discussing the condition of the African. The host said, "The African is in need of racial pride." He continued, "We need to love *we*. We are so busy loving everybody else. We need to love *we*." He spoke about a need to work as a group for liberation because of those who were getting rich on their labor. He invoked the name of Marcus Garvey. I had not expected to hear such a call for racial pride in Africa. However, when I looked around I could see that my African sisters and brothers were just as brainwashed as we in America were. The struggle for black liberation is global. The struggle continues.

In Cape Coast, we went to the Kakum National Park created to protect Ghana's rain forests. I bravely took the canopy walk, a series of seven swaying bridges made of ropes and wood slats, hanging above the trees. It was an awesome sight. The forest was picturesque. The guide showed us the tree used to make the mortar and pestle they used to make "foo foo," the doughy food they eat with soup using their fingers. We saw many trees they used to make medicine to treat many ailments from upset stomach to leprosy.

While waiting for others to complete the canopy walk, I observed several groups of children from different schools who were on field trips. They were neatly dressed in uniforms of brown pants or skirts with yellow, gold, or orange shirts. It was a joy to talk to them and observe them. They were quiet and orderly. Education is not mandatory, and it is not free past middle school. Many of the young children do not go to school because there are not enough teachers or facilities. The children work in the markets or follow tour buses looking for an American "parent," someone who will sponsor them to come to the United States or who will send them money for school

The highlight of our Roots Tour was a visit to Elmina. Since some people were fearful of taking the canopy walk and moved through it very slowly, that delayed our trip to Elmina; therefore, we skipped lunch and headed there immediately after the last person finished. The twin castles, Elmina and Cape Coast sat, in infamous splendor above the Atlantic Ocean. The buildings were white washed and very large however not at all akin to the castles of Europe. They also housed no king or queen, no royalty.

Europeans traders had built the castles in the 1600s to store their ill-gotten goods-- gold, ivory and spices. They later became holding places for the goods they used and those they exchanged for Africans who would become slaves. They housed the captured Africans in the castles until they could load them like cargo onto the ships to cross the Atlantic.

There were two groups, and I was in the group that went to Cape Coast Castle first. The guide greeted us in one of the dungeons and welcomed us back to Africa. He said a prayer and poured a libation to God and to the ancestors. A sister bent down, scraped and collected some soil from the packed dirt floor, no doubt filled with the blood, sweat, urine, and feces of our ancestors, and she put it into a vial to carry back to the United States of America. After the guide finished his prayer, she brought this guttural voice from the depths of her soul and spoke her message. It appeared as though she channeled an African woman who came with the message that, "We must remember, so we never forget." The woman wanted us to tell the story of our ancestors and their struggles. She said, "Go back and tell the story." It was very emotional. The sister collapsed after delivering the message. As she was coming back into herself, she walked like an aged African woman laden with many burdens. Many in the group cried and some later expressed anger at what the Europeans had done to our ancestors. I had grieved many times over the injustices done to us and had come to accept the past trying to make some sense of why slavery happened. I walked silently throughout the castle feeling as my ancestors must have felt, inhaling their essence that still lingered, and listening for echoes from my past.

We then toured Elmina Castle. I stood on the ground where my ancestors walked, bare feet torn and bleeding from their trek up the coast. I peered into the male dungeon and felt my fathers' helplessness as they heard the cries of their children, wives, sisters, aunts, cousins, and mothers. I entered the female dungeon and felt my mothers' vulnerability, shame, and humiliation from just being women. I stood where they brought my mothers to serve as sport for the Europeans. Their virtue and pride was stripped from them like old clothes. I cried inside my soul for all the generations of me.

The tour ended. We walked back through the "Door of No Return." One by one, our African tour guides greeted us. They welcomed each of us back to Africa, the Motherland-- "Welcome home my brother. Welcome home my sister." What an amazing feeling to be welcomed, and to feel welcome.

That was powerful symbolism. It was so emotional. Some cried. I felt I was carrying all of my ancestors back home where they belonged. I had never felt that sense of belonging to a place as long as I had lived in the United States of America. I felt at home in Africa.

Back at Coconut Grove that night, I attended a lecture on the unity of Africa and African Americans. The lecturer talked about how wealthy Africa is, yet she begs for food. He said they need tools and farm equipment like tractors, so they can work the land on a larger scale. He also discussed the African way of family unity with all generations living and working together. The generation gap does not seem to be a factor there. He mentioned the safety of the children in the villages. Africans still respect the elderly and acknowledge their ancestors. They take pride in their children and seem not to have discipline problems as we have in America. The children are not raised on junk food, sugar and caffeine-laden soft drinks, and they have little if any exposure to the influences of television, movies, video games, and music. They have the run of the village, a constant supply of fresh air and work.

On Saturday, we departed Coconut Grove at six in the morning and traveled to Assin Apimanin Traditional Area for the Enstoolment Ceremony for Dr. Barbara King, minister of Hillside Chapel and Truth Center in Atlanta who became Nana (Chief) Yaa Thumwaa I. The title Chief was traditionally bestowed upon males; women were honored with the title Queen Mother; however, Dr. Barbara King was made chief.

When we arrived at our adopted village, many of the women and children were standing along the road to greet us. They were waving handkerchiefs and wearing tee shirts with Dr. Barbara's image on them. The officials were not ready to greet us; therefore, our busses turned around and took us to the river where the Africans had their last baths before boarding the ships for the Americas and other foreign lands. We also saw the graves of two former slaves who Dr. Na'im Akbar and others brought back from the United States and carried through the infamous "Door of No Return," thus completing the circle.

Upon returning to the village, our host greeted us and took us into the ceremonial area as we danced to ancient rhythms. The King and Chiefs were wearing beautiful Kente and Ashanti robes with lots of gold jewelry. The ceremony was private with Dr. Barbara and her entourage and the king and chiefs, but the program and celebration were open to all. The event took place in an open field flanked by chairs on both sides for spectators; the chiefs and other dignitaries sat at one end. There was much drumming and dancing.

A group of well-rehearsed and beautifully costumed children performed two dances for the king. The African children were so delightful with gorgeous skin, nice smiles, and friendly faces. I found the Ghanaians to be very friendly people. As soon as the children finished and other drumming started, many women made their way to the field and began dancing and beckoning us to join them. A few African men danced. Our guide Sly said, "Most men don't dance because they don't want to look foolish and because some women do not want their husbands dancing."

Many of us attended church on Sunday at the Etherean Mission with Brother Ishmael Tetteh and his congregation. It was "Remembrance Day." For them it was, "a day to remember the past fortunes and successes; the people, events and circumstances led to them. You uplift your spirit to see and experience God." They believe that " people without Spiritual, Historical and Cultural heritage are dead." Their celebration was rich with African customs and rituals. It was a day for remembering the ancestors and realizing our connection with them. Some of the songs were in English and some in their native language. There was much singing. When offerings were taken, we marched around the collection basket barefoot and dropped in the money.

All of the young children sat quietly and orderly on the left side of the church. If they needed a drink, there was a bucket of water and a cup located in the aisle just for them. There were pallets for the small ones who fell asleep. Women were attractively dressed and coifed. Some wore African attire and some wore western. Many of the men had on Kente and Ashanti robes. All looked prosperous. Late model cars filled the parking lot. The membership did not look like most of the Africans that were in the streets, marketplaces and villages. They did not look like the people who lived in the mud huts with thatched roofs.

The church was metaphysical or New Thought. It aimed to bring out the best in the individual by teaching prosperity in all aspects of life. The Minister admonished the congregation to access the power within and to accept the kingdom of God here and now.

The African masses are bogged down in a morass of self-effacing doctrine and foreign culture. They worship the European image of Jesus and embrace the missionaries' message of submission, humility, and patience. Religion has all but destroyed the spirit of our African brothers and sisters. It has robbed them of their history and culture and taught them to wait on God. Brother Tetteh has been on a mission for many years to raise the consciousness of Africans by teaching them how to activate the God power within as opposed to the traditional teaching of God who is skyward in heaven. If God is within, you can experience heaven here on earth. Heaven is the highest state of consciousness where love and compassion guides all your actions. You live in peace. He also taught that God infinitely loves and his universe cannot consist of a devil.

Metaphysical teachings are not new. They are the teachings of the Christ based in love and compassion. They bring out the best qualities in the individual. The African continent and the world could benefit from this empowering teaching. Africans, African Americans and Africans in other prosperous nations must lift the Motherland out of this quagmire of ignorance. Africans must realize that they are the founders of civilization, the architects of ideologies. They allowed the missionaries to strip them of their history and to tell them that their customs and culture were from the devil and not in harmony with the teachings of Jesus. It is the responsibility of the African to rise up, throw off the invisible chains of ignorance and apathy from their minds and spirits, and realize that God is within them.

After church, Joel and I hired a cab and did some touring on our own. We had our driver take us to the football game at Accra Stadium, the same stadium where, in 2001, at least 126 people died. It happened when the police fired tear gas into the crowd to quell some disorderly conduct. Williams, our cab driver, said he was there when it happened.

Since there was a big football game in progress, we decided to attend. Williams accompanied us as we made our way through the crowd and squeezed through the gate they closed behind us to prevent those entering who couldn't pay. They do not allow seating in the section where the people died otherwise the stadium was packed. While making our way into the arena, we passed concessions of kabobs, various chicken parts on a skewer, and others made with cow intestine. The sights and smells were quite unlike those we were used to when attending a football game in America. There were no scents of popcorn, hot dogs, and hamburgers or chicken fingers, and French fries.

The match was exciting, but we only stayed for a short time simply to enjoy the experience of attending. I was sorry to learn that the Black Stars, the home team, did not win.

Williams took us to a restaurant/bar where we sat on the terrace overlooking the Atlantic, drank fresh juices, and learned much about daily life in Accra. Williams, like many Africans, talked of going to America. For him, it would be for a short time. He said he would like to work in America and earn enough money to start his own business in Accra. He told us how difficult it was to save money because they earn so little. He said his wife took care of the children and the household, but she also made garments to sell. I met his wife and two young sons and baby daughter as they sat at a nearby service station waiting for him to get off from work. Williams and many other young Africans are always looking for some foreigner to help them get to America or to Europe.

On Sunday, it hit me that the tour was almost over, yet I had no desire to go back to the foreign shores of the United States of America. I felt that I could easily stay right there in Ghana, as had many other African Americans over the years. I liked being surrounded by black people and seeing black faces in the hotels, shops, marketplace, craft villages, restaurants, tourist attraction, and everywhere. I knew I was home. I went back to Africa for all of my ancestors—my mothers, fathers for generations back-- my aunts, uncles, cousins, brothers and all. I am grateful to God for the experience. I imagined much, but this was more. I went back to commune with my ancestors. I did.

I arose Monday morning thinking that it was my last day on the African continent, in the country of Ghana and the city of Accra. It had been educational and cultural, a spiritual experience that I would treasure for a lifetime. I knew it would not be my last trip to Africa, to my past, my African spirit, and my ancestors. I felt that I was born for that time and now that time was almost over and there would be tomorrow. I was there, and I thanked God daily. I thanked God for health, safety, and for the beauty of Africa – the people, the land and their way of life. I thanked God for making me who I am, how I am, where I am.

We hired another cab that day so we could see more of the city. We got Gottfried, who was Williams' brother, as our driver. He took us to Woodin, a terrific fabric store filled with the most striking and skillfully woven African patterns and colors that I had ever seen. I bought several pieces. From there, Gottfried took us to Jamestown, which looked more squalid than the worst slums in America. It was bustling with its marketplace and vendors lined up along the streets with so much piled right on the side of the road —shoes and clothing made locally. Many toilet items and other goods imported from France, Belgium, England and other European countries. We drove by the prisons, one for males and the other for females. They looked horrible, awfully depressing and I imagined they had dirt floors like the dungeons in the castles and the prisoners were in chains. It looked primitive. The buildings stood on the bluff above the Atlantic.

We had lunch at the thatched hut restaurant behind our hotel overlooking the ocean. It was slightly windy and a bit cool, but wrapped in the tightly woven shawl I had bought at the Kente Weaving Village, I ordered an aborigine salad--a grilled gardenia with mushrooms and herbs in tomato sauce. It was delicious as was every morsel I put in my mouth while I was in Ghana.

I sat in the hotel lounge after lunch and listened to a young man play so many familiar tunes on the piano. The tour group gathered in the hotel lobby waiting the time of our departure. We played cards, and they served us roasted peanuts that were the most flavorful I had ever tasted. The food was always fresh. The pineapples and papaya and all the wonderful juices were enough to sustain life.

Webster defines poverty as "the condition or quality of being poor; inferiority; inadequacy; scarcity." I suppose that describes most of the region when compared to America's standard. Nevertheless, I did not feel that I was in an impoverished environment. I did not feel that I was looking into the faces of poverty when I saw my brothers and sisters of Ghana. Yes, I saw great need. However, I saw no one destitute. I saw no one idle. The cities were alive with activity—people buying and selling. What is poverty, really? Is it the absence of brick homes and nice automobiles? Is it the absence of a substantial bank account? Then by those standards, most Ghanaians are poor. Their lifestyle would probably be a turnoff to many Americans. However, what I saw and felt was simply a way of life different from my own. It was not a style competing for recognition on the world stage. I did not find myself feeling pity or sympathy for the Ghanaians as through my way was superior. I found myself trying to learn about their lives and their dreams, and immerse myself in their relaxed way of being.

Though I felt connected to the Africans on a spiritual level, I also felt disconnected because my life was on a different path. That disconnect made it okay for me to exploit the African vendors. While bargaining is a practice that is expected and welcomed, I found myself trying to get merchandise for much less than it was worth. I think that mentality grows out of the notion that the African will settle for so little. When I look around and see that they tolerate "substandard" conditions and there seems to be little effort to improve them, it is easy to exploit. I did not realize that until after I left Africa and returned to the United States.

Do Africans need help? Yes, we constantly hear about technology. Most Africans cannot compete under those circumstances. Education is not free past middle school. There are not enough Ghanaians with the skills needed to advance in today's world. Why are we black people here in America? Could it be because we came ahead of our brothers to serve as salvation for them like Joseph in the Bible story? His brothers sold him into the hands of people who would sell him into slavery in Egypt. Nevertheless, his sojourn there resulted in his family's survival when famine hit the land.

The power that has conquered this world is capitalism. It sets the standard for all else. The African is not capitalistic by nature. However, Africans can learn to make capitalism work for them.

Those of us in America who have benefited from capitalism and have resources can assist our young African brothers and sisters in education. Individually, we need to find some way to contribute to the uplifting of Africa. Some American churches and groups have built schools in their adopted village. Some are collecting books by African American writers. The Africans want to know about black people in America. They also need other books. There is so much that we can do. Ghana is wide open for all kinds of development, but it will have to come from outside.

We visited many more places than those mentioned. We toured the Center for National Culture, the Manhiya Palace, and W.E.B. Dubois Center for Pan African Culture, Kwame Nkrumah Memorial Park. We saw the graves of Dubois and former president of Ghana, Kwame Nkrumah.

Africa needs to be experienced. Especially if you are into your history and culture. More especially if you feel your connection to your ancestors. Most especially if you do not.

A BLACK MAN IN THE WHITE HOUSE

On November 4, 2008, when Senator Barak Obama was declared the 44th president of the United States of America, I said, "Gotta go. I'm going to the Inauguration."

I was determined to be on the Washington Mall when Senator Obama became Mr. Presideent. I never dreamed of seeing a Black man in the White House other than the butler. I knew it would happen one day, but not during my lifetime. I couldn't get tickets to be up close, but I was determined to join the crowds that I knew would want to be part of the historic event.

I had heard that there had been at least five black presidents in America's history – Thomas Jefferson, Abraham Lincoln, Andrew Jackson, Warren G. Harding, and Calvin Coolidge. Those men were not proudly black. They may have had a bit of African blood mixed with their European/American. However, Barack Hussein Obama is a mix of black from Kenya and white from America.

I went to Washington, DC, and stood on the Mall before the Jumbotron with thousands of others who wanted to be part of history. I had only seen inaugurations on television. Though on a large screen, this one was spectacular, more impressive than the March on Washington in 1963 and the Million Man March in 1995. I was standing there amid that surreal reality wondering how it all happened during my lifetime. Yet, I saw nothing in the atmosphere that would have led me to that conclusion before March 2007 in Selma, Alabama.

I first paid attention to Senator Obama when I went to Selma, Alabama, in 2007 to commemorate Bloody Sunday and heard him speak at Brown Chapel Church. Hillary Clinton was speaking at First Baptist Church down the same street. Although I could not get inside either church because of the crowds, I took turns listening to both.

"Bloody Sunday" is the name given to the peaceful march of about 600 people leaving Selma and going to Alabama's state capitol, Montogomery. It was a march organized by the Student Nonviolent Coordinating Committee (SNCC) for the right to vote and to protest the murder of civil rights activist Jimmie Lee Jackson. State troopers, sheriff's deputies, dogs, and a posse on horseback terrorized the marchers, beat and gassed them, injuring many as they reached the Edmund Pettus Bridge. What began as a peaceful protest that fateful Sunday turned into a bloodbath for many, including Congressman John Lewis.

That commemorative Sunday, Barack Obama captured my attention with his speech. I stood mesmerized and listened. At that moment, I knew I would support him for president because his words and the spirit behind them made him credible.

I wanted to get a glimpse of him as he left the church. As soon as he finished speaking, I went to the side door like many others. In a short time, he came out and exclaimed, "I smell barbecue. I want some barbecue." He then walked towards the crowd, and everyone rushed in to get a handshake. I couldn't get a full handshake. We only touched fingertips. But that was good enough for me to know that Barack Obama was the right man for the president. So much is communicated about an individual through his demeanor, speech, and touch.

Many dignitaries were in Selma that Sunday. The most prominent was former president Bill Clinton. I crossed the Edmund Pettus Bridge with Rep. John Lewis, former president Bill and Hillary Clinton, Dr.Joseph Lowery, and many others in the Movement. In addition, Senator Obama assisted Amelia Boynton Robinson, a civil rights icon, in a wheelchair.

When Senator Obama became Mr. President, I was there. I didn't care about the temperature barely above freezing or the massive crowd. I didn't care when someone stepped on my foot or bumped into me. I was not worried about my toes being frostbitten. They were freezing despite the footwarmers I had stuffed into my shoes. I did not care about the miles I walked to the Mall. When I got there, I knew I would not see the Obamas, Clintons, Carters, Bushes, Senators, or Representatives up close, not even Mohammed Ali. I just stood among the great crowd before the Jumbotron and gazed into a future filled with hope and promise for change. I felt connected to a moment when all seemed good and optimistic. I was there, and it was there--the spirit of all things being possible. It moved through the masses of people of all ages and colors, which ranged from the blackest of Africa to the whitest of Europe. It was there, moving with a soft hum., gently and steadily, the spirit of optimism and the promise of hope and change.

I saw many people but didn't notice their faces, just bodies moving with purpose, quickly heading down streets looking for an entrance to the most fabulous Mall in America to see the man who had worn because of their vote. He was the one to jump-start the economy, mediate warfare, implement change and give hope.

He was the one to bridge the chasm between worlds – black, white, mixed of diverse ideologies and visions. He was the one to clean up the mess of the ages. He was not the second coming of the Messiah. He did not come on the clouds in radiant glory or on a white horse. However, the sun did push through the gloom at the right moment to greet him and shine its radiance upon him as he became president. This new leader seemed to represent the people to chart a course to change the ebbing tides of pessimism, doubt, and apathy into a free-flowing sea of "Yes We Can." It is up to us, the people, to save us. Yet, an effective leader can extract that good within us, motivate, and bring it out into this world of our making and refashion it for posterity. We must protect the earth, air, and water for our progeny. We also owe them a functioning government and society. We owe them cities and countryside with good roads and safe and sound infrastructure. We owe them a better country than we knew. Each generation must be better than the one that came before. I know that President Obama is not a miracle worker any more than we are. But we can heed his call to service and participate in programs to save the environment.

I was completely present at the Inauguration that Tuesday afternoon, January 20, 2009. I stood in the crowd feeling what my ancestors must have felt packed in the dungeons of Cape Coast castle, then packed spoon fashion in the ships, rocking to and fro over the waves of the Atlantic. I closed my eyes and thought I felt surging waters as my body swayed back and forth when anyone pushed through the tightly woven mass. The crowd was vast and close. My body felt warm, yet an occasional breeze eased through and caused me to wrap my scarf higher around my face.

On the Sunday before the Inauguration, I attended the concert at the Mall. I was a mile from the event, which was at the Lincoln Memorial, but it didn't matter. The crowd's spirit was upbeat. Every artist did their best. I sang along with Pete Seeger and Bruce Springsteen as they sang "This Land is My Land." For the first time in my life, I felt that America is my land. I understood Michelle Obama when she said, "For the first time in my adult lifetime, I am really proud of my country. And not just because Barack has done well, but because I think people are hungry for change. And I have been desperate to see our country moving in that direction."

It took me more than 60 to reach that conclusion. Finally, however, after being relegated to the margins of society for most of my life, on that Sunday and Tuesday, Inauguration day, I felt that America was indeed my country.

Monday was a day to answer Mr. Obama's call to volunteer. What a day! I participated in assembling care packages for servicemen and women. The packages contained personal care items, phone cards, and chewing gum. They needed fifteen thousand volunteers to work in shifts to undertake the tasks. It was well-organized and enjoyable.

I had the honor of shaking hands with soon-to-be Attorney General Erc Holder, treasury secretary Timothy Geitner, Massachusetts Governor Deval Patrick, and others. Mrs. Obama and Mrs. Biden had left before I arrived for my shift. After I finished, I joined thousands of others in writing letters of encouragement and thanks to military personnel stationed in Iraq. Volunteers received bags from Target with water, other goodies, and a thank you card from President Obama and Vice President Biden.

When the new President spoke about the founding fathers, I felt connected to them as I never had before when listening to other African Americans talk of them. It was because Obama had a white mother, and the physical connection seemed more authentic.

Tuesday, January 20, 2009, President Barack Hussein Obama said, "Today I say to you the challenges we face are real. They are serious, and they are many. They will not be met easily in a short period. But, know this, America – they will be met."

"On this day, we gather because we have chosen hope over fear, unity of our purpose over conflict and discord.?

I was hopeful then.

AFTERTHOUGHT – MY LIFE IN PIECES

I published a memoir in 2014 after experiencing a life-threatening health challenge. I did it to pass on some of the stories from my youth, primarily to my children and grandchildren. Though life in America was somewhat different then, matters concerning race were still plaguing the country, especially with the election of President Barack Obama, a man of African ancestry. He had much opposition while occupying the residence that many citizens thought should be occupied by a white man. Not a woman, even one as capable and qualified as Senator Hillary Clinton. Only a white man should be president. A Black Man in the White House was too scary for them. Descendants of Africans were never to rise to that height in America.

In retrospect, those race problems seem almost trivial now because, in 2016, the 45th president came on the scene with a blatant, unapologetic white supremacy agenda represented by the slogan "Make America Great Again." It signaled a return to the past of my youth. As I heard his message, I understood it and feared what would come next.

In the introduction, I warned people to "Understand history. Be determined that the painful aspects of history never be repeated. Close your eyes, mind, and heart to it, and you will live it (reliving it for some). Think voting rights, think education, think housing, think employment, think women's rights, think gay rights, think slavery. Think! Think! Think!"

That is still my admonition since many in public office are changing school curricula and banning books. They are restructuring history to fashion a more favorable narrative about their ancestors. Also, they do not want their children to feel pain about their past.

I can trace my family in America back to the 17th century, yet I am not a fully enfranchised American. If I were, the right to vote would not be an issue. Yet, periodically, the Voting Rights Act has to be renewed. It scares me that that right and others can be suspended or eliminated with a pen stroke. Presently, voting rights are challenged, books are banned, and women's reproduction rights are overturned. In addition, the LGBTQ+ community is constantly under attack, and their marriage rights are threatened.

That time has come and much sooner than I could have predicted. I now fear that democracy will soon be a relic of the past. Those four years the 45th president was in the White House were challenging for me; however, they may pale if he is reelected. I don't see America falling for the okey-dokey again and voting for such an ill-equipped person to lead this great nation. They were seduced by a television star and fooled in 2016, but I believe they are wiser now.

I didn't know how much I appreciated the United States of America until January 6, 2021, when I watched as the Capitol, the seat of democracy, was attacked by rebels, conspiracy theorists, radical republicans, and others. Then, I was afraid that that was the end of the era. Now I wonder if it was only the beginning of the destruction of democracy.

This year 2022, is ending, and the insurrection instigator, the 45th president of the United States of America, and other leaders have not been held to account. Isn't that what this "rule of law" nation requires? I don't think America wants to set such a precedent of jailing a former president. However, the former president must be held accountable for his actions toward this country.

Since the mid-term elections have ended and things did not go as many predicted, some feared America could regroup and look forward with the pain and confusion of the recent past in the rearview mirror. But only if they practice Sankofa, an Akan word from Ghana, West Africa, that means "Go back and fetch it." The Adinkra symbol for Sankofa is a bird flying forward with its head turned, looking back. It signifies that we should constantly move forward in life yet look back to the past for what is beneficial – what history can teach us to live better in the present. History, the past, is a natural teacher. If honored and obeyed, we can escape much hardship, pain, and suffering.

Today, America is looking back. But not in a way as to learn from the past and not repeat it. Many are looking back longingly. They are looking for a time that was but can never be again. It was the time that I had already experienced when white men ruled America. They owned everything and had all the best jobs, homes, possessions, and power. Others were subservient second-class, including white women, to an extent.

Nearing the end of my journey, I do not want to relive the America of my youth. America has come too far to turn around. Will we save democracy for generations to come? Empires only last for a short while; the average is about 250 years. So is it time to try a new form of governing? I fear for my children, grandchildren, and succeeding generations. What kind of America will they inherit?